BURUNDI'S NEGATIVE PEACE

The Shadow of a Broken Continent in the Era of NEPAD

First Edition
Kale Ewusi, PhD
Africa Strategy Group International

- With -

Ebenezer Derek Akwanga Jr. Bsc
*School of Graduate Studies
Norwich University*

Order this book online at www.trafford.com
or email orders@trafford.com

Most Trafford titles are also available at major online book retailers.

© Copyright 2010 Kale Ewusi, PhD & Ebenezer Akwanga, Jr. BSc.
All rights reserved. No part of this publication may be reproduced, stored in a retrieval system, or transmitted, in any form or by any means, electronic, mechanical, photocopying, recording, or otherwise, without the written prior permission of the author.

Printed in Victoria, BC, Canada.

ISBN: 978-1-4269-2355-5 (sc)
ISBN: 978-1-4269-2354-8 (dj)

Library of Congress Control Number: 2010900339

Our mission is to efficiently provide the world's finest, most comprehensive book publishing service, enabling every author to experience success. To find out how to publish your book, your way, and have it available worldwide, visit us online at www.trafford.com

Trafford rev. 1/18/2010

www.trafford.com

North America & international
toll-free: 1 888 232 4444 (USA & Canada)
phone: 250 383 6864 ♦ fax: 812 355 4082

This book is dedicated to the evergreen memories of our mothers who sowed but did not live to reap

Rose Eposi Ewusi
Yaya Hilda Enanga Mbongo
And our wives who took over the baton
Marie Ewokolo Kale Ewusi nee Nganje
Agnes Akwanga nee Abungwi

- And -

Geneviva, Coretta-Scot, Yoti,
Lonie and Leonard-Spencer,
Our children whose constant love,
smiles and affection kept us awake
To complete this piece of work on time

Contents

List of Acronyms xi
Acknowledgment xiii
Forward xix
Theoretical Framework xxiii
    Structural Conflict Theory xxv
    Psycho-Cultural Conflict Theory xxvi
    Modernization Theory xxviii
Chapter One 1
The Nature Of African Conflicts 1
    Introduction 2
    Political History of Burundi 8
        Political Institutions 13
    The Era of the First Republic 1966-1976 15
    The Era of the Second Republic: 1976-1987 18
    The Third Republic (1987-1992) 19
    The Fourth Republic 1993 -1996 20
    Origin of the New Partnership for African
    Development 21
    NEPAD and African Conflicts 26
Chapter Two 31
**Sources And Dynamics Of African Conflicts: A
Literature Review** 31
    Conflicts in Africa: An Overview 39
    Sources and Dynamics of African Conflicts 44

Politics without a Social Compact 45
NEPAD AND CONFLICT RESOLUTION 51

Chapter Three 55
The Burundi Peace Process: An Evaluation 55
SOUTH AFRICA AND THE BURUNDI PEACE
PROCESS 57
The Mandela Mission 58
Mandela's Approach to Negotiation 61
The Arusha Accord: The role of the South African
National Defence Force 63
The Zuma Mission 65
Peace in Burundi: Looking Beyond Zuma 68

Chapter Four 71
**African Solutions To African Conflicts: A Historical
Perspective** 71
OAU and Conflict Resolution: Foundational Principles:
A Hindrance to Intervention 72
The OAU and Border Conflicts 75
OAU and Colonial Secession Conflict 82
The OAU and Racist Regimes 86
*OAU and Conflicts resulting From Challenges to
legitimacy of Power.* 92
*The OAU and Conflicts Involving External
Intervention* 92
The OAU and Religious and Ethnic Conflicts 94
*Summing –up the OAU's Performance in African
Conflicts* 94
The African Union: Prospects for Conflict Resolution . 96

    Features of the African Union 96
        Challenges and Prospects of the African Union 97
        African Regional Organizations and Conflict Resolution: An Assessment 99
        ECOWAS and Conflict Resolution 102
        ECOWAS Security Mechanism 102
        SADC And Conflict Resolution 109
        SADC Conflict Resolution and Prevention strategy ... 110
        ECCAS AND CONFLICT RESOLUTION 112
        IGAD And Conflict Resolution 114
        IGAD In Somalia 116
        IGAD Conflict Early Warning and Response Mechanism (CEWARN) 118
        EAC and Conflict Resolution 119
        SECURITY COOPERATION IN THE EAC 120

Chapter Five 123

Root Causes Of African Conflicts: Not Conspiracies .. 123
    African Diversity 125
    Historical Legacies 125
    Internal Factors 129
    External Factors 130
        Economic Motives 131
    Specific Situations 132

Chapter Six 135

The Burundian Conflicts: Specific Dynamics 135
    History: The Main Pretext 136

    Summing up Burundi's Historical Conflict dynamics ... 150

Chapter Seven 151
Implications And Dimensions For Sustainable Peace .. 151
    Shifting Actors 152
    A Militarized Regional Society 153
    Arms and Ammunitions Trade 154
    Scarce Resources and demographic Stress 154
    Regional Demographic Fluidity 155
    The construction of Knowledge and Identities 156
    Violent Psychology 157
    The socio-political dimension 158
    The anthropological, Sociocultural and psychological dimension 160
    The Economic Dimension 164

Chapter Eight 169
The Verdict 169

List of Acronyms

AMIB – African Mission in Burundi
AI – Amnesty International
AU– African Union
CDP – Christian Democratic Party
CEWARN – Conflict Early Warning Response Mechanism
CNLC – Congolese National Liberation Committee
COMESA – Common Market for East and Southern Africa
COPAX – Conseil De Paix Et De Security en Afrique Central
DRC – Democratic Republic of Congo
EAC – East African Community
ECA – Economic Commission for Africa
ECCAS – Economic Community of Central African States
ECOWAS – Economic Community of West African States
FNL- National Liberation Front
GHAI – Greater Horn of Africa Initiative
ICJ – International Court Of Justice
JSC – Joint Security Committee
MAP – Millennium Partnership for the African Recovery Programme
MRU- Mano River Union
MINUCI – United Nations Mission in Cote D'Ivoire
NEPAD – New Partnership for Africa's Development

NAI – New Africa Initiative
NFD – Northern Frontier District
OAU – Organization of African Unity
OPDS – Organ for Politic Defence and Security
SADC – Southern African Development Community
SADCC – Southern African Development Coordination Conference
TRAUMA CENTRE – Centre for the Rehabilitation of Victims of Violence and Torture
UNAMSIL – United Nations Mission in Sierra Leone
UNM-EE – United Nations Mission for Ethiopia and Eritrea
UNM-L – United Nations Mission in Liberia
UNM-RWS – United Nations Mission for Referendum in Western Sahara
UNOBS – United Nations Mission in Burundi
UNOCI – United Nations Mission in Cote D'Ivoire
UNOM – United Nations Mission in Democratic Republic Of Congo
USAID – United States Agency for International Development

Acknowledgment

1.1 EWUSI AND AKWANGA JR

A book of this nature is unquestionably the product of many people as well as organizations. The book is inspired by the desire to sanctify our God given talent hatched when we met in form one at the Lycee Bilingue de Buea in 1982 and eventually moved to Government High School Limbe in 1985. I am grateful for **Amnesty International** for sticking with Ebenezer during his travails with the government of La Republique du Cameroon. Without them, he could have been alive for us to reconnect and work on this project and the other projects on the pipeline. Without boasting, most of our classmates would remember that we were the best History students. Ninjo Paul – our History teacher and friend is still alive to confirm this. Although we met as classmates, we eventually discovered that we were relatives by accident. Therefore, this is our first joint project and we are proud to announce that, there are many more on the way.

In this light we wish to first of all thank our wives. They may not have contributed a single idea in the book but their relentless support through our travails has been the shoulder on which we have stood, so people can see us.

1.2 SAMUEL

John Kennedy ones said 'Mankind must put an end to war or war will put an end to mankind... War will exist until that distant day when the conscientious objector enjoys the same reputation and prestige that the warrior does today' Will mankind put and end to war? Will war come to end in Africa? That distant day has not come. In Burundi, the rebel leaders still have the reputation and prestige of a warrior and therefore, sustainable peace is farfetched. The search for not just peace but sustainable peace in Burundi is because I consider war to be as outmoded as cannibalism, chattel slavery, blood feuds and dueling, an insult to God and humanity and a daily crucifixion to Christ. In this journey, I wish to thank my very special brothers and friends – Paul Ewusi for his never ending love and assistance, Eric Ewusi and wife Jofie for their love and loyalty, my junior brother Engr Koffi Ewusi, my special sister and first lady of Wovia Dina Dikanjo. Academically, I have benefitted form the wise counsel of my friend and former Fulbright colleague, Prof Weisfelder of the University of Toledo Ohio, my former students at the Peace Studies Program at North West University, South Africa for believing in me, especially the most accomplished of them: Mr Thapelo Madumane – Second Secretary at the South African Embassy Guinea Bissau and Mr. Mpho Mfolwe- First Secretary at Botswana Embassy in England. Senior Researchers: Ignatius Mabula and Tumisang Mangole of South Africa's Department of Foreign Affairs. You guys have been my pride. I can at least bask in the glory of having produced soldiers of peace like you. Much of the information was collected from research travels sponsored by the national Research Foundation in South Africa and the United Nations Project to strengthen the capacity of African regional organization for conflict resolution and peace building. I am privileged to have walked this road and benefit from the wise counsel of Prof Hassan Kaya of the Indigenous

Knowledge Systems in the North-West University in South Africa. He held my hand through that darkness and taught me the virtues of hard work. I would be nothing without him.

Kale Ewusi, Washington DC 2009

1.3 EBENEZER

Nathan Sharansky and Ron Dermer wrote in *The Case For Democracy* that, "...the struggle for peace and security in the world is not linked to promoting democracy. The road to peace is seen as paved with good intentions, goodwill, and faith in the brotherhood of man." Africa has been torn apart for the past seventy years by wars emanating from the least of disagreement between two tribes or people compel to live and die together by the niceties of colonialism, whose onslaught on the continent created artificial physical demarcations, respected only at the behest of the Club of Dictators. These brutal tyrants more often have today become partners for peace, not because they cherish the whole notion of a peaceful society, but because they must play the role of the good boys in other to prolong their stay in power. It has become a continent in which those who truly aspire for peace are more often than not prepare to place a wolf and lamb in the same cage hoping that things would be better. This methodology has proven to be futile as *Burundi's Negative Peace* would show.

In preparing this book, we have drawn on a wide variety of sources, some totally neglected in discussing the Burundian Civil War, or used for purposes of gratifying one segment of this brutal and senseless carnage that took away more than 700, 000 lives within two decades. My special and utmost thanks goes to the formidable human rights group, Amnesty International who became my parents, my family, the friends and allies who abandoned me in those very dark days of political imprisonment. Truly, without them, without the series of Urgent Actions on my behalf issued by AI, the relentless campaign for my freedom and the unconditional release or fair trial for all of us prisoners of conscience, I would not be co-authoring this book today. Nothing I write here truly expresses the appreciation which I carry in my heart. I would always be indebted to them as long as life permits.

My thanks go to Cherrod Pate *"the priceless"* whose unbelievable smile and care for so brief a moment gave me reason to complete this book in time. When it comes to thanking of friends and colleagues, I scarcely know where to start: Edwin Mekanya Kamara, Nicole Melissa Morel, Michel Hong, Tanteh Adeline Alia, Paddy Menkem Nembo, David Nkemtita, Daniel Eyong Abungwi, Nelson R Mabngah and Tafie Marcel Tabi. No expression of thanks to them can ever suffice. To my brother and comrade-in-the-struggle, Lucas Cho Ayaba, I say thank you for always being there when I need you most. You remained a true brother and friend in the selfless struggle to purge our continent from ruthless regimes whose tentacles of violence and large scale human rights abuses have no frontier. To Prof. and Mrs Tazoacha Asonganyi, Bibiana Taku, Chiefs Fuasonganyi and Fuatabong Taku and Mr and Mrs Bedefeh for being there for me in time of need.

To Kelly Morgan Ilona, Mike O'Reily, Bryna K. Subherwal, Ulana Moroz and to all the great men and women around the world for the Individual-At-Risk Campaign for Amnesty International, I want you to know how special you are to the men, women, political activists, human rights defenders and simple citizens around the globe whose life like mine often have a rendezvous with the monster called tyranny. To Emilia Guthierez, Field Organizer for Amnesty International, Washington DC, my sister Nina Helmy-Kamal and my most cherished friends from the land of the Queen of Sheba, Betemekdes Belachew and Yonathan Amezene for their inspiration.

To Peter Kum Che Mebeng, a distinguished human rights campaigner, long-time activist for universal rights and Executive Director of Trauma Center, and to the great men and women of Trauma Center whose selfless sacrifices gave hopes and aspirations for a new day to thousands of Burundian and Rwandan refugees, I want them to know that this book is for each and everyone of them. They will always be in my heart.

It is also my pleasant duty to wholeheartedly thank my good friend and admirer, Sir Nigel S. Rodley, Professor of Law and Chair of the Human Rights Centre at the University of Essex, and Member of the United Nations Human Rights Committee whose works as the former Special Rapporteur of the Commission on Torture frightened the Yaounde Civilian Junta to keep me alive, thus making the realization of this book to be true. I owe my life a great deal to him and to Amnesty International. And to Irene Khan, the indefatigable Secretary General of Amnesty International whose unyielding crusade against poverty as a troubling human rights issue might finally be the curtain raiser in Burundi's quest for a lasting durable peace.

Upper Marlboro, Maryland
November 2009.

Forward

THIS BOOK EXPLORES the largely unknown area of negative peace in Africa and specifically Burundi in the wake of the manner in which conflicts are resolved in the continent. The use of mediation among warring parties, the implementation of ceasefire agreements, the establishment of a transitional government and the organization of elections has been the conflict resolution trajectory that has been religiously applied in resolving African conflicts.

What then is the missing link? The authors of this book fervently believe that, the above mentioned techniques do not lead to sustainable peace. In fact it leads to negative peace which is not peace at all. The peace studies theorist, Galtung, decreed that 'Peace is not the absence of violence, but peace of mind'. This is absolutely true to all civilized nations. The question which arises then is that what have Africans left out in their conflict resolution story? The response seems to us that, Africans most times under pressure from the international community, or regional organizations, have consistently failed to address the root causes of conflicts.

Considering that the root causes are most times not addressed, the tensions still persist even within future governments that succeed the conflicts. Furthermore, the international community is always quick to quit countries graduating from conflict without building the institutions which can sustain the peace.

Against this backdrop, this book explores the following issues under the following chapters.

Chapter one deals with the nature of African conflicts. Most conflicts in Africa are grounded history and the very nature in which the states came into being. The overriding reason often quoted for African conflicts has been the role of colonialism. It is authoritatively stated that, the colonial masters failed woefully to take into consideration the ethnic, linguistic and tribal nature of the African people in their configuration of the African state. The consequence of this was the establishment of states with relatives of people and parts of tribes across the border. The failure to clearly demarcate the borders by the colonial masters also led to border conflicts. Other issues dealt with include, the territorial ambitions by some African heads of state as well as the need to secure resources from other areas.

Chapter two examines some of the vast literature on African conflict and conflict resolution. There is a huge body of literature on conflicts in Africa. This literature is incisively adapted to the study. It will assist the reader to identify the relevant literature and assist other researchers in the Area to select what is usable or not. Literature review serves the purpose of identifying gaps which may come to play in dealing with a particular topic. It also serves to acknowledge the existence of work done in the area of study. Therefore the student of African conflict will find chapter two very handy in understanding the theoretical explanation of the sources and dynamics of African conflicts.

Chapter three evaluates the Burundi Peace Process. The Arusha Accord is seen as the key to peace in Burundi. But this study looks at Arusha as the starting point for the consolidation of viable peace in Burundi. Because of the fact that Arusha has been considered to be the baseline for peace in Burundi, the chapter looks at the shortcoming of the accord in relation to sustainable peace in Burundi. The simple fact that Arusha prescribes a type of peace based on ethnic lines in a country which had no ethnic problems before colonialism, is dangerous for long term peace.

The reason is that it would eternally sanctify the ethnic trajectory of the country which was a colonial misdeed. Furthermore, the accord fails to deal decisively with socio-economic problems created as a result of the conflict. Therefore although recent developments point to the integration of the rebel groups which initially failed to join the Arusha Accord, it does not guarantee sustainable peace. The authors hold that, it is the calm before the storm. We believe that, provided the issues of land, education, poverty, and unemployment are not dealt with Burundi will either in the short run or long run relapse into conflict again.

Chapter four on it part, takes a historical look at how Africa has dealt with the problem of conflict. In this area, we look at conflict resolution by the defunct Organization of African Unity which existed between 1963 and 2001. Recognizing that, the OAU was jealously tailored to preserve independence than to resolve conflict, the resolution of African conflict fell squarely in the hands of sub regional organizations. Therefore, we look at how these sub regional organizations dealt with conflict and built security organs in order to enhance peace in the regions. We note that, the recognition of the work done by these regional organizations earned them a place in the new African security architecture. We therefore historically trace the work done by both the Organization of African Unity and the sub regional organization.

Chapter five traces the root causes of African conflict which is critical to the sustainable resolution of African conflicts. We argue that the failure to indentify the root causes of conflicts and address them will not lead to sustainable peace. Therefore this chapter examines the root causes of the conflicts with a view to providing solutions.

Chapter six examines the specific dynamics of the Burundi conflict. The importance of this is the fact that, it provides us with understanding of the cycle of violence between the ethnic groups which eventually led to the conclusion by mediators that, it is an ethnic problem. The cyclical violence has led to deep hatred from both ends with protagonists interpreting and misinterpreting any actions from the other group.

Chapter Seven is the final chapter. This chapter examines the implications and dimensions of not only the type of peace prescribed and promoted in Burundi but the long term implications of the peace. The peace may be sustainable if certain conditions are met in a sustained manner. For now, certain factors such as war weariness, the new international institutions such as the African Union and NEPAD may prevent the outbreak of violence at a certain level but does not necessarily lead to sustainable peace which Galtung will call positive peace. In some instances, the country may fall into the category of acceptable dictatorship like in Kagame's Rwanda where the political stability is more acceptable than genocide.

KE and EDMA Jr.

Theoretical Framework

The main objective of theoretical perspective is to explain the theoretical foundation of the research topic. A theory is regarded as a systematically related set of statements including some law-like generalizations that are empirically testable. It is possible to perceive a number of common characteristics of a theory viz; abstractness, logic, propositions, explanations, relationships and acceptance by the scientific community. It is therefore important to base a study on a particular theory.

Further more, the primary function of this part is to attempt to explain or to account for particular phenomena, which is viewed as explanatory. It is this explanatory function, which distinguishes a theory from related but non explanatory concept such as descriptive, typology and models.

The main theoretical concepts used in this study are derived from the general theory of conflict but also from infra-theories encompassed in it such as structural and psycho-cultural theories. At the macro-level, the modernization theory analyzes the economic and social structures that shape the incentives of the society are used and at the micro-level the political agent theory addresses the preferences and interaction among the political agents. Scholars of conflict theory have written extensively about the sources of conflict, but have usually, according to their respective disciplines merely looked at and emphasized only one specific source as the real explanation of the cause of conflict while sometimes undermining or diminishing the importance of others.

Therefore, in order to develop an argument, originally based on the previous general concept and to provide for the reader a precise conceptual roadmap for this study a theoretical clarification is required. An attempt will be made to develop an argument through an in depth exposition of the two major infra-theories, namely structural conflict theory and psycho-cultural or socio-psychological conflict theory, which are direct off-shoots of protracted social conflict theory.

Limiting the argument to these theories does not imply the application of a reductionism approach, on the contrary these theories encompass different issues related to the emergence and evolution of protracted ethnic conflict, which allows for greater understanding of the issues in question and have an impact on the socio-economic development of the state.

Part of the argument in this study is that, different factors are responsible for the emergence and development of protracted social conflicts in Africa and Burundi in particular. These factors – economic, political, institutional, cultural, geographic, demographic, psychological, military and colonial, can be broken down into two main categories, despite the eclecticism of the terminology found in the literature, as structural objective conflict and psycho-cultural i.e subjective conflict .

STRUCTURAL CONFLICT THEORY

Structural conflict is essentially defined as an outcome of incompatible interests based on the competition for scarce resources; it is objective because it is defined as largely independent of the perceptions of the participants and emanates from power structures and institutions. It emphasizes that in order for conflict to manifest itself, 'proximate' factors will have to operate as triggers.

The proximate causes of conflict are those that transform potentially violent situations into deadly conflicts. This theory further facilitated the configuration of the otherwise coherent Burundi society into racial and ethnic groups. It therefore informs the stages that led to the massacres as espoused by American human rights scholar, Dr Gregory Stanton, namely, classification, symbolization and dehumanization respectively.

Practically, this theory is made evident when the Tutsi perceived the Hutu intellectuals masterminded the rebellion that fuelled ethnic tension in 1972. The Hutu intellectuals were thus perceived as a threat to the Tutsi ethnic dominance. Lemarchand (1994:302) notes that 'the Tutsi administration responded by staging brutal attacks on every single Hutu with more than primary school education".

Kenny (2002) further lamented on the killings of Hutu intellectuals by noting that 'Tutsi death squads went into high schools, picked out all Hutu pupils and made them kneel down and then smashed their skulls with sledgehammers. Thousands of Hutu intellectuals fled the country and many found refuge in neighboring Rwanda that was ruled by Hutus.

PSYCHO-CULTURAL CONFLICT THEORY

The psycho-cultural conflict theory deals with the internalization of issues through emphasis of the role of culturally shared and deep 'we-they' oppositions. This leads to the conceptualization of enemies and allies although to a great extent these oppositions between the Hutu and Tutsi were not culturally shared.

Burundi's protracted social conflict was facilitated, animated and driven by the constructed Hutu identity because of the underlying fear of extinction. Memories of past Hutu persecutions were reconstructed so that the Hutu ethnic group was seen to be vulnerable. FNL, FDD- ABASA propaganda expressed this 'fear of extinction', the 'fear of dying off', the 'fear of the future'- fears of which seemed to underlie the threat of a loss of Hutu identity. This threat, real or imagined, emanated from purported history of annihilation, humiliation, oppression, victimization, feeling of inferiority, persecution and other kind of discrimination.

The polarization that resulted provided the political capital for the post independence leadership that always thrived on underscoring the perceived differences of constructed ethnicity illustrated by the following: Kaybanda (1959), 'Two nations in a single state- two nations whom there's no intercourse and no sympathy, who are as ignorant of each other's habits, thoughts and feelings as if they were dwellers of different zone, or inhabitants of different planets.

Habyarimana (1991), 'The unity of ethnic group is not possible without the unity of the majority. Just as we note that no Tutsi recognizes regional belonging, it is imperative that the majority forge unity, so that they are able to wade off any attempt to return into slavery"

The first stage, classification can be described as the cultural and racial distinction between the three categories of Burundi so that we have the Tutsi Caucasians, the Hutu Bantu Negroid and the Twa pigmoids. The second stage symbolization, affirms the classification by attributing symbolic characteristics that could be physical or otherwise.

For instance, the size and shape of the nose became symbolic and the very names that were used to describe a group were through stereotypes and clichés. As described by Sasserath (1948) a Belgian Doctor, the Tutsis are 1.90 or 1.80 meters tall, they are slim and have straight noses, high fore heads and thin lips. They seem distant, reserved, polite and refined. The Hutu are a different people 'possessing all characteristics of a Negro: flat noses, thick lips, low fore heads, brochycephlic skulls. They are like children, shy and lazy and usually dirty'.

The third stage, dehumanization is about denial of the humanity of others. It started with the Twa, who according to Dr Sasserath, were a small minority of pigmies hunting and foraging in forests and were regarded as inferior to Hutus and Tutsis. 'The Twa keep themselves apart and are treated with contempt by the rest of the population'. On the other hand, psycho-cultural conflict theory defines conflict in terms of psychological and cultural forces that frame the beliefs about the self, others and behavior. Psycho-cultural or perceptual or subjective explanation of protracted social conflict does not exclude other explanation. However, it may be argued that ethnic conflict as seen in Burundi can only be understood, and ultimately resolved, by addressing psychological elements. As Horowitz (195:181-182) maintains the sources of ethnic conflict are not to be found solely in the psychology of juxtaposition, but they cannot be understood without a psychology, an explanation that takes account of emotional concomitants of group traits and interactions

MODERNIZATION THEORY

In discussing the influence of conflict on the socio-economic development of a state country, with relevance to Burundi, a modernization theory has been frequently used. Although it is rarely mentioned today in the political science field. The basic assumption of the modernization theory is that developing countries are on the way towards an ideal-type developmentalist model. Max Weber argued that cultural values, beliefs and interests distinguish two types of human beings, traditional and modern, with latter amenable to change and confident on the ability to bring the change around.

According to Williams (1994) the development of all societies lies in five stages which develops consecutively: (1) the traditional society, developed with limited production functions; (ii) the preconditions for the take off, embracing societies in transition process; (iii) the take-off, where growth becomes the normal condition in a society; 9iV) the drive to maturity, when modern technology expands over the whole front of the economy, social and political activities; and finally (v) the age of high mass-consumption, in which a large number of persons gain command over consumption, transcending basic food, shelter and clothing.

In this the Burundians started as a traditional society which relied on indigenous life, like farming. After colonization and influence from outside they started to change from traditional to modern life and practiced commercial farming. Their social structured life ruled by traditional leaders was transformed from the monarchical rule to political leadership, which has been dominated by military dictatorship.

Burundi's economic performance over the period 1960-2000 has been catastrophic. The usual economic factors determining growth are endogenous to political objectives, suggesting that politics and conflict explains the dismal performance. Economic development has been shaped by the occurrence of violent conflict caused by factions fighting for the control of the state and its rents. In this regard performance and development of socio-economic performance will not improve unless the political system is modernized from the dictatorial regime playing a zero-sum game to a more democratic and accountable regime.

Chapter One

THE NATURE OF AFRICAN CONFLICTS

"Every morning in Africa, a Gazelle wakes up. It knows it must run faster than the fastest lion or it will be killed. Every morning a Lion wakes up. It knows it must outrun the slowest Gazelle or it will starve to death. It doesn't matter whether you are a Lion or a Gazelle... when the sun comes up, you'd better be running."

Anonymous

INTRODUCTION

The excitement of the struggle for independence that permeated the African continent in the second half of the 20th century, has generally failed to provide the political, economic and social dream of the African people. After three decades of independence, characterized by political dictatorship and poor economic performance most African countries undertook political and economic reform measures and instituted multiparty governments. This was partly due to the fall of communism in Eastern Europe and the emergence of a new political dispensation dominated by western liberal democratic principles[1].

In spite of the above political changes, the close of the 20th century has witnessed, ongoing traumas in various parts of Africa in the area of economic decline, health hazards and increasing civil war which have taken a heavy toll on the people of the continent[2]. A case in point is the great lakes region of Africa where the Burundi conflict has been ongoing and has become so protracted. Accordingly[3],

---

1   Naomi Chazan, Peter Lewis, Robert Mortimer, Donald Rothchild, Steven J.Stedman (1999) Politics and Contemporary Society in Africa. Lynne Rienner Publishers. For a more detailed study of the precarious nature of Africa's conflicts also see, Donald Rothchild & Naomi Chazan in " The Precarious Balance: State and Society in Africa.
2   Oliver Ramsbotham, Tom Woodhouse and Hugh Miall (2005) Contemporary Conflict Resolution, Polity Press. For a more incisive knowledge of the nature of African conflicts, also see other publications by Miall Hugh et al, such as " Contemporary Conflict Resolution: The Prevention, Management and Transformation of Deadly Conflicts
3   Patrick Ryan and Michael langone (1990) examine the protracted nature of conflicts in the article titled 'Religious Conflict Resolution: A Model for families in the International Cultic Studies Association. Also see Patrick Ryan in Coping with Trance States.

protracted conflicts such as the Burundi conflict is usually conflicts between ethnic groups. They usually appear unsolvable. Such conflicts have typical preconditions that play important roles in shaping their origin and account for conflicts in societies characterized by multi communal compositions.

Azar and Moon[4] confirm that these conflicts flourish in environments of high politico-economic underdevelopment and manifest themselves over communal identity needs. The roots of these are to be found at the interlocking nexus of underdevelopment, structural deprivation and communal cleavages. These characteristics aptly describe the nature of the conflicts in Burundi, Rwanda, to a lesser extent Somali. It is against this backdrop that, a series of devastating political and human disasters have continued to rock the continent of Africa.

Disasters in the form of civil wars, famine, health hazards, genocide and ethnic cleansing as well as cancerous political instability which have seen gross violations of human rights and dignity have become part of the daily life of Africans. These scenes have been variously explained with the blame lying squarely on internal factors such as bad governance, corruption and external factors such as colonialism, neo-colonialism as well as super power politics.

Accordingly, Africa's conflicts have included those, which date as far back as the immediate post independence era such as the Sudanese civil war, the Angolan and

---

4 For the identification of the bureaucratic-managerial and legal formalist approaches to conflict resolution see Edward Azar and Moon in Interactive Conflict Resolution.

Mozambique.[5] Others emanated from military usurpation of power in the form of coup d'états during the first decade of independence as in Ghana, Nigeria, present day Democratic Republic of the Congo, Togo, and Central African Republic[6].

Most of these countries have witnessed political instability and for those that are now democratic, are governed by former military dictators now 'born again democrats' with a tendency for the use of force and human rights abuse[7]. At the end of the cold war it was expected that, a more serene and peaceful atmosphere was going to prevail considering that, some of the conflicts originated from allegiance to the two prevailing ideologies inherent in the cold war. That was not the case, for, apart from the resurgence of conflict in traditional areas of contention, where cold war

---

5   Mozambique and Angola are very important examples of African countries which were bedeviled by cold war conflicts in Southern Africa. In Angola, the major protagonists were UNITA and the MPLA while in Mozambique it was Frelimo and the Renamo. For more on the Angolan Civil War refer to Fernando Giumaraes, The Origins of the Angolan Civil War: Foreign Intervention and Domestic Political Conflict, Macmillan 2001.
6   There was a wave of military coups in post independent Africa which created the phenomenon of coups as the means of political succession. In Ghana, Kwame Nkrumah was overthrown, while in Nigeria, the government of Nnamdi Azikiwe and Tafawa Balewa was also overthrown. In the DRC, Togo and Central African Republic, Colonel Mobutu, General Eyadema and Emperor Bokassa usurped power.
7   In the 1990's with the introduction of multipartyism, many African countries previously ruled by military dictators introduced multiparty elections and the rulers resigned from the army and became civilian leaders and won the elections on the basis of incumbency. Presidents Blaise Compaore of Burkina Faso, Dennis Sassou Ngueso of Congo Brazzaville, Eyadema of Togo, Mathew Kerekou of Guinea all fall within these framework.

considerations had kept pent-up pressures in check, the immediate post cold war period has coincided with the emergence of new forms of conflict.

This category of conflicts prevalent in Africa tagged post cold war conflicts include: the genocide in Rwanda, civil war in Burundi, Somalia, Sierra Leone, Liberia, the Democratic Republic of the Congo, Uganda and the political crisis in Zimbabwe. These are the prevalent conflicts in the era of the New Partnership for Africa's Development and African Renaissance which greatly affect peace and sustainable development in these countries and the continent at large.

They have led to new problems such as human displacement, poverty and the death of millions of innocent people[8]. Nevertheless, an incisive look into the causes of conflicts in Africa and their resolution will reveal a catalogue of initiatives by both international and regional organizations. These initiatives towards conflict resolution and sustainable development have revealed the complexity and variability of the conflicts[9].

It is worth noting that, certain patterns and trends are discernible in African conflicts. Foremost amongst these is the characteristic widespread acceptance of force as an appropriate dispute settlement procedure, as was the case in the Eritrea-Ethiopian war. This trend inspired the call by

---

8 For a more comprehensive understanding of the nature of African Conflicts, see Adebayo Adedeji (1999) Comprehending and Mastering African Conflicts: The Search for Sustainable Peace and Good Governance.
9 Also see Alfred Nhema and Paul Zeleza in their book The Resolution of African Conflicts: The management of conflict resolution & Post conflict reconstruction, Ohio University Press.

the former United Nations Secretary General Kofi Annan when he said

'Africans must demonstrate the will to rely upon political rather than military responses to problem'
This tendency to react instinctively to a challenge with force appears particularly prevalent in a broad band of territory stretching from West Africa to the Horn of Africa, where many of the governments such as in Niger, Nigeria, Central African Republic, Congo-Brazzaville, and Rwanda headed by former military leaders some of whom are 'born again democrats' Related to this trend, is a deplorable practice of searching out civilians during these conflicts and subjecting them to the most heinous atrocities either gratuitously or for some perceived perverse purpose.

As pointed out, in such conflicts which most times are domestic, the main aim increasingly has been, the destruction of not just the armies but the civilians as well as entire ethnic groups, with women and children often singled out as prime targets of terrorism. These practices are common in the conflicts in Liberia, Sierra Leone and the war waged by the Lord's resistance Army in Uganda.[10]

A further regrettable development is the growing commercialization of African conflicts. War has become big business in which the prime motivation of an emerging class of entrepreneurs is the accumulation of wealth to either finance the war effort or for personal gains. According

---

10 The former Ghanaian born Secretary General of the United Nations Kofi Annan was very vocal in the quest for diplomacy in the resolution of African conflicts. In a speech in Addis Ababa on the 2nd May 1998, he called for African Leaders to reduce military expenditure to free up resources for development.

to the United Nations Secretary General, *'profit from conflicts in Africa'* is high on the list of the protagonists of the war.

This is typical of the Liberian crisis where control and exploitation of diamonds, timber and other raw materials was one of the principal objectives of the warring factions.[11]. At another level, lower ranks of the warring factions are often driven to a life of extortion, looting and plundering as a means of surviving. This is frequently the case with irregular forces such as the *Kamajors* in the Sierra Leonean conflict, where private militias hired by warlords but not paid, roving bands of unemployed demobilized soldiers who have turned to banditry, such as the *interahamve* in Rwanda[12].

Africa's conflicts have been worsened by the 'spill over effect' in which case there is the growing tendency of conflicts spilling across borders as states intervene militarily in their neighbors affairs. The Congolese conflict is a locus classicus of such a conflict in Africa that saw the intervention by Uganda, Rwanda, Zimbabwe, Namibia and Angola. This has been blamed on the porosity of state boundaries, which facilitate the movement of not only refugees but also drug dealers and arms merchants [13]. The current United Nations Chief Ban Ki-Moon describes in unambiguous terms the

---

11   Elias, T.O examines the African legal framework on Conflict Resolution within the context of the Organization of African Unity in his book ' The horizons in International Law
12   Rene Lemarchand's description of the magnitude of Burundi's conflict in 'Burundi: Ethnic Conflict and Genocide' is a dire reflection of the nature of African conflicts.
13   Read the article by Salim El Hassan titled 'Managing the Process of Conflict Resolution in Sudan' in Nhema and P Zeleza's (ed) of The Resolution of African Conflicts: the management of Conflict Resolution.

role of neighboring states in exacerbating African conflicts in the following words:

'...the role that African governments play in supporting, sometimes even instigating conflicts in neighboring countries must be candidly acknowledged'.

POLITICAL HISTORY OF BURUNDI

Burundi is a small central African country of about 8.988,091 people (July 2009 Est.)[14] comprising of four major ethnic groups namely- Tutsi, Hutu, Ganwa and Twa. It is one of the world's poorest countries. After her neighbor Rwanda, it is the most densely populated country in Africa. At an annual GDP per capita of $ 400 (2008 est.), it is among the world's poorest countries and after her neighbor Rwanda is the most densely populated country in Africa[15]. This central

---

14 CIA World Fact Book: Burundi, Political
15 For a historical understanding of the Burundi read in detail the account offered by Angelo Barampama, Fribourg (CH) Universite de Fribourg in Le problem ethnique dans la societe Africain en mutation. In his description of the nature of justice in the Burundi society he states 'Quoi qu'en disent ceux qui présentent les *Bashingantahe* comme des juges toujours intègres, il est un fait que cette justice était généralement rendue à la tête du client. Cette réalité transparaissait particulièrement en cas de justice pénale. Ainsi lorsqu'il y avait un meurtre, la famille du meurtrier se rachetait (*kwicungura*) en payant à la famille de la victime *indihano* (prix du sang) qui consistait en vaches dont le nombre variait selon les exigences de la famille éprouvée et son rang social. Selon une étude d'Angelo Barampama, le verdict variaitsuivant que l'auteur du meurtre ou la victime était Hutu ou Tutsi. Quand un meurtre était commis sur un membre d'une famille, la pratique consistait souvent à venger la victime en assassinant un membre de la famille du meurtrier. Pour marquer son désir d'échapper à la vengeance, la famille du meurtrier pouvait aussi demander au chef de servir d'intermédiaire pour

African country has been embroiled in civil disputes and political instability for most of post independence period.

The seeds of discord that led to the Burundi conflict were sown by the Belgian colonialists in 1961, following the assassination of Prince Rwagosore, the leader of the Independent Party called the Union for national progress- a multi-ethnic political party after the victory of the party in the first legislative elections against the Belgian supported Christian Democratic Party. [16]

Contrary to her neighbor Rwanda, Burundi was able to achieve independence in relative calm. When she achieved full independence in 1962, in the context of weak democratic institutions, the Tutsi King Mwambutsa IV established

---

réparer le crime en payant des vaches. *Quand un Hutu tuait un Tutsi, il devait payer 14 vaches. Quand un Tutsi tuait un Hutu, il ne payait que 7 vaches. Mathématiquement donc, la vie d'un Tutsi valait deux fois la vie d'un Hutu.* Si le crime était commis par un Ganwa sur un autre Ganwa, la réparation se faisait par la guerre entre les deux familles jusqu'à la victoire du plus fort.

16 For a colonial perspective on the roots of the Burundi conflict see the detailed dissertation of Baganzicaha in ' Les evolues au Burundi a la veille de L'independance, Paris. Also see Zenom Nicayenzi in his description of the various classes and their role on the Burundi traditional society when he states that "Désormais, la contribution du Mushinganthe est mesurable. L'étudiant qui travaille avec assiduité et discipline et contribue à faire baisser les tensions ethniques dans le milieu de formation, celui-là est un véritable Mushingantahe et son apport peut être mesuré et évalué. L'homme ou la femme qui atteint les meilleurs résultats contre le minimum de dépenses au sein de l'entreprise et fait preuve d'un esprit de fraternité, celui-là est un Mushingantahe. Le Burundais, au sein de son quartier ou sur la colline, qui tend constamment à améliorer les conditions de vie de la population grâce à sonapport moral, intellectuel et social, voilà un homme excellent et efficace, donc un Mushingantahe'

a constitutional monarchy comprising equal members of Tutsi and Hutu. During Burundi's 43 years of independence from Belgium beginning from 1962 till date, over ten Heads of State have governed the country.

Most of them took power following military coups. Assassination of leaders also became a popular occurrence (See table 1)

Table1: Succession of governments and leaders in Burundi

Period in Office	Head of State	Political lineage	Ethnic Group
The Republic of Burundi			
1962 to 1966	King Mwambutsa IV, King	Monarch	*Tutsi*
1966	King Ntare V Ndizeye V, King	Monarch	*Tutsi*
28 November 1966 to 1 November 1976	Michel Micombero, President	Mil/UPRONA	*Tutsi*
2 November 1976 to 10 November 1976	Jean-Baptiste Bagaza, Chairman of the Supreme Revolutionary Council	Mil/UPRONA	*Tutsi*
10 November 1976 to 3 September 1987	Jean-Baptiste Bagaza, President		

3 September 1987 to 9 September 1987	**Pierre Buyoya,** Chairman of the Military Committee of National Salvation	Mil/UPRONA	*Tutsi; 1st Term*
9 September 1987 to 10 July 1993	**Pierre Buyoya,** President		
10 July 1993 to 21 October 1993	**Melchior Ndadaye,** President	FRODEBU	*Hutu*
21 October 1993 to 27 October 1993	**François Ngeze,** Chairman of the Committee of Public Salvation	Mil	*Hutu; in rebellion*
27 October 1993 to 5 February 1994	**Sylvie Kinigi,** acting President	UPRONA	*Tutsi*
5 February 1994 to 6 April 1994	**Cyprien Ntaryamira,** President	FRODEBU	*Hutu*
6 April 1994 to 25 July 1996	**Sylvestre Ntibantunganya,** President	FRODEBU	*Hutu*
25 July 1996 to 30 April 2003	**Pierre Buyoya,** President	UPRONA	*Tutsi*
30 April 2003 to 26 August 2005	**Domitien Ndayizeye,** President	FRODEBU	*Hutu*
26 August 2005 to present	**Pierre Nkurunziza,** President	CNDD-FDD	*Hutu*

It is argued that, in such a highly contested political terrain the Tutsi minority emerged as rulers much to the discontent of the Hutu majority.[17]

All positions of power and wealth were reserved for the Tutsi minority. That fuelled ethnic tensions and in 1972, the Hutu staged a rebellion to protest against what was perceived to be Tutsi oppression. On the other hand, the Tutsi perceived the rebellion as being masterminded by the Hutu intellectuals. The Hutu intellectuals were thus perceived as threats to their ethnic dominance and maintain that, the Tutsi administration responded by staging brutal attacks on 'every single Hutu with more than primary school education'

He further states that, 'Tutsi *death squads went into high schools, picked out all Hutu pupils, made them kneel down, and*

---

17 Esterhuysen (1998). But for a more exhaustive description of governance issues in Burundi see also JB Ndayizigiye in his account of the humiliation and conflict in Burundi 'The issue of governance concerns the ways in which the Burundi society has been governed and is being governed, the distribution of the contested authority and resources within the society, and most of all the legitimacy of the authority in the eyes of Burundi society. The sources of power have always been authority, human resources, skills and knowledge, intangible psychological and ideological factors, and material resources and sanctions (Burgess, 1994, p. 19). According to Ian Doucet, there is a link between good governance and legitimacy in producing networks of social relationships, which are stable and durable (1998, p.7). Between the Hutu majority population and the Tutsi minority power, relationships are retained by coercion and maintained by the threat and the use of force, not legitimized by both parties.

then smashed their skulls with a sledge hammer'. As a result thousands of Hutu intellectuals fled the country and many found refuge in neighboring Tanzania and Rwanda especially as the latter was ruled by a Hutu. The appalling conditions of Burundian refugees in Tanzania drew the attention of the United Nations High Commissioner for Refugees who appealed to the international community to put pressure to end the suffering of the Burundian civilians. It was against this background that, efforts were made towards a peaceful solution and the establishment of a transitional government in Burundi.

Political Institutions

It is believed that, the existence of social crisis in a country is a manifestation of the inability of the country's leadership to regulate inevitable conflicts among members of a group and different social components[18]. In Burundi there appears to be a natural antagonism between the governors and the governed which often take violent turns. Political power is always jealously guarded, and in situations where the power happens to be the main source of revenue, the struggle becomes bitter.[19] Since the era of constitutional monarchy, up

---

18 Samuel Amoo's article on the OAU and African conflicts: Past Successes, Present Paralysis, Present Paralysis and Future Perspectives' aptly describe the nature of political conflicts in Africa. Institute of Conflict Analysis, George Mason University.

19 This state of affairs is more aptly explored by Reyntjens F in 'Again at the Crossroads: Rwanda and Burundi, Upsala: Nordiska Security Review. Vol5 No 5. According to him, the political evolution of Rwanda and Burundi must be seen in a broader regional geopolitical context. The presence of the Rwandan and Burundian armies in the DRC is the expression of the extraterritorial extension of these countries civil wars. While the Burundian armed conflict runs parallel to very fragile negotiations, the Rwandan regime remains closed to any idea

to the semi-presidential regime which followed those of the single party, Burundi society was characterized by extreme violence. According to the 1962 independence constitution, Burundi was a constitutional monarchy along the lines of the former colonial master- Belgium.[20] The *Mwami* who prior to independence had embodied all legislative, executive and judiciary powers lost all the powers under this constitution. The government was characterized by a Prime Minister as Head of government appointed by the "Mwami" but was accountable to the parliament. The 'Mwami' appointed the members of government on the recommendation of the Prime Minister.

But in reality executive power rested in the hands of the Prime Minister[21]. This sowed the seeds of chaos in the

---

of political dialogue. The Burundian talks where the facilitator Nelson Mandela induced a forceps delivery, ended in August 2000 with the signature of an accord which is really a non-accord

20 Menard JF in 'L'état en Afrique Noire' examines the configuration of pre-colonial Burundi society in relation to political power distribution. This brings out the evidently weak institutions which under normal circumstances were not tailored to absorb the shocking conflict. He further indicates that, the constitution was masterminded by the colonialists and therefore had everything to do with the whims and caprices of Belgium. This has been a major source of conflict in a good number of African colonies especially the former Belgian colonies of Rwanda, Burundi, and present day democratic Republic of the Congo.

21 The evolution of the conflict after 1993 was not only linked to weak political institutions. The violence which succeeded the elections is well described by Lemarchand who states in his Book, Burundi: Ethnic Conflict and Genocide that in a headlong rush for multiparty democracy, for a brief moment, Burundi stood as one of the most promising candidates. He further describes the brief

nascent administration. The political base of the country which included the traditional authorities was eroded by the Belgians at independence. The Parliament on its own was bicameral composed of the National Assembly and the senate. Whereas the parliamentarians were elected through direct universal suffrage, the Senators were elected through electoral colleges. The initial problem for the monarchy was how to run the parliament. The problem was exacerbated by dissension within the UPRONA party which seriously undermined parliament and led to the formation of factions.[22] In 1965, the pluralist elections further polarized existing divisions heralding a coup d'etat in October 1965. That coup consummated the irreversibility of the cycle of political violence and repression further exacerbated the situation.

THE ERA OF THE FIRST REPUBLIC 1966-1976

Ndikumana (1998)[23] explains that, during this period, Burundi functioned without a constitution which finally

---

period of democracy in this words 'One of the most remarkable transitions to democracy yet seen in Africa and a model for all aspiring democracies' but within two years, tens of thousands were dead and hundreds of thousands forced into exile. Burundi has become one of Africa's intractable basket cases. In the wake of the wreckage created by the failed putsch of October, 1993, Burundi is second only to Rwanda on the list of states subject recurrent bouts of ethnic insanity.

22 Lemarchand (op cit)
23 Ndikumana L (1998) Institutional Failure and Ethnic Conflict in Burundi, African Studies Review, Vol 41 (i)Pg 29-41. For a more comprehensive examination of the causes of the conflict it is instructive to explore the Leonce Ndikumana, in 'Distributional Conflict, The State and Peace building in Burundi where he states that The nature of endogenously generated group dynamics determines the type of preferences (altruistic or exclusionist),

came into being on 11 July 1974. This Republic was more committed to ensuring equality amongst the population by involving them in the management of public affairs. The dominant party UPRONA also became the sole party at independence upon the integration of the Union of Burundi Women (UFB), the Rwagosore Revolutionary Youth (JRR) and the Union of the Burundi Workers (UTB).

This amalgamation of political parties gave UPRONA the monopoly of political activity, thus making it the party of the state with its attendant confusion of legislative and executive powers.[24] The 1974 constitution confirmed this

---

which in turn determines the type of allocative institutions and policies that prevail in the political and economic system. While unequal distribution of resources may be socially inefficient, it nonetheless can be rational from the perspective of the ruling elite, especially because inequality perpetuates dominance. However, because unequal distribution of resources generates conflict, maintaining a system based on inequality is difficult because it requires ever increasing investments in repression. It is therefore clear that if the new Burundian leadership is serious about building peace, it must engineer institutions that uproot the legacy of discrimination and promote equal opportunity for social mobility for all members of ethnic groups and regions.. Burundi, ethnicity, civil war, distributional conflict.

24 Ngaruko, F and Nkurunziza JD (2000) An Economic interpretation of Conflict in Burundi, in journal of African Economies: Mimeo: The World Bank. This study which was commissioned by the Economic Commission for Africa states thatIt shows that conflicts in Burundi have resulted from a combination of poverty, governance policies of exclusion and the fight for the control of the country's limited resources. The public sector being the main source of financial accumulation, Burundian bureaucracy is analyzed in detail and is found to be a predatory bureaucracy which cares for its own interests. In order to avoid the recur- rence of war in the country, it is

state of affairs. It formalized the principle of a single party controlling the wheels of state, including the judiciary. This made the party General secretary the de facto Head of state and government with legislative powers also. It can be ascertained that, this massive concentration of power in the hands of a single individual is a source of conflict in itself. The result of this arrangement was ethnic dictatorship, regionalism and corruption. The nation was thus set on the road to violence. It is also true, that the military regime set up in 1965 was no exception.

Furthermore, the 1969 and 1971 plots instead created a climate of violence which revived the conflict. Indeed the Hutu rebel attack of 1972 against the Tutsi population, with the confirmed objective of establishing a Hutu regime of obedience, coupled with the repression of Hutu intellectuals, is an important stage in the build up of the Burundi conflict. This led to the mass fleeing of refugees into neighbouring states such as Tanzania.

The institutional machinery also contributed to this episode. The authorities were overwhelmed by the disturbances created and the occasion was propitious for the settling of accounts with adversaries. Power was deeply entrenched in tribal division and the national conflict was inflamed. On

---

recommended that Burundians, with the assistance of other fellow Africans and the international community, first of all break the cycle predation-rebellion-repression. Secondly, the paper recommends that a solution be found to the country's endless problem of impunity whereby criminals responsible for some of the most horrendous crimes have never been prosecuted. The paper remarks that the challenge of bringing peace to Burundi is tall, but that the current mediator, former South African President Nelson Mandela, is probably the best but last hope Burundians can count on to enjoy a peaceful future

the 1st of November 1976, the Burundians had an opportunity for renewal of a state which had fallen deep into tribalism, and nepotism through a military coup.

THE ERA OF THE SECOND REPUBLIC: 1976-1987

There were two phases in the second republic. The first being from November 1976 to 1982 and then to 1987. During the first phase, there was the restoration of peace and social justice. Citizens were involved in public affairs through UPRONA and there was the resuscitation of affiliated movements. A remarkable occurrence during this period was also the return of some refugees. Accordingly[25] the problem began when authoritarianism set in during a conflict between the President and his Prime Minister over power sharing. This was amplified by an increase in the latent conflict between church and state.

---

25 Filip Reyntjens traces the root of the challenges of the second Republic in his background to the article titled 'Burundi: A Peace Transition after a Decade of War' when he states that 'The protracted conflict is structural in nature and caused by unequal distribution of economic resources and political power which in effect results in relative deprivation and differential access to life chances and choices, including education, subsistence, security, leadership and participation. The state of affairs has been sustained by often illegitimate repressive and discriminatory regimes which use political favor and rewards and manipulate cultural and ethnic differences or other identity factors to galvanize local support and consolidate their hold on power.

The issue of the President controlling both the executive and legislative arms of government with a judiciary which was far from independent created an unpalatable situation. In spite of the passing of the constitution in 1981, it was obvious that, the form of the constitution was not the reason for the exacerbation of the tension, but it was rather the practice.

The second phase of the second republic started with the promulgation of the 1981 constitution. Between 1981 and 1987, in spite of a decade free of massacres and killings, the level of frustration and ethnic exclusion was extremely visible. Therefore on the 3rd November 1987, there was yet another military coup led by Major Pierre Buyoya, which ushered in a new republic.

THE THIRD REPUBLIC (1987-1992)

This era was characterized by a serious search for solutions and the drive towards the democratization of the country. It culminated in the promulgation of the 1992 constitution. Unfortunately, this period also coincided with bloody events such as the cases of Ntega and Marangara in august 1988 and Cibitoke in 1991 where tensions between local authorities and the administration led to a civil war. In spite of the fact that, the government had been warned, government nonchalance and Hutu resistance to state authority further led to a deterioration of the situation.[26]

---

[26] The key characteristics of the Burundi civil war are described by Paul Collier and Nicholas Sambanis. They hold that each episode of violence in Burundi resurfaces the same unresolved issues of poor governance that are related to all the previous wars. Governance failure and all the unresolved prior conflicts explain the recurrence of violence. All wars except for the 1993 episode have been prompted by Hutu acts of rebellion in protest against

This ushered in a climate of civil disobedience and a perceptible refusal of the grassroots population to submit to State authority. This state of affairs could be partially attributed to the general wind of change blowing across the continent after the collapse of the Soviet Union, but to say the least it was encourage by Hutu extremists of the PALIPEHUTU party. It was clear that, the regime was ready for power sharing among the different components of the nation especially with its inclusion of some undeclared partisans of the Hutu in the government. But the agitations were preponderant and greatly weakened state authority[27].

THE FOURTH REPUBLIC 1993 -1996

This period saw the emergence of the first Hutu President Melchoir Ndadaye in the democratic elections of 1993. He was assassinated in October 1993 after only one hundred days in office. Since then, some 200,000 Burundians have perished in widespread, often intense ethnic violence between Hutu and Tutsi factions. Hundreds of thousands have been internally displaced or have become refugees in neighboring countries.

Burundi troops, seeking to secure their borders, briefly intervened in the conflict in the Democratic Republic

---

their perceived exclusion. In response the Bururi Tutsis have used the Tutsi dominated army to repress the rebels, resulting in even greater exclusion and deeper resentment which fuels the next episode of violence.

27 Reyntjens in his work 'Talking or fighting: Political evolution in Rwanda and Burundi, explores attempts at resolving the conflicts in both countries. He states that, although there have been numerous incidents and confrontations between the army and Hutu rebels in Burundi, a tendency towards the reduction in the intensity of the civil war has continued.

of the Congo in 1998.²⁸ A new transitional government, inaugurated on 1 November 2001, signed a power-sharing agreement with the largest rebel faction in December 2003 and set in place a provisional constitution in October 2004. In 2005 a majority Hutu government was elected. The new government led by President Pierre Nkurunziza signed a South African brokered peace treaty with the last rebel movement but still faces monumental challenges, clouding prospects for a sustainable peace.²⁹ Therefore the modernization of the present African society is faced with different obstacles. Amongst them is the Burundi situation, which is, for some, a mere ethnic problem, and to others an eminently political problem, whilst for others still, it is a socio-economic problem. Its several dimensions accord it a worthy example as a typical African conflict, which as contemporal as it is, will impact on attempts at the rebirth of Africa in the area of conflict resolution through the principles New Partnership for Africa's Development.

ORIGIN OF THE NEW PARTNERSHIP FOR AFRICAN DEVELOPMENT

It is well known that what is now the NEPAD is a product of Presidents Thabo Mbeki of South Africa and Abdoulaye Wade of Senegal who concurrently drafted two separate documents. These documents were the Millennium

---

28 Amnesty International confirms that in spite of that, there continued to be widespread massacres perpetrated against unarmed civilians by the Burundian army as well as armed opposition groups.
29 The 2005 elections which brought president Pierre Nkurunziza to power is well articulated by Arid Stenberg in his work Titled ' Burundi: Parliamentary elections, July 2005, University of Oslo.

Partnership for the African Recovery Programme (MAP)[30] and the OMEGA Plan respectively.

The MAP, although initially conceived by President Mbeki, was drafted with the support of the Presidents of Nigeria Olusegun Obasanjo and Algeria Abdulaziz Boutleflika. At a latter stage, there was the involvement of Senegal and Egypt in the process of merging the two documents. The MAP received its first endorsement at the Extraordinary OAU summit in March 2001 in Libya, which at the same time declared the establishment of the African Union to replace the OAU (Nabudere, 2002)[31].

---

30 This was an initiative of President Thabo Mbeki of South Africa to move the continent towards the path of development.

31 Prof Dani Nabudere critically examines the historical lapses inherent in the NEPAD program. He describes the program as a failure of African leaders to detach themselves from the colonial link. He laments "This rich African heritage, which has been despoiled, looted and plundered by the same "development partners" throughout the last five hundred years in which Africa has continued to be dominated and subordinated, instead of being the basis for Africa's own development and transformation, became for NEPAD leaders, just a cheap basis for yet" another begging" from the same exploiters under the illusion that they will support a "Marshall Plan" for Africa's redevelopment! Instead of building on this negative experience of European domination for self transformation, the leaders instead blame the state of Africa's predicament on the African "weak capitalist class." They are not even able to understand that the same exploiters fought against the emergence of an African capitalist class so that they could enrich themselves on Africa's resources. It is as if the history of colonization was momentarily being forgotten while African leaders were busy handing over Africa for a new colonization. No wonder that Tony Blair, capturing on this self-effacement by the NEPAD.

The MAP was right from the beginning a detailed project for the economic and social revival of Africa involving a constructive partnership between Africa and the developed world. On its part, the OMEGA Plan[32] of President WADE was presented to the France-African summit in January 2001 and formerly launched in June 2001 at the International Conference of Economists on the Omega Plan. The merging of the two documents gave birth to the New Africa Initiative (NIA)[33][34] later named the New Partnership for Africa's Development (NEPAD). In its preamble the NIA, stated that, the initiative was Africa's strategy for achieving sustainable development in the 21st Century.

In addition to that, it is important to note the document called 'Compact for African Recovery', which is the product of the Economic commission for Africa (ECA). In the process of articulating the Compact document and the related consultations, it also emerged that the development of the MAP and the Omega Plan was for the same purpose. Thus the Compact became an important document for cementing the two African documents of MAP and Omega plan.

According to the Compact document (2002), Africa must put into effect the requisite political reforms in order to attract the necessary investment for economic growth. Thus Compact engendered the propositions of MAP and Omega plan with good governance as the pivot from which enhanced partnerships with the donors was to be envisioned (Mbeki, 2002).[35] Therefore, NEPAD contends that,

---

32 This was a concurrent plan developed by Senegalese President Abdulaye Wade for the Development of the continent
33 New Africa initiative.
34
35 President Thabo Mbeki of South Africa indisputably crafted, publicized and worked hard to implement the New Partnership

the quality of governance is critical for poverty reduction because poor governance leads to the vicious circle of impoverishment, conflict and capital flight. On the other hand, it adds that 'in a globalizing economy, international capital seeks; secure rule governed countries for investment. This then sets the tone for what NEPAD stands for.

The program itself contains a vision, a perspective and the outlines of a plan for the rejuvenation of Africa. It clarifies the objectives and approach to development projects. The priority areas of NEPAD include:

---

for African Development. His explanation is lengthily quoted by Prof Nabudere when he states that "During the year 2000, we spent sometime meeting the political leadership of the developed world-the North. Accordingly, in May we met Prime Minister Blair and President Clinton in London and Washington D.C., respectively. We also met the then Governor George W. Bush in Austin, Texas. In June, we were part of the Berlin meeting on progressive governance. ... In the same month, we visited to participate in and addressed the meeting of Nordic Prime Ministers. Again in June, we addressed the meeting of the European Council held in Portugal, which was attended by all heads of government of the EU. In July, together with Presidents Obasanjo and Bouteflika, we met heads of state and governments of G7 in Tokyo, and had the opportunity to hold bilateral discussions with the Japanese Prime Minister, Yoshiro Mori. While in Tokyo, we also met the President of the World Bank, Jim Wolfensohn. Later, in Pretoria, we also held discussions with the Managing Director of the IMF, Horst Kohler. In September, we addressed the UN Millennium Summit and had an opportunity to meet Presidents Putin of Russia, among others. Before this, we had also interacted with the UN Secretary General, Kofi Annan, who committed the UN to co-operate with us as we worked on the MAP"

- Creating peace, security and stability, including democratic governance, without which it is impossible to engage in meaningful economic activity.

- Investment in Africa's people through a comprehensive human resource strategy.

- Harnessing and developing Africa's strategy and comparative advantages in the resource based sectors to lead the development strategy.

- The diversification of Africa's production and exports.

- Increasing investments in the information and communication technology sector, in order to bridge the digital divide;

- Developing financial mechanisms

It is worth noting that these laudable objectives are only achievable in an atmosphere of peace and stability, which is not the case in Africa. As the President of South Africa concedes: *'The renewal of our continent cannot take place in conditions of war and conflict'*.[36] There fore NEPAD envisages

---

36 President Mbeki worked hard to resolve conflicts and develop Africa in the spirit of NEPAD than any other African Leader. He explains the reasons for his action plan in this terms 'In effect this initiative, this new partnership-the NEPAD ... Acknowledges that the current approach to pursuing developing in Africa simply has not worked and that there's not enough to show for billions of dollars and decades of development assistance. I think also that the authors of the New African Initiative understood full well that they had to do something about it and something fast because tolerance both inside

both Africa wide and regional initiatives in conflict resolution and prevention as key to bringing about peace and security within the continent. As a matter of fact, achieving peace and security is a monumental task, which faces the NEPAD. This task is compounded by a lack of political will in most African countries that have adopted multipartyism albeit through pressure but have failed to establish credible democratic institutions and root out corruption.

Furthermore the problem of good governance, which is absent in most African countries, has resulted in conflicts. Coupled with these, issues of religion, ethnicity, poverty, disease and sometimes power struggle continue to dominate the reasons for conflicts in Africa.

One of these cancerous conflicts which are of monumental challenge to the NEPAD is the 'Burundi Conflict'.

NEPAD AND AFRICAN CONFLICTS

It is important to note that, the commitment to conflict resolution in Africa form part of a broader context of goals set by the NEPAD. Some of the goals and philosophies that

---

and outside Africa for this constant demand that we reward failure and continue to reinforce it without much reinforcing of success was a paradigm that simply had to change. So NEPAD offers a different kind of paradigm. It offers the prospect of concentrating engagement on those countries that are prepared to take political and economic decisions necessary to make this new plan work. And the prospect of reinforcing success in the Botswana's, the Namibia's, the South Africa's, the Mozambique's, the Mali's and Ghana's and Senegal's and lots more'

form part of the African renaissance have implications regarding what approach should be taken to promote peace on the continent.[37]

By the same token, the NEPAD proclaims that Africans must take their destiny into their own hands. When applied to the handling of conflicts, this aspect of NEPAD insinuates that Africa should resolve its own conflicts and that it should develop and strengthen its own conflict management strategies.[38] Therefore, it is apparent that, there is a strong commitment on the side of the NEPAD not only to the prevention of conflicts and the resolution of existing conflicts such as the Burundi conflict.

The Burundi conflict has become one of those conflicts whose resolution has eluded both the United Nations Organization and the Organization of African unity. The mediation attempts by eminent personalities such as

---

37 For a better understanding of philosophy of partnerships for development see in detail Susan Mathews in 'The Right to Development, Global Partnerships and Peer and Partnership Review, Tilburg University, Netherlands. But Professor Nabudere differs from the philosophy put forward by Mathews. He criticizes the relationship between NEPAD and the G8 group of countries. According to him 'The African people have once again been made objects and instead being subjects of their transformation. Indeed, it is becoming clear that it is through the G-8 "personal representatives", that the G-8 will dictate their recolonisation of the continent. NEPAD is already being used to exert pressures for African leaders to accept worse political conditionalities than those, which were imposed under Structural Adjustment Programmes.

38 Prof Nabudere's criticism of NEPAD's ability to inspire the building of African resolution strategies holds water if one looks at the history of African Leaders in terms of absence of political will in confronting Africa's problems.

former President of South Africa Nelson Mandela and former Deputy President of South African Jacob Zuma now President have not materialized in what Africans believed would be a sustainable solution to the conflict.[39]

Conflict resolution as an important element of the NEPAD, implementation committee has reaffirmed its conviction that peace and security are necessary preconditions for sustainable development. It therefore decided to set up a sub committee on peace and security to focus on conflict management, prevention and resolution within the context of the NEPAD process.[40]

It is against this backdrop that this examines the Burundi conflict as one of the conflicts in Africa, which will impact on the implementation of the New Partnership for Africa's development (NEPAD). Its multi-dimensional nature, the continued deterioration of the conflict despite efforts from both prominent individuals and international organization, the seemingly lack of political will of the leaders, the constant split of rebel groups to form new

---

39 Jacob Zuma was sacked by President Mbeki as Deputy President of South Africa and therefore mediator and replaced as mediator by the former South African Minister of Safety and Security Mr Charles Nqakula.

40 This move was to be supported by the economic commission for Africa document which was conceived for the development of the continent called the Compact document. It states 'According to the Compact document, "the quality of governance is critical for poverty reduction" because "poor governance leads to vicious circle of impoverishment, conflict, and capital flight." On the other hand, it adds: "in a globalizing economy international capital seeks secure, rule governed, countries" for investment. This then set the tone for what was to follow as the NEPAD was "panel- beaten" into a saleable investment document acceptable to the donor community.

groups and therefore put forward new demands and its spill over effect in the region have rendered peace in the region unsustainable and will affect the development of the region in particular and Africa as a whole which is the goal of the NEPAD.[41]

---

[41] The plan envisages both Africa-wide and regional initiatives. Conflict prevention and the eradication of infectious diseases are examples of programmes that will be continental in scope. Economic development initiatives, such as the development of agriculture and agro industries, economic infrastructure, the promotion of competitiveness and economic integration will be managed at regional or sub-regional levels

Chapter Two

SOURCES AND DYNAMICS OF AFRICAN CONFLICTS: A LITERATURE REVIEW

Arms on armor clashing bray'd horrible discord, and the madding wheels of brazen chariots rag'd: dire was the noise of conflict.

John Milton (1608 - 1674)

INTRODUCTION

This chapter discusses the different perspectives of the causes of conflicts in Africa and specifically the Burundi conflict as well as conflict resolution in Africa through institutions within the context NEPAD. For a start it is important to examine some of the definitions of conflict. According to Wall and Callister (1995)[42] conflict as something that exists when two or more groups make mutually exclusive claims to the same resources or positions, and war is a means of allocating the same resources to resolve conflict. More common is those who simply define conflict as a situation in which two or more human beings desire goals which they perceive as being obtainable by one or the other, but not both. Putting into place appropriate mechanisms for conflict management and resolution requires an understanding of the causes and nature of the conflicts.

Considering that most conflicts in Africa are protracted and ethnic in nature rather than purely strategic, theorists like Azar (1990:145)[43] stated that in order to manage and hopefully resolve these kinds of conflicts, a comprehensive approach that identifies and tackles their multiple causal factors is necessary. He used the term protracted social conflicts " to suggest the type of ongoing and seemingly irresolvable conflicts especially in the developing countries of Africa".

Ryan (1990)[44] defined protracted conflicts as "usually conflicts between ethnic groups which have been going on for some time,

---

42 The article by James Wall Jr and Ronda Robert Callister (1995) Conflict and it Management, examines the causes of conflict, its Core process and its effect. Journal of Management, Vol 21, No 3, 515 558 (1995)
43 Azar E (1990) The Management of Protracted Social conflict: Theory and Practice. Aldershot and Dartmouth
44 Op cit

and which may appear to be irresolvable to the other parties caught up in them. Protracted social conflicts have typical preconditions that play important roles in shaping their genesis and account for the conflicts to arise in societies characterized by multi communal compositions. According to Azar and Moon (1996:305)[45] these conflicts flourish in environments of high politico-economic under development and manifest themselves over communal identity needs. The roots of these are to be found at the interlocking nexus of under development, structural deprivation (political, economic social and psychological) and communal cleavages.

Moreover it is assumed that social, political and economic inequalities usually take the form of ethnic discrimination in kinds of society. In fact "structural victimization" is perceived to affect some groups disproportionately or to benefit others. It is this juncture of actual physical and psychological deprivation that structural victimization bursts into hostile and violent actions.

According African conflict analysts, the causes of conflicts in Africa are complex, and frequently so thoroughly intertwined with a range of social, economic and political factors that isolating individual variables can be extremely difficult. In the past, economic issues were often held to be at the root of violent conflict, and it was these issues that seemingly propelled communist-inspired insurgencies during the cold war. Similarly, the "hierarchy of needs" approach which was particularly fashionable in the 1970s pointed to economic issues being the paramount factors in achieving development and preventing conflict.[46]

---

45 Op cit
46 Jorge Arbache describes the role of social, economic and political factors in African conflicts 'Conflicts are more frequent during growth deceleration episodes than during normal times, whereas major conflicts are less frequent during growth acceleration and

Today it is generally understood that the causes of violent conflict are more complex. In general, there is some agreement that the root causes of conflict include poverty, economic dependence, weak states, ethnic discrimination, international rivalries, and foreign interventions. "Environmental security", including competition over diminishing resources, is also being pointed at. Sub-Saharan Africa and particularly Burundi is widely regarded as a development failure and large parts are embroiled in deadly conflict.[47] It is worth pointing out that, the causes of conflict in the developing world is corroborated by the fact that socio-economic factors do not on their own cause conflict, instead they interact with other issues like governance to intensify or prolong it.

On his the other hand it has been demonstrated that in countries where the interests of particular groups such as the military are threatened, violent responses often follow. He argues that, if improved civil and political rights are not accompanied by social and economic improvements, the military will surely intervene. He shows that externally imposed structural adjustment policies are likely to run

---

deceleration episodes than during normal times. The correlation coefficients suggest that economic collapses are associated with minor conflicts, and that major conflicts hamper chances of growth acceleration. Given the severity of the conflicts in Africa, it may have unprecedented regional governance and political consequences, and may eventually fuel governance reform reversals. Because poor governance and conflicts are likely to hold back growth recovery and vulnerable groups are exposed the most to them, these issues cannot be overlooked by any agenda seeking to protect Africa from the adverse impacts of economic crisis'.

47 For a comprehensive view of the causes of conflict in the third word, see the full article by Frerks GE & Douma P (1999) The Causes of Conflict in the third world, synthesis Report. Wageningen University Netherlands.

counter to the democratic impulse of the society, because they are seen as a source of economic hardship. Therefore, he argues that, the west is tacitly creating conditions for military intervention in African democracies by insisting on economic conditionality without providing resources to prop up the democratization process.

A question arises whether conflict in itself causes state collapse, Zartman,[48] responds to this question counter intuitively that, on the contrary, violence is the result of state collapse. He explains this in more details when they assert that 'poor performances of the states functions are broad causes of collapse'. Further more, state tyranny and state incapacity are two sides of the same coin, with both ultimately destroying the legitimacy and infrastructure of the state. As the inevitable power vacuum transpires, violence ensues, and vice versa.

Like Zartman, Rotberg[49] focuses on state institutions as the central element in the state collapse. In a description of the criteria for state collapse, he focuses upon the return of the state to the center of the political and social stage. Although many point to the over extension of the state as the root of collapse, he argues that, it was the militarization of politics and the failure of a state in performing its primary function of delivering the common good which results in the erosion of the states purpose and causes its ultimate disintegration. The militarization of Burundi politics and the failure to

---

48 To examine the relationship between conflict and state collapse see William Zartman (2000) on Traditional cures for modern conflict: African conflict medicine.
49 Prof Robert Rotberg's examination of the causes and consequences of state failure is legendary. Also see his article on False Unity in Zimbabwe (2009) Op Ed Boston Globe.

deliver public good across ethnic lines is a major factor in the resolution equation.

Anderson[50] offers one of the most original examinations of the consequences of violent conflict. Rather than simply focusing on the tragedy of war, she looks at winners and losers. "Warlords" for example enjoy economic gains from control of resources, which are the basis of patronage networks, and will thus seek to prolong the war.

Reno (2002)[51] shares this analysis, but also strongly argues that, collapsed states are an important component of the global economic system, as warlords, freed from the constraints of statehood, run their territories like very bloody business. Influenced by world systems theory, he argues that, these collapsed states are symbiotic from uncontrolled and monopolistic access to natural resources such as oil and germs.

Deng (1995)[52] too demonstrates that, the impacts of war or conflict are not evenly spread through out society. Her study of the cost of war is as original as it is startling. Burundi has fought most of its conflicts in its soil and thus represents an excellent case study of the costs of war to a victor that in large part escaped horrific suffering. She analyzed the

---

50 See Mary Anderson 'Humanitarian NGOs in Conflict Intervention' in managing global chaos, ed Chester Crocker, Fen Hampson and Pamela Aall (Washington DC, United States Institute for Peace Press 1996) pp 343 -354
51 William Reno, Armed Rebellion in Collapsed States. Also see John Heilbrunn, 'Paying the price of Failure: Reconstructing Failed and Collapsed States in Africa and Central Asia, Perspectives on Politics 2006, 4:1:135-150 Cambridge University Press.
52 Francis Deng's 'War of Visions: Conflict of Identity in the Sudan' describes the impact of war in the Sudan. For more on this area, also see below

direct and indirect costs to Burundi, including corruption, an inflated military, disgruntled public, an undermined economy, and cuts to education and health services.

Nordstrom (1995)[53] explores not only how violence deconstructs societies, but also how those caught in its grip employ tremendous creativity to survive against all odds. She writes

"For the vast majority of Burundians, war is about existing in a world of suddenly divested of lights. It is about a type of violence that spills out across the country and into the daily lives of people to undermine the world, as they know it. A violence that is severing people from their traditions and their futures severs them from their lives. It hits at the heart of perception and existence. And that is of course, the goal of terror warfare: to cripple political will by attempting to cripple all will, all sense."

Nordstrom[54] perceived that to better understand the process of dehumanization, in conflicts one must see what it means to be human within a particular cultural context. In Burundi, this is grounded in family and community life, parameters that disintegrated as the war progressed. She recognizes that, African cultures do not make sharp distinctions between self and the society; in this context, the destruction of the community in Burundi has been accompanied by psychological chaos.

This is countered by tremendous creativity in survival strategies. She documents several examples of Burundians

---

53 Carolyn Nordstrom's 'Shadows of War: Violence, Power, and International Profiteering in the Twenty First Century. California Series in Public Anthropology, 10.
54 Op Cit

reordering the world through the creation of symbols, society and culture. This is interesting especially if one looks at the ways in which traditional healers developed rituals to take the violence out of people and reintegrate them into society.

Another dimension of the Burundi equation is the hope and optimism portrayed by Abramson (1998)[55], in his documentary, where he sheds very little light on the conflict itself. His interview with former child soldiers and healers at a rehabilitation center reveals the suffering of children abducted by the FDD and the FNL and forced into sexual slavery and shows the center's efforts to rescue and reintegrate them into a society that has come to fear them.

According to Boshoff (2004)[56], the security situation in the parts of Burundi remained volatile and reports of robberies and attacks have increased in frequency. Approximately 20 000 residents have been displaced into the hills further east of the city of Bujumbura as a result of fighting between the government of Burundi soldiers and the rebels. The civilian community has been the victims of the conflict as they are the ones who suffer because of the insecurity in Burundi caused by the volatile situation of the conflict. The scarcity of food has caused people to resolve into committing crimes so that they could provide for themselves and their families.

---

[55] This documentary directed by Neil Abramson sheds light on the impact of conflict on women and girls in West and Central Africa and UNICEF response
[56] Details Henry Boshoff's report on the Security situation in Burundi can be found on the asap@iss.co.za titled Burundi: Situation Report 2004.

Martin (1992)[57] blames this on the high rate of arms proliferation which is highly uncontrollable. He states that these weapons end up in wrong hands and are used to commit crimes around Burundi because of the state of insecurity and the inability of the government to counteract against law breakers on his part Brogan (1998:3)[58] blames the 'Germans and the Belgians ignorance in not looking at the roots and culture of the Burundian people (Hutus and Tutsis) during colonialism and in the course of granting independence as well as preparing them for a post colonial state. This conflict has its root in the Burundi civic and ethnic complexion including the political dominance of one group over the other.

CONFLICTS IN AFRICA: AN OVERVIEW

According to Amoo (2003)[59], the memories of Africa's elite are either very short or the ambition for power is so overwhelming that, they are not fazed by the dire prospects of a Sierra Leone, Liberia, Somalia or Rwanda. Indeed in language and tactics, the continents elite threaten each other with such dire prospects. Their ambition is frighteningly simple: power or conflagration! Sadly, we seem to cherish our role as the perpetual objects of charitable concern. Our discussion of these challenges will lead us to examine related and crucial issues, such as the position, sources, dynamics and impact of conflicts and violence on the continent of Africa.

---

57 Susan Martin in her moving article 'Burundi: Out of sight, Out of mind' deals exhaustively on the refugee situation caused by the conflict.
58 Patrick Brogan, Rwanda and Burundi in World Conflicts, London, Bloomsberry.
59 Op Cit

The search for stability in the era of NEPAD, based on good governance and peer review, and strategies for healing and reconciliation as a foundation for civic peace within a democratic dispensation. Nathan (2001)[60] holds that, the end of the cold war saw the international community reveling in the cliché of "peace dividend". It never happened. The period between the cold war and the mid 1990's coincided with a world wide increase in the number of violent conflicts, invariably over ethnic and religious identity especially the destructive cauldron in the great lakes region of East Africa.

Africa may have been marginalized in almost every aspect of global socio-economic development; but sadly not in the arena of pathological brutality during conflicts. Conflicts in Africa have become synonymous with images of obscene brutality and despair. Wole Soyinka is right when he deplores that *"we can no longer speak of wars on the continent, only arenas of competitive atrocities".*

Amoo (2002)[61] goes further by noting that, of the chaotic mix of complex wars in West Africa, Sierra Leone in particular, represents one such arena of competitive atrocities, where the limbs of children, even of babies, have been brutally chopped off in the name of some struggle to bring the blessings of democracy to the people. This particular arena of atrocity has turned African culture and indeed, the essence of humanity on its head. As chillingly depicted in the Economist (1999),

"Children kill their parents, cannibal gangs roam the countryside; and chaos rules, barbarism flourishes...something primal has happened: both a political order and a moral order has collapsed"

---

60   Nathan Op Cit
61   Op Cit

In the horn of Africa, central Africa, West Africa and elsewhere in Africa, states and non state actors have been pursuing lethal agendas with brutality and abandon for over a decade. Well armed militias and rebels have proliferated, particularly in the great lakes region. These rebels and militias operate under various forms of collective identity, mostly ethnic and lay claim to distributive justice, inclusion or control of a state. Reason why the saying goes that,

"When the twentieth century began, the world was an assemblage of imperialistic, nationalistic states competing over rights and powers to rule people. As it draws to a close, it became an assemblage of peoples struggling over rights and power to rule states"[62]

---

62 Patrick Chabal descriptions the evolution of the nation state in Africa in his essay ' Power in Africa: An Essay in Political interpretation 'Power in Africa casts a fresh look at contemporary Black African politics. It reviews the merits and failings of existing interpretations of Africa's post-colonial society and proposes a new approach to its understanding. It has two main aims. First, to present a comparative conceptual framework which places Africa's politics within their appropriate historical context? Second, to offer an explanation of what is actually happening in Africa--beyond the clichés of a dark continent perennially in crisis. No one can deny that today Africa is in crisis. Wars, coups, famines and violence stalk the continent and fill the pages of our newspapers. Africa's debt is astronomical, economic development has virtually ceased, corruption is endemic and force seems the chief instrument of politics. Our understanding of that crisis, however, has often been hampered by the conceptual frameworks we have used to explain it. Power in Africa develops a political analysis which attempts to construct a plausible interpretation of Africa's contemporary predicament.

This has been the condition of the many regions of Africa at the end of the twentieth century. Currently the most persistent challenge to stability and development in Africa is the proliferation of civil wars and intra-state conflicts, often engulfing whole regions in a chain reaction of violence. Fate, with little help from Africa's elite, seems to be playing a cynical game with the lives and hopes of the long suffering masses. The euphoria and hope at independence in the 60's dissolved quickly in the face of venal regimes and the epidemic of military coups.

Hopes were raised again in the late 1980s: democracy or participatory, transparent, accountable governance appeared to be embraced at last on the continent. Cases abound such as in Burundi and Congo Brazzaville where successful elections were held in 1993.[63] Soon thereafter massacres and conflicts ensued and persist till today. Elections were on

---

63 For a comprehensive overview of elections and conflict in the great Lakes, see Timothy Sisk and Andrew Reynolds when they contend that 'Elections have emerged as one of the most important, and most contentious, features of political life on the African continent. In the first half of this decade, there were more than 20 national elections, serving largely as capstones of peace processes or transitions to democracies. The outcomes of these and more recent elections have been remarkably varied, and the relationship between elections and conflict management is widely debated throughout Africa and among international observers. Elections can either help reduce tensions by reconstituting legitimate government, or they can exacerbate them by further polarizing highly conflictual societies. This timely volume examines the relationship between elections, especially electoral systems, and conflict management in Africa, while also serving as an important reference for other regions. The book brings together for the first time the latest thinking on the many different roles elections can play in democratization and conflict management.

the agenda in the peace process in Rwanda before 1994, and then the genocide intervened and threw the whole of the Great Lakes region into an intractable turmoil.

Angola took one look at election results and reverted to old, dangerous habits. Elections were going to herald a new era in post- Barre Somalia. Nigeria annulled her own elections as a convenience to military rule till the dictator of the day conveniently dropped dead. Ghana returned to a democratic state in 1979 but not before the bloodiest interregnum in her history, when the most educated and fortunate of her youth clamored for more blood leading to a very short duration of her democracy.

While conflicts are not limited to Africa, the continent has experienced an especially large number of conflicts and complex emergencies. During the 1990s it was estimated that, conflict and violence claimed over three million lives in Africa with 160 million Africans living in countries in the throes of a civil war.

Historically, from 1989 to 1993, Africa averaged fifteen small and large armed active conflicts each year. This was second only to Asia and these figures did not include massacres in Burundi and the genocide in Rwanda in 1994. In 1995, 26 countries were impacted by complex emergencies worldwide, 12 were in Africa. 12 of the 18 great domestic slaughters between 1955 and 1994 were in sub Saharan Africa, with eight in the Greater Horn - Sudan, Somalia, Uganda, Rwanda and Burundi. In the DRC alone, more than 2.5 million people have died since the war began in 1998, many of them as result of malnutrition and preventable diseases. Shamefully though, 65% of the population are undernourished in one of the most naturally endowed places on earth[64].

Zartman (1999)[65] points out that, the increasing regionalization of conflicts in Africa poses additional challenges. Conflicts in the core problem areas in the great lakes region, for example, are primarily internal in nature but the fact is that the various domestic political conflicts have not remained self-contained, nor have they always been self generated. The stakes of conflicts in many regions of Africa may indeed be internal but their origins and ramifications have involved an entire region. Conflicts in Africa now tend to be more virulent and destructive, and less amenable to management because their implications lie within both the state and the region.

SOURCES AND DYNAMICS OF AFRICAN CONFLICTS

Even though intra state conflicts in particular are a global phenomenon, their specific dynamics need to be understood. Four structural conditions may be identified as the critical source of violent intra-state conflict in Africa. These are authoritarian and oppressive rule; the marginalization of minorities and occasionally majorities; socio-economic deprivation and inequity; and weak states that lack the institutional capacity to manage political and social conflict effectively. The potential for violence rises when these

---

64 Irobi EG (2005) confirms this state of affairs by stating that 'The conflicts in these countries are mostly between ethnic groups not between states. If not checked, ethnic conflicts are contagious and can spread quickly across borders like cancer cells. Ted Gurr and Monty Marshall have written that most African conflicts are caused by the combination of poverty and weak states and institutions.

65 Zartman (Op Cit)

conditions are present simultaneously mutually reinforced and exacerbated by other structural problems. In Africa, such problems include unstable civil-military relations and the proliferation of arms. To this list, can be added the criminal complicity of local and international actors in perpetuating civil wars for the purpose of controlling natural resources such as oil, diamonds and gold.

Much regrettably, we are confronted with a paradox whereby democratic practice is increasingly becoming a potential source of violent conflict in the fragile new democracies in Africa. It is common in several new democracies bitter, zero-sum (win or lose) struggles among the political elite with threats of destruction through impeachment; intemperate and inflammatory language in political discourse; deep polarization to the level of a house divided against itself; and lightly veiled threats and incitement to chaos. Indeed, in several of the new democracies in Africa, the political elite are hurling threats of damnation at one another and the state as if it were harmless confetti. All such developments confuse and frighten the populace while they can motivate the ambitious to unconstitutional misadventures.

POLITICS WITHOUT A SOCIAL COMPACT

According to Amoo (2003)[66] in several regions of the continent, the one vital issue that confronted countries at independence, and persists as a principal source of conflict, is the absence of a viable social compact to govern relations between the diverse groups within the state while recognizing and ensuring each group's need for identity, security and participation. In the absence of a social compact responsive to the socio-political realities of

---

66 Amoo (Cp Cit)

a nation state, there is no basis for national consensus about the means and ends of government; and raises doubts as to the legitimacy of the formal government in power.

Olukoshi (1999)[67] pursues this argument, by noting that, independence dispensations and new political systems were crafted without a social contract negotiated and acceptable to the mosaic of groups that constituted the new state. The independence dispensation was invariably an agreement between the nationalist leaders and the departing colonial power for the former to take over the successor state. No agreement was drawn up among the ruled or even the between the ruled and the rulers, but among the new rulers in the name of the ruled. In this sense, the independence constitutions were not only alien but, even more importantly, lacked legitimacy in the eyes of most of the ruled. Some of the ruled have perceived their identity, destiny and security to be under siege since then. Hence, we are confronted with the proliferation of violent conflicts in several regions of the continent.

Nathan (1999)[68] posits that, the earlier generation of the continents leadership adopted the mantra of 'blame tribalism' for all woes, prescribing and rationalizing authoritarianism, the one-party state, and coerced total integration as a panacea for conflicts and a development necessity. These leaders enjoyed an historical advantage of concurrence from cold war leaders and the intellectual formulations on modernization theories of the time. The brutal application of their African prescription failed to resolve or even mitigate conflicts. At best it created the type

---

[67] Olukoshi (Op cit)
[68] See Laurie Nathan in Mediation of African Conflicts: The gap between mandate and capacity.

of serenity one finds in a cemetery, whose whirlwind the continent began to reap beginning in the 1990's, when the Ghosts of yesteryear began to haunt the continent with vengeance.

Stanvenhagen (1990:26)[69] noted that some African conflicts are caused by disputes over resource sharing, arising from gross disparities in wealth among different groups within the same country and the consequent struggles for reform of the economic systems to ensure equitable distribution of economic power. In cases like Burundi ethnicity determines access to the resources of the country.

According to Shelton (1997)[70], Africa has been affected by a complex array of problems that have not been remedied for the last decades because of colonialism, socio-political problems that have evolved in the post-colonial war and ethnic differences and hatred. On the whole, violent conflicts in Africa have over the decades been pervasive, intense and protected, and have its origins related to race, land, labour and political rights that predominantly occurred as a result of European conquest and colonial domination over Hutus and Tutsis. When Belgium was prepared to grant Burundi independence, the minority Tutsi had been preferred over the majority Hutu. Subsequently conflict ensued between Hutus and Tutsis after independence.

Lemarchard[71] has noted that "behind the murders of political opponents, the systematic cleansing of urban and rural districts, the armed attacks on refugees and internally

---

69 Stavenhagen Rudolfo in 'Ethnic Conflict Management
70 Read complete article by Garth Shelton 'Preventive Diplomacy and Peace Keeping: Keys for Success. African security Review, Vol 6 No 5
71 Lemarchard (Op Cit)

displaced persons, and the ambushes of civilians, lies the conviction held by both Hutus and Tutsis that unless the other crimes are retaliated against the retribution, planned annihilation will inevitably follow". Miall [72] states that " in the context of the divide and rule policy, the colonial administration injected and imposed a caricatured, racist vision of Burundian society, accompanied by prejudices and clichés relating to morphological considerations designed to set the different components of Burundian population against one another on the basis of physical characteristics and character trait.

It also introduced identity cards which indicated ethnic origin, thus reinforcing ethnic awareness to the detriment of national awareness. This also enabled the colonizer to accord specific treatment to each ethnic group in accordance with its theories, thus manipulating the existing system to its advantage by resorting to discriminatory practices".

On the eve of independence, the colonizer sensing that its power is threatened, intensified divisive tactics and orchestrated socio-political struggles which lead to ethnic conflict and massive and deliberate killings, widespread violence and exclusions. In fact the current version of 'blame tribalism' as a political refuge looks for more sophisticated rationalizations.

Democracy is an alien and western construct unsuited to the culture, history, values and ethnic diversity of African states. This argument confuses the form of democracy, which must be adapted to local circumstances, with the essence of democracy which seeks to entrench rights and freedoms that are universal. Good governance should

---

72 Hugh Miall (Op Cit)

be nothing less than a democratic regime of government which is adapted to the realities, the values and the needs of the groups involved.[73]

Realistic constitutions and efficient governance structures, developed through negotiations, could have managed the group differences and divergences, the aspirations and the need for security. Rather the political elite in most African states have spent the last forty years on invalid definitions of problems and dysfunctional prescriptions. Often unity was decreed, organized, monopolized, enacted, and enforced as the primary strategy of conflict management.

Latter day revolutionaries all over the continent used the military to usurp the sovereign rights of the people in order

---

[73] Said Ajenumobi confirms the challenges of Democracy and Good governance in Africa when he states that' the demand for political participation and the involvement of the people in the choice of their leaders and decision-making which constitutes the critical hub of political democracy (Sorensen, 1993) is not a new phenomenon in Africa. The anti-colonial project was constructed and legitimized on this basis. As such, the current democratic effervescence in Africa could be regarded not as a process of "democratic birth", but to use the words of Richard Joseph (1990) is a process of "democratic renewal". Although the urge for good governance is implicit in this process of democratic renewal as we earlier noted, however, the conception and usage of the term "good governance" in recent times came from the World Bank. Given the virulent political resistance which greeted the implementation of the Structural Adjustment Programmes (SAPs) in Africa and the growing concern with their apparent failure by the World Bank, there was a slight shift in strategy by the Bank towards domesticating the policy and finding an appropriate institutional and political framework within which to situate it in the domestic economies of African countries. The emphasis therefore shifted to "good governance

to bring democracy and development. Africa got neither; rather conflicts among demand and demand bearing groups were exorcised, denied and suppressed[74]. The result has been horrendous.

In the new dispensation, the New Partnership for Africa's development will have to grapple with these conflicts. This scenario will in the course of time vindicate the new cream of African leaders with their new found determination to extricate Africa from conflicts, poverty and underdevelopment. One of these challenges is the Burundi conflict which has been raging for more than a decade and

---

[74] This is clearly stated in African Democracy forum in its editorial thus 'Democratic progress seems increasingly evident in Africa. Many long-time dictators and authoritarian regimes in Africa have been removed by break-through elections and with tireless efforts by democracy and human rights movements. More countries in Africa have begun holding elections on a regular basis. Women have started attaining leadership positions in government, political parties, the business sector, and in their communities throughout the region. The 2007 adoption of the African Union's Charter on Democracy, Elections and Governance symbolizes the increasing recognition by many African states of the importance of democratic values and practices. Despite this progress, however, many new democracies in the region have not lived up to the expectations of those who welcomed the advent of democratic governance. In some countries, elected leaders have simply failed to put sufficient democratic practices in place. In others, corruption continues to plague all levels of government. And new democracies have often failed to accommodate differing political points of view, ethnic and religious diversity, and territorial division. All of this represents serious failures in establishing sustainable democracy. Therefore, while many advances in democracy can be celebrated, it is clear that much hard work remains to be done on the practical level of making democracy work.

in which the major promoter of NEPAD- South Africa has been mediating for almost a decade.

NEPAD AND CONFLICT RESOLUTION

At the outset the NEPAD commits itself to conflict resolution. This is exemplified in a speech by President Mbeki (2002)[75] of South Africa in which he stressed that;

'a permanent solution of the self-serving promotion of ethnic, religious, racial and narrow nationalist interests that are responsible for many conflicts within and between countries in Africa'.

These characteristics form a good description of the Burundi conflict under discussion. This view is important, as supporters of the NEPAD are keen to see Africa being portrayed in the right light.

According to Oppelt (1999),

'Africans are sick and tired of being sold globally as the motherland of skulls and dismembered bodies'.

The view was echoed by South African deputy President Jacob Zuma (2002)[76], in a speech at the launch of the South African chapter of the African Renaissance in which he said

---

[75] Speech by President Thabo Mbeki during the Launch of the African Union, Durban South Africa.
[76] Jacob Zuma is now President of South Africa. He was Deputy President of South Africa from 1999 to 2005 when he was fired by President Mbeki.

'We will know that the African renaissance has been achieved once war and destruction are mere chapters in history rather than a daily reality for many Africans'.

The deputy president further identified the end of conflict as an essential ingredient for the realization of African renaissance. By the same token, the NEPAD document calls for the developed countries to materially support mechanisms for the processes of conflict resolution, prevention and management as well as peacekeeping initiatives.

In fact, there exist some major contradictions inherent in this request. It is important for advocates to clarify their position regarding the extent of involvement on the resolution of conflicts in Africa. This presents a major challenge to the NEPAD because conflicts such as that in Burundi bore benchmarks of western influence from cause to effect.

That notwithstanding, the challenge of conflict resolution by the NEPAD is exacerbated by what Ngubane (2003)[77] characterizes as a lack of political will on the part of the leaders in Burundi whose analyses of the conflict is tainted by a dichotomous and distorted vision.

Characteristically, the entire continent, has witnessed not less than 28 conflicts in sub Saharan Africa alone during the last two decades. Of these, 17 states in Sub Saharan Africa face conflicts whose roots stretch to the armed struggles of the pre-independence era. These conflicts need to be addressed through a radical revision

---

77 Ben Ngubane served as Chair of the NEPAD Ministerial Council for Science.

of the prevailing methods, which should concentrate on revisiting the root causes of the conflict. This should be followed by a progressive move towards an objective evaluation of the cultures, the dynamics and the actors concerned. This does not only require political will but vast financial resources (Azar, 1990)[78].

Through NEPAD Africa looks to the West for financial aid in order to resolve its conflicts. But the foreign aid has its own problems, which include insincerity, alienation of the recipient and reinforcement of the myopia surrounding how best to adopt it[79].

The path, which needs to be followed by Africa, will require the fusing of liberal democratic idealism with scientific realism, which emanates from a deep insight into African nationalism and refined by modernism. Without this, the impediment of conflicts will keep haunting Africa's drive towards renewal. All the commitments to peace by African leaders are usually not accompanied by discussions and actions. It is one thing to declare the end

---

78 Azar (Op cit)
79 Holt VK &Shanahan MK, in their report African Capacity-Building for Peace Operations state that 'African multinational organizations have reshaped themselves, setting out to organize more operational responses to conflict and post conflict situations. The AU has an ambitious agenda, deploying two peace operations since 2003 and considering additional missions. ECOWAS has retooled itself, sent out multiple peacekeeping forces, and moved forward to develop a sub regional standby force for future missions. Both organizations are working to build more capable headquarters staff and peacekeeping forces in concert with their member states, the international community, and the United Nations.

to conflict and quite another to devise a strategy for the eradication of war on the continent[80].

---

[80] Professor Ben O. Nwabueze's book, *Democratization* (Nwabueze 1993), is the best place to begin for a wide-ranging and textured examination of democratization in African societies. "Democratization is not only a concept, nor is it synonymous with multi-partyism," Nwabueze writes, "it is also concerned with certain conditions of things, conditions such as a virile civil society, a democratic society, a free society, a just society, equal treatment of all citizens by the state, an ordered, stable society , a society infused with the spirit of liberty, democracy, justice and equality." The stated thesis of Nwabueze's book is that democratization, "in the fullest sense of the term, requires that the society, the economy, politics, the constitution of the state, the electoral system and the practice of government be democratized

Chapter Three

THE BURUNDI PEACE PROCESS: AN EVALUATION

"After climbing a great hill, one only finds that there are many more hills to climb."

Nelson Mandela

The Burundi Peace talks began in 1995 with the Late Tanzanian President Julius Nyerere as the mediator. For a long while Nyerere tried to bring peace to the ethnic ridden Burundi yet the blood bath continued. The stature of Nyerere as one of Africa's most respected leader and as one of the pioneers of Africa nationalism did little to convince the warring Tutsis and Hutu about the irrationalism associated with conflict. Nyerere's inclination to socialist principles made him less popular with the Western countries under the cold war equation. Diplomatically they denounced his ideology and gave little or no support to his efforts to bring peace in that country.[81]

---

81 See the Joint Communique of the Fifth Regional Summit on the Burundi Conflict which states as follows 'The Regional Summit received a comprehensive report from the Facilitator of the Peace Process, Mwalimu Julius Nyerere on his efforts to facilitate a negotiated settlement to the conflict in Burundi including his recent endeavours to convene on 25th August, 1997 in Arusha, Tanzania, a meeting of all parties to the conflict. The Regional Summit expressed its regret that in spite of all these efforts, there has been no progress in the negotiation process. It expressed, in particular, its disappointment over the refusal of the Government of Burundi to take part in the first session of all party negotiations in Arusha. The Regional Summit recalled the previous decisions taken in Arusha I, II, III and IV Regional Summits. The Summit reaffirmed that the objective of the negotiations is to achieve a new dispensation based on the principles of democracy and security for all. In this respect, it is expected that the negotiating parties will come up with transitional mechanisms towards the attainment of this ultimate objective. The Regional Summit decided to maintain the existing sanctions and to ensure their scrupulous application. In this regard, the Summit decided to create a Special Secretariat comprising representatives of all the participating countries working under the Regional Sanctions Co-ordinating Committee,

After his death Former South African President Nelson Mandela took over as mediator. With the support of his successor, Thabo Mbeki and Ugandan President Museveni, Mandela immediately committed himself and South Africa to strive to bring peace to Burundi which had been ravaged by ethnic confrontations.

SOUTH AFRICA AND THE BURUNDI PEACE PROCESS

In 1994, Nelson Mandela became the first black President of South Africa, marking the end of white minority Rule. A year earlier, a civil war had broken out in Burundi between the Tutsi ruling minority and the Hutu majority. The conflict was fueled by other conflicts in neighboring Rwanda, Democratic Republic of the Congo (DRC) and Uganda. In 1999 President Nelson Mandela was invited to serve as mediator of the peace negotiations, which had been set in motion by the organization of African unity after the death of Nwalimu Julius Nyerere

This marked the beginning of South African involvement in the resolution of the Burundi conflict. Since then South Africa has not reneged from the process. A key thesis put forward for South African engagement in Burundi is that, South Africa's engagement in the Burundi peace process

---

to monitor compliance by all the participating countries. The Regional Summit was informed of Mwalimu Julius Nyerere's position to step aside as Facilitator of the Burundi Peace Process. The Summit was firmly of the view that the continued role of Mwalimu is crucial for a negotiated settlement of the conflict in Burundi. It reaffirmed its confidence in the Facilitator and urged him to continue.

forms part of a far larger jigsaw of peace it is trying to construct in central and eastern Africa[82].

The Mandela Mission

When Nelson Mandela took over the mediation of the Burundi conflict, he built on the foundations already laid down by Julius Nyerere. His mediation culminated in the signing of the Arusha Accord by the Tutsi dominated government and the Hutu dominated parties on August 2000. The Arusha Accord provided for a process of transition in which power would be shared between Tutsis and Hutus in a lead up to democratic elections[83].

---

82 South Africa has played a particularly prominent role. South African involvement in the Democratic Republic of Congo, and Burundi within the context of bringing African solutions to African problems represent an alternative strategy of conflict resolution, the same strategies are simply being promoted by new actors. South Africa has pursued several worthy initiatives in the DRC and Burundi, which have made a positive contribution to conflict resolution in those two countries. Nonetheless, the conceptual underpinnings of South African involvement, namely a reliance on liberal notions of peace and politics, have closely followed the prescriptions promoted by other international actors. The efforts made by South Africa, yet suggest that South Africa should broaden its definitions of peace, and look beyond liberal conceptions of success and failure in its interventions in the DRC and Burundi

83 On Monday 28 August 2000, 13 of the 19 parties involved in the talks signed the Arusha Peace and Reconciliation Agreement for Burundi. Eight African Heads of State and two Heads of Government, the President of the United States of America, Bill Clinton, three European Ministers, the Secretary General of the Organisation of African Unity (OAU), the Deputy Secretary General of the United Nations, and many other figures traveled to attend this solemn ceremony.

It was however an imperfect agreement and was been roundly criticized by some observers for failing to secure the adherence of important Hutu rebel movements which continued to wage war against the government. None the less, for good or ill, it provided a broad framework for continuing efforts to end the war. Although always complicated and perpetually subject to delays, these appear, at long last, in 2004, to be bearing fruit in terms of securing the agreement for outstanding rebels to join their fellow country men in constructing peace through a shared political process.[84] There are important considerations which seek to underscore the reasons for Mandela's leadership in forging a peace agreement between the conflicting parties in Burundi. The appropriateness of his mission is based on his own personal example in dealing with similar issues in the context of South Africa's transition to democracy. According to Bentley & Southall, the points of convergence[85] are;

---

84 Mandela delivered scathing criticisms of the Tutsi delegations and attributed their refusal to sign to the fact that they were not in touch with the realities of Burundi, as most lived in exile. "Some of these leaders... have never been imprisoned... never been in regroupment camps or refugee camps," Mandela said. "They have no real empathy with Burundi people." The criticism had a certain effect, however. A day after the historic event, two more parties signed on to the accord. On 12 September -just one day before the deadline for all parties who wanted to be involved in the transitional institutions to sign - all the remaining parties committed to signing the accord. Despite the fact that all 19 parties involved in the Arusha process are now on board, the accord has still met with a lot of criticism. Within the diplomatic community in particular, fears abound that the accord may not hold. Many liken the Burundi situation to that Rwanda in 1993 where an accord was disregarded and genocide soon followed. But regional leaders are adamant that the situation is different and that the worst will not happen.
85 The appointment of President Mandela as the facilitator after the death of Julius Nyerere was also based on the parallels between the Burundi conflict and the South African anti apartheid struggle.

Like Burundi, pre-1994 South Africa had a pre-democratic dispensation characterized by the rule of a minority shored up by the support of a powerful security apparatus that was able to operate with virtual immunity and that was regularly accused of systematically violating the human rights of political opponents. The Tutsis in this scenario are compared to the South African whites.

Both South Africa and Burundi are societies in which political tensions and mistrust are exacerbated by deep divisions along 'racial' or 'cultural' lines. South Africa, like Burundi, has issues of distribution and concentration of wealth along racial lines to confront, as well as the historic reservation of certain professions and educational advantages for the ruling minority.

Both South Africa and Burundi also face difficult questions of national unity and democratic participation. Finally, the appropriateness of amnesty for those who have misused positions of power and perpetrated acts of violence and terror for political ends is an issue which confronted post-1994 South Africa and which now faces Burundi. A truth and reconciliation commission, as was established in South Africa, was agreed upon for Burundi at Arusha, yet remains one of the most problematic aspects of the current transition.[86]

For one, the Burundi conflict was based on a minority Tutsi ethnic group governing the country while, in South Africa, it was a minority white race governing the country. Therefore the conflict was built around majority versus minority equation.

86 There is ample proof that truth commissions including the more ambitious truth and reconciliation commissions cannot by their nature deliver restorative justice because they most often move away from delivering criminal verdicts (retributive justice) toward truth seeking and reconciliation. These alternative

Mandela's Approach to Negotiation

From the beginning of his involvement, Mandela earned the reputation of being a tough, but fair negotiator. Contrary to Nyerere's intellectual approach to the negotiations, Mandela was more hands on and down to earth from the beginning.

He first and fore most harnessed the backing of the international community in order to provide the process with legitimacy, backing and resources. At his very first plenary meeting with the Burundian delegations in Arusha in 1999, he informed them that he had invited King Fahd of Saudi Arabia, President Chirac of France, President Obasanjo of Nigeria and Bill Clinton of the USA to attend the next plenary as well as President Mkapa of Tanzania and Museveni of Uganda (Chair of the regional summit), Salim Salim as Secretary General of the OAU.

He then proceeded by bringing an all inclusive strategy in which all the other rebel groups excluded from the talks during Nyerere's period as negotiator were included. The rebels' previous exclusion which was regarded as the weakest link in the negotiations thus resolved, and early meeting of the CNDD-FDD took place and by March 2000 he had secured the agreement in principle to enter into negotiations albeit with conditions, of not only the CNDD-

---

forms of justice mean that the work of truth commissions falls in Martha Minnows (1998) phrase, somewhere in the morally, politically, and emotionally fraught continuum between vengeance and forgiveness. The issue of the complexity and multiplicity of truth is a central one linking the problematic demands of justice and the hopes for reconciliation. It is also the arena in which the parties' competing versions of history and the politics of memory play themselves out.

FDD, but also the FNL. This earned him the respect and praise of President Buyoya who himself agreed to meet with the rebel leaders in South Africa. It is important to note that, in spite of the fact that, the talks did not culminate in the rebels signing the Arusha Accord[87] and the consequent prevarication led Mandela to continue the talks without them, the very fact that, he did make considerable efforts to include them was extremely important in enhancing the legitimacy of the subsequent Accord.

In a bid to avoid the perception of forcing a South African solution down the Burundian throat, his approach was, 'this is how we did it in South Africa, so draw your own conclusions and borrow what you think might be useful in your situation'. He was ready to analyze the conflict in ethnic terms there by compelling the Burundians to face the problem of ethnicity more honestly.

---

87 The purpose of the Burundi peace agreements was to respond to the root causes of the country's conflict, namely the political and economic exclusion of the larger part of the population and healing the rifts between the various groups. These causes were mainly addressed through instituting mechanisms for power sharing, as stipulated by the Arusha Agreement. Various challenges resulted in a delay in the implementation of certain aspects of the agreements, which have either not been fully implemented or are yet to be implemented. As for the effectiveness of the agreements, the newly-established institutions, though democratic, are still facing critical challenges. These include: political stabilization, security stabilization, reconciliation, fighting impunity, the lack of resources, and poverty. Nonetheless, broadly speaking, the relevant agreements have been implemented to a large extent, and have had a positive impact on the overall peace process in Burundi through attempting to address the root causes of the conflict.

This led to the idea of ethnic power sharing solutions such as the idea of a revolving Presidency between Tutsis and Hutus. In situation where he encountered difficulties he would hold bilateral with on the one hand, UPRONA and the military and on the other with FRODEBU. Unafraid to use blunt language (which initially came as a shock to delegates who were not used to such directness) Mandela would then stitch together an agreement which he would then present to the smaller parties as fait accompli.

Mandela finally emphasized the need for the peace process to be underpinned by the necessary financial assistance to address the immediate humanitarian and longer term development needs. This push for funds culminated in an international donor's conference in Paris in December 2000 following the signing of the agreement on 28 August 2000.

According to Van Eck, nobody else could have gotten away with what he managed to achieve in such a relatively short time. None the less Nelson Mandela played a critical role in pushing the peace process forward and his efforts have been complemented and sustained by South Africa's wider foreign policy in Africa.

THE ARUSHA ACCORD: THE ROLE OF THE SOUTH AFRICAN NATIONAL DEFENCE FORCE

By October 2001, Mandela successfully secured agreement on the deployment of South African troops as peacekeepers in Burundi, from a cautious President Mbeki and an initially reluctant General Siphiwe Nyanda (Commander-in-Chief of the SANDF), as well as backing for the venture from UN chief Kofi Annan. The initial task of the troops would be to protect returning politicians forced to exile by the war in the run up to the installation of the transitional government, which was to go ahead despite the absence of a ceasefire[88].

They were also expected to train a local Burundian force to take over from them. In spite of initial resistance to this deployment, Mandela managed to persuade the Defence Minister, President Buyoya and obtained official backing from a Security Council resolution of 29 October 2001. This did not impute a UN operation despite Un endorsement and therefore the operation was under the auspices of the AU with South Africa essentially assuming the sole responsibility with financial assistance from Belgium and the EU.

It is note worthy that, the mission of the SANDF later transformed from a protection force to a peace keeping force. This was due to the eventual merger with troops from Ethiopia and Mozambique to become the AU's African Mission in Burundi (AMIB), which would have the responsibility for, amongst other things, disarming rebels moving into the cantonments, feeding them and ensuring their security, assisting their demobilization and monitoring the peace. AMIB was also likely to become centrally involved in the difficult and dangerous task of integrating elements of the different militias into anew Burundian Defence Force.

---

88 These developments also coincided with the deployment of South African troops in Burundi in October and November 2001 with a view to protecting about 150 Burundian political leaders who returned from exile to participate in that country's power-sharing Transitional Government. In the early months of 2003, the number of South African troops deployed in the above-mentioned missions stood at about 900 SANDF servicemen and women.

Whilst the burden on the SANDF was, in theory, to be eased with the proper establishment of AMIB following the arrival of Ethiopian and Mozambican troops the SANDF is likely to be challenged as the mechanics of the peace process unfolds. Furthermore, the absence of major casualties in combat from the SANDF does not guarantee the inevitability especially in the highly unstable circumstances of Burundi which is under going what is an extremely contested transition.

It is something of a tribute to the SANDF's success in facing the daily challenges that, the South African troops came to feel appreciated by the Burundian public[89].

The Zuma Mission

After the signing of the Arusha Accord, President Mandela withdrew from active involvement in the Burundi peace process. The baton passed over to Former Deputy President of South Africa Mr Jacob Zuma. His major task was to use his mediation skills to cajole the Burundian politicians into implementing the Arusha agreement and to forge a lasting political settlement.

Drawing from his vast experience in mid wifing the political conflict between the ANC and the IFP in KwaZulu-Natal, he was to play a major in encouraging the transitional government and the different rebel factions to underwrite the Arusha process. Zuma displayed great patience in an arena where his role was often contested by regional governments and he cajoled, flattered, twisted and bullied

---

[89] Towards the end of 2002, the South African National Defense Force (SANDF) also clearly linked South Africa's military-strategic objectives to "promoting security", which was defined as "the provision of external deployment or support to enhance security in support of decisions by the executive".

unwilling politicians into taking the risks for peace.[90] Yet this was in a context of a transitional period during which the status of the Arusha Accord as a basis for viable political settlement was to be rudely and violently challenged.

As facilitator of the transition process, Zuma worked hard to organize direct negotiations between the Burundian government and the various rebel groups which refused to sign the Arusha Accord. With the help of Gabon, Tanzania and UN experts, the team produced a draft ceasefire agreement which was circulated to the different parties. But unfortunately the Burundian government rejected the draft as pre-maturely making inappropriate concessions to the rebels.[91] The draft agreement was preparatory after three weeks of talks held in Pretoria in August 2002 in which the government finally signed a ceasefire with the three rebel groups.

After further extensive negotiation by Zuma and his team, the transitional government signed a mediation Agreement with the CNDD-FDD on December 2002 which was intended to lead to the finalization of a detailed ceasefire

---

90 The South African contribution is well summed up by Devon Curtis: 'It was Mandela who brokered the agreement on transitional leadership, and South African Deputy President Zuma who negotiated an end to the deadlock over security sector reform and the ceasefires.

91 The signing of ceasefire agreements between Buyoya's government and many Hutu rebel groups did not end hostilities. Fighting persisted and many Hutus fled the country. In 2001, former South African president Nelson Mandela brokered the Arusha Accords, establishing a Tutsi-Hutu power-sharing government. Despite the agreement and a later ceasefire between the government and the main rebel group, the conflict still continued.

agreement and the conclusion of outstanding political and military issues. However, in mid December 2002 the CNDD-FDD refused an invitation to Pretoria to conclude the agreement. This led to loss of momentum as fighting resumed between the army and the CNDD-FDD.

Subsequently, heavy regional and international pressure for the CNDD-FDD to go to Pretoria led to the signing on 27 January 2003 between the government and the three rebel groups of an additional memorandum of understanding establishing a Joint Ceasefire Commission. Failure of the ceasefire to hold led to continuing violence and continuing negotiations.

As a result the CNDD-FDD suspended further negotiations citing continued hostilities, the blockage of humanitarian aid and lack of consultation on the intended troop deployment into Burundi. But a renegotiation at a two day regional summit under the auspices of Presidents Museveni and Mkapa of Uganda and Tanzania respectively and Deputy President Zuma, the belligerents recommitted themselves to implementing the ceasefire and ending ten years of war.[92]

---

92 Despite remaining unrest in the country, which called for assistance from the South African security forces, on November 1, 2001, Burundi established a fragile Transitional Government that shared power without a cease-fire. After the onslaught of the transitional government of Burundi (TGOB), there were several cease-fire agreements which are listed below. In October of 2003 the African Union established the African Union Mission in Burundi (AMIB), which was to set up the disarmament, demobilization and reintegration (DDR) process. This was replaced by the UN Mission in Burundi (ONUB) in June of 2004 and preceded the October 2004 commencement of the Arusha Agreement, which ended the period of the transitional government and called for national elections

At a moment when the Burundi transition was yet to be resolved, Deputy President Zuma- the facilitator of the Burundi peace process was sacked from the position of Deputy President of South Africa following a case of corruption involving his financial adviser. In the last ANC policy review conference he requested to be relieved from his position as deputy Head of the party. Although this was rejected, there were wider implications on his activity as the facilitator of the Burundi Peace Process[93].

Peace in Burundi: Looking Beyond Zuma

The mediation in the Burundi Conflict was started by men of unquestionable authority such as Julius Nyerere and after his death, Nelson Mandela. For the latter he exuded personal authority and charisma and at that time enjoyed the added aura of being an African President who had

---

93 The ANC-Cosatu-SACP 'tripartite alliance', got into an unsavory wrangle about the position of Jacob Zuma, deputy president of the ANC and dismissed deputy president of the country. Zuma's dismissal by Mbeki in June of 2005 led to acrimonious exchanges between the alliance partners and left a void in the Burundi peace process considering his role as mediator. The wrangle led Mbeki to ask for an internal (ANC) commission of inquiry to determine whether there is a conspiracy in government or ANC circles to get rid of Zuma prior to the 2007 ANC national conference, where a successor to Mbeki is to be elected. It is common knowledge that Zuma was implicated in the infamous Shabir Shaik trial regarding corruption in an armaments deal in 1999-2000. Zuma was due to stand trial in October of 2005 on corruption charges and possible income tax invasion. The fact that court proceedings against Zuma and possible appeals were still pending at the 2007 ANC national conference. This made the leadership succession crisis in the ANC all the more acute. However Zuma won the elections against Mbeki and became President of the country in 2008.

voluntarily stood down from office. On the contrary Zuma came in with less admirable credentials and his authority was contested by the regional leaders.[94] But as Deputy President of the powerful and influential South African state he gradually built some authority. His sacking as deputy President and subsequent arraignment to court on corruption charges left him with a bad reputation and less moral standing to continue as the mediator. This not withstanding the transition government was established and elections were held in 2005 after the establishment of an interim constitution.

Chapter Four

AFRICAN SOLUTIONS TO AFRICAN CONFLICTS: A HISTORICAL PERSPECTIVE

"For Africa to me... is more than a glamorous fact. It is a historical truth. No man can know where he is going unless he knows exactly where he has been and exactly how he arrived at his present place."

Maya Angelou

OAU AND CONFLICT RESOLUTION: FOUNDATIONAL PRINCIPLES: A HINDRANCE TO INTERVENTION

A bird's eye view of the charter of the OAU indicates that, it was inspired by the anti-colonial struggles of the 1950's which was devoted to the eradication of colonialism and the denunciation of abuse of Africa by non-Africans. The importance the charter placed on the safeguarding of sovereignty, territorial integrity, and independence was viewed as being essential in order to consolidate the African States' hard won independence and struggle against neo-colonialism in all its forms.[95]

According to Naomi et al (1999) the same anti-colonial sentiments that made the OAU such an effective political body, the drive for independence has become the albatross around the neck of African states, which suffocated their potential to fight against the abuse of human rights and led to conflicts in many parts of the continent.

This was so because the concept of sovereignty and independence implied non-interference in the internal affairs of member states. Therefore conflict resolution under the OAU relied on the emphasis by the organization for cooperation by member states for the peaceful settlement of disputes through negotiation, mediation and conciliation. As a result of this apparent shortcoming, it was discovered as early as 1979, when the committee on the review of the charter was established that, there was a need to amend the OAU charter in order to gear it more accurately for the challenges of a changing world.[96]

---

95 Organization of African Unity Charter 1963 Art III (3)
96 Despite numerous attempts since 1979, OAU Member States could not agree on amendments to the 1963 Charter Eventually an Extraordinary Summit of the OAU held in Sirté, Libya on 9

The foundational deficiency for conflict resolution has relegated the achievements of the OAU in that respect to a lame duck. It is important to point out that, part of the problem is as a result of the crisis of the composition of the Heads of state and Government wherein their accession to power is ranges from political assassination, civil war, coup d'etat and for a few through democratic elections and yet subscribe to the same charter which condemns such methods of accession to power.

Never the less, in a bid to evaluate the role of the Organization of African Unity in regional conflict resolution and dispute settlement, it is important to categorize the mammoth challenges that the organization faced in the area of conflict resolution during its four decades of existence.

Elias[97] classifies post colonial African conflicts in two categories, firstly, those that can be regarded as inherited as they emanate from the rights and obligations that devolved in the new states in the course of the application of state succession and secondly, those that are the results of post independence alignments mainly in the economic and technical spheres.

Furley (2003) on his part, categorizes post colonial conflicts into internal or intra state conflicts and inter-state conflicts. Inter - state conflicts are caused mainly by border disputes emanating from the legacy of colonialism. As for intra state conflicts, they seem to have a myriad of causes ranging

---

September 1999 (Sirté Declaration) called for the establishment of an African Union in conformity with the ultimate objectives of the OAU Charter and the provisions of the Abuja AEC Treaty giving rise to the Constitutive Act of the African Union in Lome, Togo on July 11 2000.

97 T.O Elias (ibid)

from ethnic animosity caused by the divide and rule tactics of the colonial regimes in Africa such as the Hutu-Tutsi conflicts in Rwanda and Burundi, to the historical differences between groups.

In evaluating the role of the OAU, the question arises as to how the OAU fared in the area of dispute settlement in Africa. This evaluation will be based on the categorization of African conflicts into seven types and analyzing the role of the OAU in those conflicts.[98] They include;

- Inter-state Conflicts arising from the colonial legacy of artificial borders

- Conflicts Emanating from colonial State succession

- Conflicts Involving Illegitimate and racist Regimes resulting from delayed decolonization

- Internal conflicts arising from secessionist Movements

- Internal conflicts Resulting from Challenges to the legitimacy of the Authority in Power

- Conflicts Involving External Intervention

Conflicts with strong Religious and Ethnic Underpinnings

---

98 For more on African conflicts please see Oliver Furley where he states that "**the 1990s have so far seen no diminution in the number of conflicts in Africa, and most forecasts predict a further increase...**"

The OAU and Border Conflicts

The OAU was confronted by two major border conflicts in this sphere. The first included the Algerian- Moroccan Border Conflict. This was the first test case on the capacity of the infant OAU to resolve conflicts. It was also a microcosm of other border conflicts which bedeviled the continent in that it illustrated the legacy of colonialism. The actual conflict erupted in July 1962, when Moroccan troops tried to occupy various areas in the disputed frontier zone after the referendum that ushered in Algeria's independence. Morocco claimed that, this area formed an integral part of its Kingdom. The Algerian government responded through military force[99].

The genesis of the problem could be traced much earlier to the beginning of French colonial rule in the Maghreb region. Morocco had existed as a distinct entity for more than a thousand years when the French conquered and occupied Algeria in 1930. To serve their own interest, the French avoided demarcating the boundary between Morocco and Algeria; Indeed France signed several treaties with Morocco without attempting to fix a boundary between the two entities.

This boundary issue and the Islamic concept of 'umma[100]', denoting a nation as a community of believers, as

---

99 Three factors contributed to the outbreak of this conflict: the absence of a precise delineation of the border between Algeria and Morocco, the discovery of important mineral resources in the disputed area, and the Moroccan irredentism fueled by the Greater ideology of the Istiqlal Party and Muhammad Allal al-Fassi.

100 The phrase *Ummah Wahida* in the Qur'an (the "One Community") refers to all of the Islamic world unified. The Quran says: "You [Muslims] are the best nation brought out

distinguished from the western concepts of a nation with an ascertainable territory encouraged Morocco to harbor irredentist ambitions. Thus when the French were forced by the Algerian war of independence to withdraw from Algeria in 1962, the seeds of conflict had been geminating for a long time.

During that war of liberation, Morocco decided to submit the border dispute to the United Nations Security council, while Algeria, favoring an African solution, took the dispute to the OAU. Even Morocco's allies in the Security Council persuaded it to seek an African solution first. Emperor Haile Selasie of Ethiopia and President Modibo Keita of Mali organized a meeting in Bamako to negotiate a ceasefire. Although the negotiated armistice was short-lived, the meeting produced the famous Bamako communiqué[101] which consisted of a five-point plan with the following goals;

The immediate end of hostilities

---

for Mankind, commanding what is righteous (Ma'ruf - lit. "recognized [as good]") and forbidding what is wrong (Munkar - lit. "unrecognized [as good]")...." On the other hand, in Arabic *Ummah* can also be used in the more Western sense of nation, for example: *Al-Umam Al-Muttahida*, the United Nations

101 Agreement reached at Bamako on 30 October 1963 by His Imperial Majesty Haile Selassie I, Emperor of Ethiopia, His Majesty Hassan II, King of Morocco, His Excellency Ahmed Ben Bella, President of the Republic of Algeria, His Excellency Modibo Keita, President of the Government of Mali and Head of State.

- The creating of a committee composed of Algeria, Moroccan, Ethiopian and Malian military officers which would define a demilitarized zone.

- The supervision of security and military neutrality in the demilitarized zone by Ethiopian and Malian observers;

- The request fro an extra ordinary meeting of the OAU council of ministers, for the purpose of creating a committee of arbitration to effect a definitive solution of the Algerian- Moroccan dispute and

- The cessation of hostile propaganda attack.

The requested extraordinary meeting of the OAU council of ministers was convened in Addis Ababa in November 1963 to discuss the conflict. In examining the arguments by both disputants, the council of ministers was in a quandary because both parties had equally strong but irreconcilable positions.

Characteristically, the council avoided dealing with the substantive issues raised by both parties and instead appointed an ad hoc committee composed of Ivory Coast, Ethiopia, Mali, Nigeria, Senegal, Sudan and Tanzania, designed to bring about a definitive solution to the dispute. The parties attended several of the commissions meetings, none of which appears to have decisively changed the status quo. However, the two governments announced on February 20, 1964, that they had signed an agreement and resumed diplomatic ties.

A series of negotiations culminated in a temporary treaty of cooperation and solidarity between the two countries. It would be erroneous to credit the end of this conflict solely to OAU efforts. There is no doubt that the ad hoc committee facilitated the negotiations that preceded the settlement. The final settlement of the conflict, however appears to have originated from the protagonists. Be that as it may, a conflict which exhibited signs of future catastrophe in a fragile continent had been successfully resolved.

The second border conflict within this realm was the Ethiopia-Somalia-Kenya border conflict[102]. This conflict

---

102 The conflict was caused Somalia's unwillingness to recognize political boundaries drawn by British, French, and Italian colonists, in conjunction with Ethiopia. Since independence, successive Somali governments had sought to reincorporate those Somalis living in Ethiopia, Kenya, and Djibouti into Greater Somalia. (Under the Siad Barre regime, the five-pointed star on the Somali flag represented the northern and southern regions of the republic and the "unredeemed territories" in Kenya's North Eastern Province, Ethiopia's Ogaden Province, and Djibouti.) In 1960-64, for example, guerrillas supported by the Somali government battled local security forces in Kenya and Ethiopia on behalf of Somalia's territorial claims. Then, in 1964, Ethiopian and Somali regular forces clashed. By late 1964, it had become obvious that the initial campaign to unify all Somalis had failed. Ethiopian forces had established superiority over the Somalis in the Ogaden, in part because of Ethiopia's ability to conduct air raids on Somali territory. In Kenya the government relied on assistance from British counterinsurgency experts to control Somali guerrillas in what was then the Northern Frontier District (NFD). In late 1964, Kenya's president Jomo Kenyatta and Ethiopia's emperor Haile Selassie signed a mutual defense agreement aimed at containing Somali aggression. The two countries renewed the pact in 1979 and again in 1989. These factors, in combination with the opposition of the Organization of African Unity to Somali aims and defense costs that amounted to 30 percent of the national budget in the mid-1980s, forced Mogadishu to reconsider its territorial ambitions.

which involved the plight of the Somalis is perhaps the best example of the arbitrary manner in which the European colonial powers went about dividing Africa. While it is impossible to give here a full account of the history of the establishment of the colonial state in the horn of Africa, suffice it to say that, the Somali people are spread across the borders of Ethiopia, Djibouti and Kenya.

The protests of this Somali balkanization went unheeded; despite consistent Somali objections, the British colonial authorities signed treaties with Ethiopia which transferred the Ogaden region occupied by Somalis to Ethiopia. In addition, when the British granted independence to Kenya in 1963, they ignored the wishes of the predominantly Somali inhabitants of the Northern Frontier District (NFD) of Kenya to be unified with Somalia.

Consequently, the irredentist stance taken by Somalia immediately after independence in 1960 was neither unexpected nor surprising. The western Somalia Liberation front, acting in close collaboration with the Somali government, called for self determination for Somalis in Kenya and Ethiopia. The determination of the Somali to gain autonomy, and their resentment of what they viewed as British betrayal, was registered in March 1963, When Somalia broke off diplomatic relations with Britain. Tensions reached their peak in 1964, when Somali nationals raided Ethiopian and Kenyan army and police posts. Earlier attempts by Somalia to introduce the dispute for discussion at the OAU inaugural conference met stiff opposition from Ethiopia and the matter was shelved[103].

---

103 Most OAU members were alienated by Somali irredentism and feared that if Somalia were successful in detaching the

However, due to the continued incitement of the Ethiopian Somali population, Ethiopia requested an extraordinary session of the council of ministers to discuss what Ethiopia considered aggression by Somalia. The Somali government also requested that the dispute be included on the agenda of the extraordinary session. Both disputants were asked to present their cases before the council of ministers when it met on February 12, 1964.

Regrettably the resolution passed by the council of ministers did not address the substance of the problem, but simply implored both sides to settle their differences amicably in accordance with the OAU charter. Unfortunately, the next extraordinary Council of Ministers meeting that took place in Lagos, Nigeria did not address the heart of the dispute either. While Somalia pointed out the importance of self determination for Somalis, the words of the Ethiopian delegate capture Africa's fears to revise its colonial boundaries on the basis of ethnicity,

'if we seek to redraw the map of Africa on the basis of so called tribal or racial or ethnic affinities, we will have cast ourselves adrift on a wild sea in a voyage that can only end in disaster'

Considering the above statement, both sides were urged to respect each others territorial integrity and to continue to respect the ceasefire. The diplomatic efforts of president

---

Somali-populated portions of Kenya and Ethiopia, the example might inspire their own restive minorities divided by frontiers imposed during the colonial period. In addition, in making its irredentist claims, the Somalis had challenged two of Africa's leading elder statesmen, President Jomo Kenyatta of Kenya and Emperor Haile Selassie of Ethiopia.

Kaunda of Zambia led to the signing of a memorandum of understanding to end tensions.

Unfortunately, a new government led by Siad Barre[104] took over power in Somalia. Although he did embark on expansionist policy, at the 21st meeting of the council of ministers in May 1973, Somalia unsuccessfully attempted to persuade the summit to formally agree that a dispute existed. That marked the beginning of a succession of events that culminated in a devastating war between Ethiopia and Somalia from 1977-78. Participation by the superpowers on both political divides escalated the war. Efforts by an OAU ad hoc committee to settle the conflict were ineffective. However, due to Somalia's denial of arms and facilities to local guerrillas, this conflict was scaled down considerably.

---

104 Mohamed Siad Barre (b. 1919 – January 2, 1995) was the military dictator and President of Somalia from 1969 to 1991. At the time of independence in 1960, Somalia was touted in the West as the model of a rural democracy in Africa. However, clanism and extended family loyalties and conflicts were societal problems the civilian government failed to eradicate and eventually succumbed to itself. The new Barre-led military junta that came to power after the ensuing coup d' etat said it would adapt scientific socialism to the needs of Somalia. It drew heavily from the traditions of China. Volunteer labor harvested and planted crops, and built roads and hospitals. Almost all industry, banks, and businesses were nationalized. Cooperative farms were promoted. The government forbade clanism and stressed loyalty to the central authorities. An entirely new writing script for the Somali language was introduced. To spread the new language and the methods and message of the revolution, secondary schools were closed in 1974 and 25,000 students from fourteen to sixteen years of age were sent to rural areas to educate their nomadic relatives.

OAU and Colonial Secession Conflict

A typical example of such a conflict has been the Western Sahara Conflict. No other dispute has shaken the very foundations of the OAU like the protracted Western Sahara conflict. Following the admission of the Sahara Arab Democratic Republic (SADR) to the OAU, a Moroccan instigated boy cot brought the activities of the OAU to a halt when the nineteenth summit conference, which was held in Tripoli Libya, failed to take place due to the lack of a quorum.

To put this conflict in perspective, the area called Western Sahara was acquired by Spain in 1884 and 1934 against the protestation of ownership by the Kingdom of Morocco. Interestingly, a third country Mauritania also claims sovereignty over this territory. After prompting by the United Nations, Spain agreed to carry out a referendum for the people to decide whether they wanted to join Morocco, Mauritania or to be under the protection of Spain. Spain's attempts to carry out the demands of the referendum from the United Nations General Assembly in 1965 and the OAU in 1972, were however preempted when largely due to Morocco's and Mauritania's diplomatic efforts the General Assembly adopted a resolution seeking an advisory opinion from the International Court of Justice[105]

---

105 UN General Assembly Resolution 3292 requested that the International Court give an advisory opinion on the following questions

I. Was Western Sahara (Río de Oro and Sakiet El Hamra) at the time of colonization by Spain a territory belonging to no one (terra nullius)?

on the status of the Western Sahara before Spanish colonialism and the legal ties between the territory in question and the Kingdom of Morocco and Mauritania.

The International court of justice found that although certain ties of allegiance existed between some tribes in the Western Sahara and the Kingdom of Morocco and also that, some legal ties existed between Mauritania and the territory, there was no sufficient evidence to prevent the

---

And, should the majority opinion be "no", the following would be addressed:

:II. What were the legal ties between this territory and the Kingdom of Morocco and the Mauritanian entity?

On October 15, a UN visiting mission sent by the General Assembly to tour the region and investigate the political situation published its findings, showing that the Sahrawi population were "overwhelmingly" in favor of independence from both Spain and Morocco/Mauritania. These findings were submitted to the Court, who published their opinion the next day. For the former question, the Court decided by a vote of 13 to three that the court could make a decision on the matter, and unanimously voted that at the time of colonization (defined as November 28, 1884), the territory was not *terra nullius* (that is, the territory, did belong to someone).For the latter question, the Court decided by a vote of 14 to two that it would decide. It was of the opinion, by 14 votes to two, that there were legal ties of allegiance between this territory and the Kingdom of Morocco. Furthermore, it was of opinion, by 15 votes to one, that there were legal ties between this territory and the "Mauritanian entity". However, the Court defined the nature of these legal ties in the penultimate paragraph of its opinion, and declared that neither legal tie implied sovereignty or rightful ownership over the territory. These legal ties also did not apply to "self-determination through the free and genuine expression of the will of the peoples of the Territory."(ICJ Reports (1975) p.68, para. 162)

General Assembly from implementing 'the principle of self determination through the free and genuine expression of the will of the people of the territory'.

This apparent rejection by the ICJ of any claims by both Morocco and Mauritania did not hinder the invasion of the territory by Moroccan forces. This forced the Spanish to cede the territory to Morocco and Mauritania. Another regional power Algeria which was the prime supporter of the Polisario front fighting Spanish occupation was outraged by this turn of events and therefore the Polisario front shifted its attacks against Morocco and Mauritania, of which Mauritania was quick to withdraw owing to problems at home.

Eventually, a council of ministers summit was held in Khartoum, Sudan after two attempts in 1976 and 1979 failed due to a lack of a quorum. This summit established an ad hoc committee consisting of Mali. Guinea, Nigeria, Ivory Coast and Tanzania to look into the conflict. At the 1979 Monrovia conference, the OAU passed a resolution calling for a ceasefire and the holding of a free referendum for the inhabitants of the Western Sahara in order to exercise their right of self determination. Meanwhile the UNO recognized the Polisario as the legitimate representative of the Saharawi people.

At the Nairobi summit in 1981, the ad hoc committee proposed a three point plan for the resolution of the conflict with the following provisions:

- Ceasefire and direct negotiations between the parties

- Establishment of a multinational peacekeeping force and an interim administration

- A referendum organized by the OAU and the United Nations.

This plan never materialized because the Implementation committee appointed to succeed the ad hoc committee failed to bring the parties to the negotiating table. As a result, in 1982, events took a new turn when in a council of Ministers meeting, the OAU Secretary-General, Edem Kodjo[106], admitted the SADR to the OAU's membership. This decision created a crisis which led to the cancellation of the Tripoli meeting and the construction by Morocco of a wall called the useful triangle while the POLISARIO also launched its most ambitious attack called the Maghreb offensive on Morocco which made the wall ineffective. At this point the arena of efforts to resolve this conflict shifted from the OAU to the United Nations.

Presently, this is one of the conflicts in Africa that cries out for resolution. The Security Council needs to develop

---

106 Édouard Kodjovi Kodjo, better known as Edem Kodjo (born May 23, 1938), is a Togolese politician and diplomat. He was Secretary-General of the Organization of African Unity from 1978 to 1983; later, in Togo, he was a prominent opposition leader after the introduction of multiparty politics. He served as Prime Minister from 1994 to 1996 and again from 2005 to 2006. Kodjo is currently the President of the Patriotic Pan-African Convergence (CPP) As Secretary General of the OAU he controversially allowed the Sahrawi Arab Democratic Republic (SADR) to be seated as a member of the OAU on February 28, 1982, over the objections of Morocco and various other African countries that supported the Moroccan position. According to Kodjo, this decision was based simply on the fact that a majority of OAU member states had recognized the SADR, but it led to a serious crisis within the OAU, with a number of member states boycotting OAU meetings. Senegalese President Abdou Diouf accused Kodjo of "mischief-making"

a formula to determine the inhabitants of Western Sahara so that the long overdue referendum can take place and the Saharawi people can live in peace again.

The OAU and Racist Regimes

The Namibian and Zimbabwean struggles for independence and South Africa's struggle against the apartheid regime fall squarely within this category. Unlike the other conflicts where the OAU had to act as a neutral arbiter, in these conflicts, the OAU directly challenged the legitimacy of these regimes. The OAU viewed these regimes as unacceptable obnoxious vestiges of white supremacy from the colonial era. The OAU's initiatives to liquidate these illegal regimes were double pronged: diplomatic war within the United Nations and financial and military support to the African Liberation movements within these states[107].

---

107 See OAU resolution on Decolonization CM/Res. 241/Rev.1 (XVII) 1971. Also instructive is Y Alimov in OAU: Ten year of Existence in which he indicates that 'The following main lines may be noted in the activities of the OAU: struggle for total eradication of colonialism on the continent; beating back the moves by neocolonialism; peaceful settlement of disputes and conflicts; development of all-round cooperation between African states; strengthening of independent Africa's international positions; struggle for peace and international security. In the past decade, the OAU has employed various methods to accelerate the liberation of the colonial peoples on the continent. Working for the speediest elimination of the survivals of colonialism, the OAU has linked this issue not only with the liberation of over 30 million Africans from colonial slavery, but also with ensuring the security of the countries already) liberated. African leaders believe that the security of their countries will be threatened as long as racist-colonial regimes exist. The OAU has given consistent political support and material assistance to national liberation organizations.

In Southern Rhodesia (now Zimbabwe), the 1964 Unilateral Declaration of Independence of the minority settler community after the dissolution of the Federation of Rhodesia and Nyasaland in 1963, hit the soft under belly of the OAU. At the Second Ordinary session of the Heads of State and Government meeting in Accra, Ghana, in October 1965 resolution was passed which recommended convening a broad-based constitutional conference that would 'obtain universal adult suffrage, free elections and independence'.

The determination of the Ian Smith white minority government to test the resolve of the council of Ministers to give the United Kingdom an ultimatum which stated that; 'if the UK does not crush the minority rebellion and restore law and order and thereby prepare the way for majority by December 1965, the member states of the OAU shall sever diplomatic relations on that date with the United Kingdom. This ultimatum was ignored by both the United Kingdom and the government of Ian Smith.

Ultimately only nine states implemented the council of minister's resolution. Indeed it is difficult to pin point the OAU's contribution to final resolution of the Southern Rhodesia conflict. However, the OAU's rhetoric and diplomatic pressure contributed to the isolation and pariah status of the Ian Smith government acquired. The regime eventually realized that, the war against the African guerilla forces that had infiltrated the rural areas of the country was unwinnable.

THE OAU AND CONFLICTS OF SECESSION

The OAU's blatant refusal through its charter to revise African borders has been a hindrance to the attempt by a good number of secessionist movements in Africa to succeed. The rationale behind this fear to revise Africa's borders is based on the genuine fear of throwing the continent into a spiral of instability. So far only Eritrea has successfully seceded from Ethiopia.

One of the first secessionist attempts which faced the OAU was the Congo crisis. This crisis was sparked off by the Belgian sponsored secessionist attempt of the mineral rich Katanga province after the Congo gained independence from Belgium with a left leaning Prime Minister –Patrice Lumumba[108]. The assassination of Prime Minister Lumumba with the connivance of Belgium, the United States and other mercenaries and the subsequent installation of the secessionist Moise Tshombe[109] shocked the OAU. The regroupment of forces loyal to assassinated Lumumba under the banner of the Congolese national Liberation committee (CNL) and the launch of an attack made matters worse.

---

[108] Patrice Émery Lumumba (2 July 1925–11 February 1961) was an African anti-colonial leader and the first legally elected Prime Minister of the Republic of the Congo after he helped win its independence from Belgium in June 1960. Only ten weeks later, Lumumba's government was deposed in a coup during the Congo Crisis He was a subsequently imprisoned and murdered in circumstance suggesting the support and complicity of the governments of Belgium and the United States

[109] He was the son of a successful Congolese businessman and was born in Musumba Congo. In the 1950s, he took over a chain of stores in Katanga Province and became involved in politics, founding the CONAKAT party with Godefroid Munongo which ran under a banner of an independent, federal Congo. In the general elections of 1960, CONAKAT won control of the Katanga provincial legislature. That same year, the Congo became an independent republic, and in the resulting strife, Tshombe and CONAKAT declared Katanga's secession from the rest of the Congo

In 1964, OAU member states threatened to walk out of a Non-aligned summit in Cairo should Tshombe be allowed to attend as he was deemed a traitor with Lumumba's blood on his hands. The conflagration which later ensued as a result of super power involvement with local protagonists as pawns created an extremely dangerous situation.

At an extraordinary session of the assembly of Heads of State and government, an ad hoc committee was appointed under the chairmanship of President Kenyatta[110] of Kenya with a mandate to reconcile the warring parties and normalize relations between the Congo and its neighbors. The OAU also called for the withdrawal of foreign mercenaries and the formation of a caretaker government as well as the holding of elections.

These calls by the OAU characteristically went unheeded and initiatives by the Kenyatta committee to reconcile the factions similarly failed. However, the eventual defeat of the CNL forces led to the emergence of Tshombe as the de facto leader. Thus the OAU displayed its impotence in yet another regional conflict. However the active involvement of extra-regional forces in this conflict absolves the OAU from any true indictment. After all, the endorsement of the OAU's call for the withdrawal of mercenaries by the United Nations Security Council went unheeded and even the United Nations peacekeeping forces utterly failed to maintain peace.

---

110 On June 1, 1963, Mzee Kenyatta became the first Prime Minister of self-governing Kenya. At midnight on December 12, 1963, at Uhuru Stadium, amid world leaders and multitudes of people, the Kenya flag was unfurled. A new nation was born. A year later on December 12, 1964, Kenya became a Republic within the Commonwealth, with Kenyatta, as the President.

Another secessionist attempt surfaced in Africa's most populous nation- Nigeria in 1967. This conflict signified a microcosm of the internal contradictions within the African nation state. The origin of the conflict can be traced to tribal inclination of Nigeria's political parties. A case in point is the fact that, the National council of Nigerian citizens (NCNC) was dominated by the Igbo of the East, the Northern People's Congress (NPC) by the Hausa people of Northern Nigeria and the action Group (AG) by the Yorubas of the West.[111]

In January 1966, a military coup engineered by Igbo Officers led to the assassination of the NPC Prime Minister Tafawa Balewa and an accession to power of an Igbo general Aguiyi Ironsi[112]. A counter coup in July led to Ironsi's assassination and the catapulting to power of Yakubu Gowon[113] from the North. This retaliation was unacceptable to the Igbo and especially the Military Governor of Eastern Nigeria Colonel

---

111 The first post-independence National Government of Nigeria was formed by a conservative alliance of the NCNC and the NPC, with Sir Abubakar Tafawa Balewa, a Hausa, becoming Nigeria's first Prime Minister while the eastern Igbo dominated NCNC leader Dr Nnamdo Azikiwe became President. The Yoruba-dominated AG became the opposition under its charismatic leader Chief Obafemi Awolowo.
112 Major General Johnson Aguiyi-Ironsi served as the Head of State of Nigeria from January 16, 1966 until he was overthrown and murdered on July 29, 1966 by rebels
113 General Yakubu Gowon (born 19 October 1934) was the head of state (Head of the Federal Military Government) of Nigeria from 1966 to 1975. He took power after one military coup d'etat and was overthrown in another. During his rule, the Nigerian government successfully prevented Biafran secession during the 1966–1970 Nigerian Civil War

Ojukwu[114]. The latter later declared the Eastern region an independent State of Biafra. A bloody civil war ensued which lasted for three years.

In this conflict, the OAU's capacity to resolve this conflict was inhibited by the charter's principle of non interference in the internal affairs of a State. Although the OAU was aware of its impotence in the face of the conflict, it did not want to appear as if it was not doing anything while a devastating civil war raged in Africa. The crisis was discussed at the assembly of heads of State and government[115]t in Kinshasa, Zaire in 1967.

The resolution passed at the end of the conference recognized that the conflict was Nigeria's internal affair, but placed the 'services of the assembly at the disposal of the federal Government of Nigeria' The conference also decided to send a consultative mission to the head of Nigeria's federal government to 'assure him of the Assembly's desire for the territorial integrity, unity and Peace of Nigeria'.

It is strange why the Head of Nigeria's government will need such an assurance from the OAU's assembly. The Assembly was not fighting to dismember, nor was it violating the territorial integrity of Nigeria. Whatever logic lay behind the assembly's confused response to the Nigerian civil war, several issues are apparent. The tension between the desire to resolve the conflict and to remain faithful to the OAU charter explains the confused state of mind and

---

114 General Chukwuemeka Odumegwu born November 4, 1933) was the leader of the secessionist state of Biafra in Nigeria (1967–1970), during the Nigerian Civil War, and previously Military Governor of the Eastern Region of Nigeria
115 The Assembly of Head of State and Government was an Art VII institution created specifically under article VII (1)

the unmitigated diplomatic blunder. On the contrary, by sending a mission the OAU had done what it had pledged not to do – interfere in the internal affairs of a state.

OAU and Conflicts resulting From Challenges to legitimacy of Power.

Most of the previously examined cases also encompass challenges to the legitimacy of power. To revisit the Congo crisis, Moise Tshombe's[116] ascension to power was considered illegitimate. This was confirmed by the OAU member states of the non aligned movement. Therefore the CNL forces loyal to assassinated Prime Minister Lumumba mobilized against the Tshombe's government, causing the civil war. In the course of time, Mobutu's ascension to power in a military coup which saw the liquidation of his opponents and the establishment of a Kleptocracy[117] which looted and plundered the resources of the Congo, was countered by rebel forces led by Laurent Kabila. Mobutu later fled to morocco where he died of Prostate cancer.

In such conflicts, the OAU found it self powerless and had to cede the resolution of the conflicts to the United Nations.

The OAU and Conflicts Involving External Intervention.

Intra- state conflicts in Africa have witnessed the involvement of external forces either from within or without Africa. Since independence these accusations have been rife. In fact it was Ghana's alleged involvement in a coup in

---

116 Moise Tsombe IBID
117 Government that extends the personal wealth and political power of government officials and the ruling class, via the embezzlement of state funds at the expense of the wider population, sometimes without even the pretense of honest service

Togo that led to the incorporation of Article III, clause five into the OAU charter. Probably, the most famous unilateral intervention by an African state into another was the 1979 Tanzanian intervention and ousting of Dictator Idi Amin[118] in Uganda. The OAU, through its Liberation committee indirectly gave aid to rebel groups who were fighting the last colonial regimes in Rhodesia, Namibia, and South Africa.

A more recent unilateral involvement by African states in an internal conflict was the military support by Uganda, Angola, Burundi, and Rwanda of the rebels of Laurent Kabila[119] in Zaire, which helped him gain the presidency. Mobutu's attempts to maintain power did not change the situation this time; he was eventually ousted by Kabila's forces.

The cold war manifested itself in Africa through superpower intervention in African internal conflicts such as the Russian and Chinese involvement in the Congo crisis in support of

---

118 Idi Amin Dada was the military dictator and President of Uganda from 1971 to 1979. Amin joined the British colonial regiment, the King's African Rifles, in 1946, and eventually held the rank of Major General and Commander of the Ugandan Army. He took power in a military coup of January 1971, deposing Milton Obote. Amin's rule was characterized by human rights abuses, political repression, ethnic persecution, extrajudicial killings, nepotism, corruption and gross economic mismanagement. The number of people killed as a result of his regime is unknown; estimates from international observers and human rights groups range from 100,000 to 500,000.
119 Laurent-Désiré Kabila was President of the Democratic Republic of the Congo from May 1997, when he overthrew longtime dictator Mobutu Sese Seko, until his own assassination in January 2001. He was succeeded by his son Joseph Kabila.

the CNL and United States and Belgian intervention on the side of the government of Moise Tshombe[120].

The OAU and Religious and Ethnic Conflicts

The Hutu-Tutsi conflict within Rwanda and Burundi are examples of ethnic conflicts exacerbated by the colonial divide and rule policy of playing ethnic groups against each other. Another similar conflict but with strong religious undercurrents is the Sudanese civil war.

In the Sudan, which is a country made up of a predominantly black Christian South and controlled by a Muslim Arabic north. Attempts by the Muslim north to implement Islamic policies like the sharia law and imposing them on the southerners led to a southern insurrection for autonomy from the North.

The OAU's response to this seemingly Africa's longest civil war has been to work with the Intergovernmental Authority on Development, a sub regional body in the Horn of Africa in mediating an end to the conflict. The OAU has avoided direct involvement for fear of precipitating a fallout between the Islamic states of North Africa and sub-Saharan states that could destroy the unity within the continental body.

Summing –up the OAU's Performance in African Conflicts

The performance of the OAU in conflict resolution can be characterized by modest success in a few cases and dismal failures in most others. It is important to identify in roads

---

120 Moise Tshombe (Ibid)

that the OAU has made and the challenges it faced in its endeavors to establish a lasting peace in Africa. Internal conflicts presented the most daunting challenges to the OAU for two reasons. First, where outside powers have been involved, the capacity of the OAU to deal with them was substantially eroded. This is explained by the fact that, extraterritorial forces, as part of the United Nations, had more resources and authority than the OAU. For instance, superpower interventions in the Congo crisis were so pervasive and overwhelming that the OAU efforts to nullify them proved fruitless.

Secondly, the OAU lacked power to intervene in internal conflicts. Article III,[121] clause two of the OAU Charter explicitly prohibits member states from interfering in the internal affairs of other member states. This provision has been conservatively interpreted and applied so that conflicts within a state are placed beyond the purview and jurisdiction of the OAU. The result has been an artificial and conceptually unrealistic dichotomy between inter state and intra- state conflicts with the OAU having jurisdiction only to deal with the former. But evidently, this distinction is unrealistic.

All intra- state conflicts in Africa have a trans-border spillover effect that cannot be ignored by other states. As the above studies show, it is impossible for the OAU to be faithful to this distinction. The OAU intervened in one way or another in each of the conflicts that could be viewed as internal as the case of the Nigerian civil war demonstrates.

---

121 Organization of African Unity Charter 1963.

The transition from OAU to the African Union (AU)[122] is in itself an attempt to address the past infirmities.

The African Union: Prospects for Conflict Resolution

On May 26, 2001, the organization of African Unity (OAU) was finally transformed into the African Union (AU) when the constitutive act of the AU came into effect. Later in July, African heads of States and foreign ministers met in Lusaka for the final OAU meeting and officially launched the African Union. The ratification by all the 53 African Nations reflected the enthusiasm of the Africans to embrace this new political and economic dispensation.

FEATURES OF THE AFRICAN UNION

The African Union is fashioned loosely along the lines of the European Union. It consists of a Central Bank[123] (yet

---

122 The African Union is an intergovernmental organization consisting of 52 African states. Established on July 9, 2002, the AU was formed as a successor to the Organization of African Unity (OAU). The most important decisions of the AU are made by the Assembly of the African Union, a semi-annual meeting of the heads of state and government of its member states. The AU's secretariat, the African Union Commission, is based in Addis Ababa, Ethiopia. During the February 2009 Union meeting headed by Libyan leader Gaddafi, it was resolved that the African Union Commission would become the African Union Authority.

123 The African Central Bank (ACB) is one of the three financial institutions of the African Union. It will over time take over responsibilities of the African Monetary Fund. The creation of the ACB, to be completed by 2028 was first agreed upon in the 1991 Abuja Treaty. The 1999 Sirte Declaration called for a speeding up of this process with creation by 2020. When it is fully implemented via Pan-African Parliament legislation, the ACB will be the sole issuer of the African Single Currency, will become the banker of

to be established), a Central Parliament[124] (already hosted by South Africa) and a centralized judicial system. Other important features will include the crystallization of regional and continental trade and an easier movement of Africans from one nation to the other. It is believed that all these elements will elevate the continent to a higher pedestal of political, economic and cultural progress.

Challenges and Prospects of the African Union

In spite of these laudable moves, there are numerous stumbling blocks facing the AU though Afro-optimists say are not insurmountable. One of the major stumbling blocks often cited is the issue of conflicts on the continent. There is an extremely high incidence of conflict in Africa which the OAU could not grapple with and which the AU cannot ignore. Intervention through peace keeping initiatives on the continent has led analysts to believe that, they have been an exercise in lip service.

It is note worthy that, the defunct OAU never carried out any intervention and her delegation of such tasks to

---

the African Government, will be the banker to Africa's private and public banking institutions, will regulate and supervise the African banking industry, and will set the official interest and exchange rates; in conjunction with the African Government's administration

124 The Pan-African Parliament, also known as the African Parliament, is the legislative body of the African Union. The African Parliament held its inaugural session in March 2004. At present it exercises oversight, and has advisory and consultative powers, which will last for the first five years of its existence, after that time period it will exercise full legislative powers. Its 265 Parliamentary representatives are elected by the legislatures of the 53 AU states rather than being directly elected in their own capacity.

regional organizations, should not be the modus operandi of the new AU. There is the need for a new approach to conflict resolution and peace building. These interventions have generally failed to bring consensus within the regions and sometimes have been belated. A case in point is the Rwanda genocide which happened at the continent watch.

Against this background, it is imperative that, the AU gives priority to conflict resolution on the continent. For this to happen, there AU needs the following;

- Firstly, she would need the unbridled support of the member states. This is important for the organization to be able to garner resources quickly and face up to challenges before they become benign. The willingness of member states to provide financial and moral support on time will preclude the organization from becoming a lame duck. At a time when enthusiasm for the new dispensation is high, member states should seize the opportunity to amass enough resources for the nascent organization. Further more acknowledgement of the contribution of smaller countries should be publicized to avoid the perception of ownership of the organization by the big powers of Africa.

- Secondly, the AU would need both political and military muscle. There is an absolute need for the AU to have the political nerve to intervene in conflict situations. The absence of a military muscle will preclude the organization form executing her duties in the area of conflict resolution and peace keeping. This was lacking in the OAU and historically in the League of Nations and rendered those organizations ineffective. For the AU to succeed, it has to avoid going down the same path. At the moment, the prospects for a brighter Africa are rife, but there is the necessity for peace in order for the AU to also realize her ambitious developmental programme.

African Regional Organizations and Conflict Resolution: An Assessment

There are about five Regional Organizations in Africa which have taken upon themselves the responsibility to guarantee peace and stability in the continent. In spite of the fact that most of them were formed as economic unions, over the years the prevalence of conflict has engineered an overhaul of these organizations to embrace the resolution of disputes.

Note worthy are organizations such as; The Economic Community of West African States (ECOWAS)[125], The Southern African Development Community (SADC)[126], The

---

125 The Economic Community of West African States (ECOWAS) is a regional group of fifteen West African countries, founded on May 28, 1975, with the signing of the Treaty of Lagos. Its mission is to promote economic integration. In 1976 Cape Verde joined ECOWAS, and in December 2000 Mauritania withdrew, having announced its intention to do so in December 1999. It was founded to achieve "collective self-sufficiency" for the member states by means of economic and monetary union creating a single large trading bloc. The very slow progress towards this aim meant that the treaty was revised in Cotonou on July 24, 1993, towards a looser collaboration. The ECOWAS Secretariat and the Fund for Cooperation, Compensation and Development are its two main institutions to implement policies. The ECOWAS Fund was transformed into the ECOWAS Bank for Investment and Development

126 The Southern African Development Community (SADC) is an inter-governmental organization headquartered in Gaborone, Botswana. Its goal is to further socio-economic cooperation and integration as well as political and security cooperation among 15 southern African states.

East African Community (EAC)[127], The Intergovernmental Authority on Development (IGAD)[128], The Economic Community of Central African States.[129] In addition to these, there is another grouping of over 17 states known as CENSAD[130], made up of West, North, Sahelian and some Horn of Africa states.

The power of Regional Organizations to act as arbiters of conflicts in Africa is founded on the following reasons;

- Proximity to the Conflict: In most cases regional organizations are made up of both countries in conflict and countries that are at peace with themselves. Political and geographical proximity allows these organizations to better analyze the

---

127 The East African Community (EAC) is the regional intergovernmental organisation of the Republics of Kenya, Uganda, the United Republic of Tanzania, Republic of Rwanda and Republic of Burundi with its headquarters in Arusha, Tanzania.
128 The Intergovernmental Authority on Development (IGAD) is a seven-country regional development organization in East Africa. Its headquarters are located in Djibouti City.
129 The Economic Community of Central African States is an organisation for promotion of regional economic co-operation in Central Africa. It "aims to achieve collective autonomy, raise the standard of living of its populations and maintain economic stability through harmonious cooperation".
130 CEN-SAD was established on 4th February 1998 following the Conference of Leaders and Heads of States held in Tripoli (Great Jamahiriya). The Treaty on the establishment of the Community was signed by the Leader of Great El-Fateh Revolution and the Heads of State of Burkina Faso, Mali, Niger, Chad and Sudan. The Central African Republic and Eritrea joined the Community during the first Summit of the organization held in Syrte in April 1999. Senegal, Djibouti and Gambia joined during the N'djamena Summit in February 2000. Others countries joined later, and still more are in the process of joining the Organization.

causes and effects of conflicts and if necessary to seek extra regional support to bring an end to the dispute. A critical example was the internal dispute in Liberia wherein under the auspices of ECOWAS, the former Liberian President Charles Taylor[131] was eased out of power and exiled in Nigeria. At the handing over ceremony, conspicuously present was the South African President Thabo Mbeki[132].

- Credibility: Generally, regional organizations are seen to be fair in conflict resolution in Africa. Their first hand knowledge of the critical issues involved in the conflicts and their ability to enlist extra-regional organizations both at the pan African and non Pan African levels are owing to the credibility they bring in conflict resolution.

But it is important to note that the ability for Regional Organizations to resolve conflicts in Africa is not smooth sailing. There are a number of constraints which are inherent on the very nature of the organizations in Africa.

- Firstly, all the regional organizations in Africa are made up of countries, some of which are large and influential owing to their economic and military might. Nigeria in ECOWAS, South Africa in SADC,

---

131 Charles McArthur Ghankay Taylor served as President of Liberia from 2 August 1997 to 11 August 2003. He was once one of Africa's most prominent warlords during the First Liberian Civil War in the early 1990s and was elected president at the end of that conflict. He was subsequently forced into exile, and is currently being held in the United Nations Detention Unit on the premises of the Penitentiary Institution Haaglanden, location Scheveningen in The Hague, and on trial by the Special Court for Sierra Leone.

132 Thabo Mbeki (Ibid)

Kenya in EAC, Ethiopia in IGAD and Cameroon in ECCAS. This situation is problematic, because, the tendency has always been that in conflict situations, the leader of an influential state takes the initiative and enlists the support of other members in a bid to launch a peace effort. The perception this brings is that, the influential states could be seen as pushing others around.

By and large, the extent to which regional organizations have and can play in conflict resolution differs a great deal. It has been judged that the most active regional organizations in the African continent, with regards to conflict resolution have been ECOWAS which has been seen in Liberia, Sierra Leone, and Cote D'Ivoire; IGAD which is active in Sudan and Somalia. At the moment SADC has established a committee on Defence and Security and there is consultation among member states on matters of Politics, Defence and Security among member states of the EAC.

ECOWAS and Conflict Resolution

This institution was originally conceived as an organization for promoting economic development in West Africa. However, insecurity began to loom large with the outbreak of the Liberian Civil war in December 1989, the Sierra Leonean war in March 1999. As a result, the organization was forced by circumstances to embrace a new role.

ECOWAS Security Mechanism

The ECOWAS mechanism for conflict prevention, Management, resolution, Peacekeeping and security was adopted at the ECOWAS summit in Lome in December 1999.The mechanism expanded two previous sub regional security initiatives: a protocol on Non-Aggression signed in 1978, and a Protocol Relating to Mutual Assistance on Defense (MAD)[133] in 1981. The first protocol called on members to resolve their conflicts peacefully through ECOWAS.

The second promised mutual assistance for externally instigated sponsored aggression and called for the creation of an Allied Armed force of the community, consisting of standby forces from ECOWAS States. The mechanism of 1999 was also shaped by ECOMOG's experiences in Liberia, Sierra Leone and Guinea-Bissau. This mechanism evolved out of the activities of ECOWAS' standing Mediation committee (SMC) established in 1990 following the outbreak of the civil war in Liberia.

The ECOWAS Mechanism of 1999 comprises six distinct bodies, designed to help contain and defuse impending conflicts. The first is the mediation and Security council, the main decision making body on all matters concerning conflict prevention, peacekeeping, security and other areas of operation. It is made of ten members who are elected to two-year terms. The second important body of the new Mechanism is the Defense and security Commission, which examines all technical and administrative issues and assesses logistical requirements for peace keeping operations.

The Commission consists of military technocrats and advises the Mediation and Security Council on mandates, terms of reference and the appointment of Force Commanders for military missions. One pressing need of

---

133 See in detail The ECOWAS Protocol relating to Mutual Assistance in Defence signed on 29 May 1981.

the ECOWAS secretariat is to appoint more staff to oversee its Mechanism. Until recently, this responsibility fell largely on three overworked Legal Affairs officers. General Cheik Diarra was appointed deputy Executive Secretary for political Affairs, defense and security in early 2001 and is in the process of increasing his staff.

The third body of the mechanism is the Council of Elders, a group of eminent persons mandated to use their good offices in the prevention, management and resolution of conflicts. The council of elders is to consist of eminent persons from Africa and outside the continent including women, traditional, religious, and political leaders appointed on an ad hoc basis. Seventeen of its thirty- two members met for the first time in Niamey, Niger, from 2to 4 July 2001. The fourth body of the Mechanism is the Executive Secretariat and particularly the Executive Secretary, who coordinates the activities of the various bodies of the Mechanism and the implementation of its decisions. The fifth body of the new Mechanism is the Early warning Observation System[134], which collects and transmits data to the ECOWAS Secretariat on impending signs of conflict. Finally, ECOMOG, a body that will consist of standby forces from its member states, is to be the peace keeping and monitoring arm of the Mechanism. ECOWAS' new Mechanism also calls for improved cooperation among its members in the areas of early warning, conflict prevention, peace keeping operations, cross-border crime,

---

134 The ECOWAS Early Warning System was a strategy adopted for the prevention and resolution of conflicts in its nascent stage before they degenerate into violent conflicts of the magnitude of those experienced in the sub-region over the past decade. The strategy aimed at saving the usual huge costs that go with resolving full-blown conflicts and undertaking post-conflict reconstruction as well averting humanitarian catastrophe.

and the trafficking of small arms and narcotics. Many of these ideas were based on ECOMOG's experiences in Liberia, Sierra Leone, and Guinea-Bissau.

Since it has already undertaken three military missions, it is important to discuss ECOWAS' military arm in more detail. The ECOWAS Mechanism calls for the establishment of a brigade-size standby force, consisting of specially trained and equipped units of national armies, ready for deployment at short notice. The force's main tasks involve observation and monitoring, peacekeeping, humanitarian intervention, enforcement of sanctions and embargoes, preventive deployment, peace building operations, disarmament and demobilization and policing activities including anti-smuggling and anti-criminal activities.

These were many of the tasks that ECOMOG performed in Liberia and Sierra Leone. The proposed sub-regional force is expected to embark on periodic training exercises to enhance the cohesion of the troops and the compatibility of equipment. It will undertake exchange programs in West African military training institutions, as well as external training involving the UN and OAU. Four thousands troops from Benin, Burkina Faso, Chad, Cote d'Ivoire, Niger, Togo and Ghana took part in war games in the Burkinabe town of Kompienga and northern Togo in May 1998, with Nigeria involved in the military planning for these exercises.

The ECOMOG force is mandated to intervene in four cases: first, a situation of internal armed conflict within a member state; second, conflicts between two or more member states; third, internal conflicts that threaten to trigger a humanitarian disaster or pose a serious threat to sub-regional peace and security, and situations that result from the overthrow or threat to a democratically elected government; and fourth any other situation that the council deems "appropriate".

While the first two scenarios were included in the ECOWAS Protocol Relating to Mutual Assistance on Defense of 1981[135], the third scenario was a conscious effort to provide legal cover for future interventions, again, based on Liberia, Sierra Leone, and Guinea-Bissau experiences In Liberia and Guinea-Bissau ECOMOG[136] intervened by arguing that the situation posed a humanitarian disaster and a threat to sub-regional peace and security. In Sierra Leone, ECOMOG restored a democratically elected government to power after its overthrow by soldiers. The interventions in Liberia and Sierra Leone were controversial and questioned on legal grounds, even by some ECOWAS members.

The ECOMOG interventions in Liberia, Sierra Leone, and Guinea-Bissau exposed the logistical weaknesses of West Africa's armies. For the foreseeable future such logistical support will have to come from external donors until the sub-region develops its own capabilities. The issue of financing is particularly important to the building of ECOMOG's standby force. The ECOWAS security Mechanism foresees troop-contributing countries bearing financial costs for the first three months of military operations, before ECOWAS takes over the costs.

The initial agreement for the ECOMOG mission in Liberia was for each contingent to fund its own troops for the first month of the mission, after which time the full ECOWAS would assume responsibility for ECOMOG. But Nigeria

---

135 Op cit
136 Monitoring Observer Group of the Economic Community of West Africa States (ECOWAS)

ended up footing about 90 percent of the costs (over U.S.$1.2 billion) while francophone countries opposed to ECOMOG mission to Guinea-Bissau. Under the ECOWAS security mechanism, a Special Peace Fund is to be established to raise revenue. Funding will be raised from member states, corporate bodies, the UN, multinational organizations, the OAU and the rest the international community.

The three ECOMOG missions demonstrated the importance of securing financial support before embarking on an intervention. Such costs can prove a disincentive to future interventions in a sub-region saddled with crippling debt burden. OAU peacekeepers from Tanzania and Uganda withdrew from ECOMOG's mission in Liberia in 1995 in large part because their financial and logistical needs were not being met. Other ECOWAS states, like Togo declined to contribute troops to ECOMOG due to the costs of maintaining peacekeepers in Liberia.

The Nigerian-led OAU intervention force in Chad between 1979 and 1881 was to withdraw largely because it lacked the funding and logistical support to sustain it. All this experiences underscore the significance of financial and logistical support for future sub-regional efforts at conflict management.

The ECOWAS security Mechanism has so far received funding from the AU and several donor governments. The OAU gave ECOWAS $300.000 for its deployments in Sierra Leone and Liberia. The European Union (EU) (2 million Euros), the U.S. Agency for International Development (USAID)[137] ($250,000) and the governments of the United

---

[137] The United States Agency for International Development (USAID) is the United States federal government organization

Kingdom, Japan (U.S.$100,000) and Germany have also made contributions in support of the ECOWAS security mechanism. Canada has contributed $300,000 for the establishment of an ECOWAS Child Protection Unit. The government of the Netherlands has also expressed an interest in funding the mechanism.

Beside ECOWAS, the Mano River Union (MRU)[138] comprised of Guinea, Liberia, and Sierra Leone also works to resolve conflict in the region through the Joint Security Committee (JSC), which was created at the Summit of MRU Head of State in Conakry in April 2000. The JSC Committee was born out of the need to address the deteriorating security situation along the borders of the three MRU states. The JSC consists of a technical Committee and a Border Security, and Confidence-building Unit, with a mandate to address and monitor joint security and border issues. One of the first tasks undertaken by the JSC, as the security situation along

---

responsible for most non-military foreign aid. An independent federal agency, it receives overall foreign policy guidance from the United States Secretary of State and seeks to "extend a helping hand to those people overseas struggling to make a better life, recover from a disaster or striving to live in a free and democratic country

138 The Mano River Union (MRU) is an international association established in 1973 between Liberia and Sierra Leone. In 1980, Guinea joined the union. The goal of the Union was to foster economic cooperation among the countries. It is named for the Mano River which begins in the Guinea highlands and forms a border between Liberia and Sierra Leone Due to conflicts involving the countries the objectives of the Union could not be achieved (see Sierra Leone Civil War, Liberian Civil War. However, on May 20, 2004, the Union was reactivated at a summit of the three leaders of the Mano River Union states, Presidents Lansana Conté of Guinea, Ahmad Tejan Kabbah of Sierra Leone and Chairman Gyude Bryant of Liberia.

the borders between Liberia and Guinea has deteriorated and tensions between the two countries have increased.

A further factor complicating the resolution of the Liberia/Guinea is the fact that members of the JSC are parties to the dispute. More fundamentally, political differences among ECOWAS member states, relating to disagreements over conflict management strategies, continue to test the capacity and resolve of ECOWAS to address conflicts in the sub-region.

ECOWAS leaders have often not spoken in unison on these issues. Although ECOWAS appeared at first to support a plan by the international community to impose sanctions on Liberia in 2001 in order to deter its support for sire Leonean RUF rebels, it later called for a two-month moratorium before such sanctions could be imposed. Following the imposition of sanctions on Liberia by UN Security Council in May 2001, some ECOWAS leaders have publicly questioned the wisdom of punishing Charles Taylor while seeking his cooperation for the disarmament of RUF rebels in Sierra Leone.

SADC And Conflict Resolution

In order to understand the role of SADC in responding to conflicts and crisis, it is important to recognize a key feature of security in this sub region: the overwhelming military and financial preponderance of South Africa. SADC's predecessor, the Southern African Development Coordination Conference (SADCC), was established in 1980 specifically to counter the economic, military and political dominance of South Africa. While its creation symbolically signaled a shift from defense against apartheid to regional cooperation, the specter of South African economic and military power continues to affect the dynamics within SADC.

SADC Conflict Resolution and Prevention strategy

In 1996, SADC created the Organ on Politics, Defense and security (OPDS). But the Organ has not achieved much in terms of promoting collective security in the region. Its strategic vision on how to address the insecurity facing Southern Africa is still undefined, and has been wrecked by divisions among its members.

The organ remains captive to the political rivalry between South Africa and Zimbabwe, countries which represented the two opposing conceptions of the functioning of the organ. Zimbabwe felt that incorporating security within the SADC Secretariat in Botswana, rather than leaving it as a specialized task for the chair in Harare, would divert the organization's attention from its main objective of economic development and integration. In contrast, South Africa argued that the organ should be placed within the structure of the SADC and run by the SADC chair.

These differences have paralyzed the operation of the OPDS. At the SADC summit in AUGUST 1997, President Nelson Mandela of South Africa, then the acting Chairman of the organization, threatened to resign from the SADC chairmanship if the OPDS was not brought under the central SADC chair. This dispute between Mandela and Zimbabwe's President Robert Mugabe,[139] who had held

---

139 Robert Gabriel Karigamombe Mugabe (born 21 February 1924) is the current President of Zimbabwe. He has held power as the head of government since 1980, as Prime Minister from 1980 to 1987, and as the first executive head of state since 1987.In 2008, his party suffered a defeat in national elections, but Mugabe

the chair of the SADC organ since its creation, led the SADC summit to suspend the organ SADC leaders then appointed a committee composed of a "troika" of Malawi, Mozambique and Namibia to identify a suitable solution to this problem.

The SADC Treaty provides little direction in resolving this problem since it does not contain any details about the nature and functioning of a security organ. Since 1997 SADC has struggled to find a solution to this impasse. Two main proposals emerged: first, to transform the organ into separate committees and work on an ad hoc basis to integrate the organ into the SADC frame work under a deputy chairperson from one of the troika countries; and second, to operate the organ on the basis of specific protocols signed by member states. The SADC summit held in 2001 finally rotated the chairmanship of the organ from Zimbabwe to Mozambique.

With the paralysis of the organ, SADC's Interstate Defense and Security Committee (IDSC),[140] established in the mid-1980s, often coordinated SADC's security efforts. SADC leaders proposed the establishment of a brigade-level standby force to which member states would contribute with units and Headquarters staff to intervene in regional conflicts. But progress on this issue has remained stalled. SADC states did, however undertake joint military exercises called "operation Blue Crane," funded by EU states. SADC has under taken police operations involving Mozambique, South Africa, and Zambia.

---

[140] retained power after running unopposed in a subsequent run-off election.

The SADC organ needs to be operationalized and strengthened if the organization is to play an effective role in conflict management. Dealing with security requires addressing three main issues. First, a common vision of security must be nurtured and strengthened within SADC. This can be facilitated through the signing of defense non-aggression pacts, promoting the protection of human rights, having a moratorium to limit arms smuggling, and creating pacts for environmental protection and the protection of vulnerable groups during conflicts.

Second, the region needs to embark on institutional development at both national and sub-regional levels to implement and monitor the various accords established by SADC. Finally, SADC must set priorities, establish a program of action in security matters, and draw up a calendar to be ratified by national governments.

ECCAS AND CONFLICT RESOLUTION

Recognizing the need to cooperate to solve common problems within a wider sub-regional grouping, the member states of the Central African Customs and Economic Union created in 1981 and of the defunct Economic Community of the Great Lakes States in 1983. Conceived as a tool to pursue economic development, promote regional cooperation and establish a Central African Common Market, ECCAS brought together eleven countries: Angola, Burundi, Cameroon, Central African Republic, Chad, Congo, Brazzaville, Democratic Republic of Congo, Equatorial Guinea, Gabon, Rwanda, and Sao Tome and Principe.

In an attempt to address the perennial conflicts in central Africa, ECCAS leaders decided to create an Early Warning

Mechanism in 1996. At a meeting in Libreville in 1997, called to discuss the political crisis in what was then Zaire, ECCAS leaders proposed the idea of an interstate security cooperation mechanism for the prevention and management of conflicts in the sub-region.

The aim of the mechanism was to establish a legal and institutional framework to promote and strengthen peace and security in Central Africa. Thereafter the Conseil de Paix et de Securite de l 'Afrique Centrale (COPAX)[141] was established under the auspices of the UN standing committee for security Questions in Central Africa. COPAX had a dual mandate: to prevent, manage and resolve conflicts in Central Africa; to undertake any necessary action to deal effectively with political conflicts; and to promote, preserve and consolidate peace and security in the sub-region.

Over the years, technical problems associated with creating ECCAS's structures, coupled with the pursuit of narrow national interests, have blocked the effective operation of

---

141 Central African states adopted a pact of non-aggression at the end of the fifth meeting of the UN Consultative Committee on Security in Central Africa held in Yaoundé, Cameroon. The pact, adopted on 9 September 1994, was arrived at after five days of meeting and discussions between military experts and ministers of Cameroon, Central African Republic, Republic of Congo, Equatorial Guinea, Gabon and Sao Tome and Principe. At a summit conference of the United Nations Standing Advisory Committee on Security Questions in Central Africa which took place in Yaoundé on 25-26 February 1999, member states decided to create an organisation for the promotion, maintenance and consolidation of peace and security in Central Africa, which would be called the Council for Peace and Security in Central Africa (COPAX). The COPAX Protocol has now entered into force.

the security mechanism. ECCAS members, for instance, do not agree on the relationship between ECCAS, COPAX and its Early Warning Mechanism. Some states argue that since ECCAS is a weak organization, the security mechanism should be an independent body, while others advocate that the mechanism work within existing institutions.

This suggests a general lack of political will among countries in a region afflicted by conflicts. The political and security environment in Central Africa has made it difficult for ECCAS to become institutionalized as a regional organization. States in the sub-region have responded to this failure by seeking membership in alternative sub-regional organizations. For instance, the DRC is a member of SADC, while Burundi and Rwanda applied to join the East African Community. Any revitalization of ECCAS would have to resolve how to deal successfully with multiple memberships of regional organizations, a phenomenon that is not peculiar to this region.

IGAD And Conflict Resolution

The Intergovernmental Authority on Drought and Desertification (IGADD),[142] comprising Djibouti, Ethiopia, Kenya, Somalia, Sudan and Uganda, was established in 1986. Eritrea joined after its independence in 1993. Initially IGADD was established to act as an early warning mechanism for alerting the international community of impending humanitarian emergencies and to coordinate resources in responding to crises on the horn of Africa. Cooperation was thus confined to issues of drought, desertification and food security. IGADD avoided addressing issues related to military security, then conceived as a prerogative of

---

142 IGADD (Ibid)

individual states and, therefore, as falling outside the arena of collective action.

However, as insecurity continued to curtail economic, social and political developments. IGAD member states started to confront these problems collectively. Out of these efforts a decision to begin to transform the security architecture in the sub region. In March 1996, sub-regional leaders signed an agreement transforming IGADD into the Inter governmental Authority on Development (IGAD). The organization's mandate was expanded to include conflict management, prevention and resolution. Under the new agreement, IGAD prioritized the pursuit the pursuit of peace and security, and had as its principal aim the maintenance of peace and security, on the horn of Africa. Specifically, the agreement provided for:

The creation of a sub-regional mechanism for the prevention, management and resolution of inter and intra state conflicts through dialogue; and collective action to preserve peace, security and stability, defined as an essential prerequisite for economic development and social progress. The agreement proposed dealing with conflicts by eliminating threats to security; called for the establishment of a mechanism for consultation and cooperation for the pacific settlement of disputes; and agreed to deal with disputes among member states within the sub region before referring them to other regional or international organizations. Demonstrating unprecedented political commitment, IGAD states pledged themselves to resolving outstanding security problems and conflicts, and to preserving sub-regional stability.

In seeking security and Peace, IGAD pursued a dual track approach. To deal with conflicts likely to polarize the organization, IGAD often creates semiautonomous ad hoc mechanism, outside of its secretariat, which are then mandated to deal with a particular issue. The secretariat on the Sudan Peace Process, based in Nairobi, is one such mechanism. The process that led to the restoration of a transitional government in Somalia in 1999 was another such mechanism.

IGAD's second peace making track revolves around its secretariat in Djibouti, which addresses issues on which its members have forged consensus, such as the establishment of a conflict early warning and response mechanism (CEWARN)[143], a campaign against small arms and a diverse range of humanitarian issues.

IGAD In Somalia

Following the failed international effort to restore peace in Somalia in the early 1990s responsibility for ending the conflict increasingly came to rest on sub-regional actors. Compared to the Sudan Peace Process, the Somali process was fluid and less structured. However, this process did reveal the potential of state and civil society actors playing complementary peace building roles.

Finally, in October 1998, in cooperation with the IGAD Forum partners Liaison Group, IGAD member states created a standing committee on the Somali peace process, chaired by Ethiopia. Based on the format of the Sudan Peace process, this committee was mandated to organize a peace process in Somalia by providing a consultative forum

---

[143] The Conflict Early Warning and Response Mechanism (CEWARN) is an initiative of the seven-member Intergovernmental Authority on Development (IGAD), playing a key role in executing one of its core mandate of promoting peace and security in the Horn of Africa region.

for negotiations aimed at reconciling and restoration of a government in Somalia.

The ensuing process involved the initial consultations among state and intergovernmental actors, namely IGAD, the Arab League, the OAU and the UN, as well as a broad spectrum of Somalis including clan leaders, Muslim clerics, warlords and members of the civil society. From March through May 2000, a series of consultations with Somali intellectuals, professionals, former politicians and representatives from the business community was organized in Djibouti by IGAD.

The last of these meetings involved 200 Somali traditional leaders and 100 women delegates. The Somali National Peace conference took place on 4 June 2000, in Ata, Djibouti. This meeting identified arms control, disarmament of militias, restoration of looted property, and determining the status of Mogadishu as priority issues. Special committees were created to address each issue. By the time the national peace conference ended on August 2000, a transitional National assembly (TNA), composed of 245 members, had been established.

A week later, members of the TNA elected Mr. Abdul Kassim Salat Hassan[144] as President of Somalia. After his inauguration in Djibouti, Salat moved his government to Mogadishu. Shortly thereafter, a new legislative assembly and a cabinet were formally established. The

---

144 Abdiqasim Salad Hassan is a prominent Somali politician. He was President of Somalia from 2001 to 2004, and previously served as Interior Minister and Finance Minister in the government of Mohamed Siad Barre.

government continues to face serious difficulties, including the challenging of its authority by warlords controlling different areas in Mogadishu and the non participation of representatives from Somaliland and Puntland. Despite these problems, Somalia was readmitted to IGAD during its November 2000 meeting.

However in spite of the uncertainties that have characterized the Somali peace process, efforts to bring the Somali question to normalcy have not ceased. In 2003 the Assembly of Heads of State and Government summit requested the African Union to assist IGAD to resume facilitation of the reconciliation process in Somalia. The summit decided to name a facilitation committee on the Somali peace process and membership included Djibouti, Eritrea, Ethiopia, Uganda and Sudan. On January 2004, leaders of the groups signed an agreement in Nairobi, Kenya, to move the talks into the final phase and pave the way for the adoption of a Transitional Federal Charter. The Charter provides the legal frame work for a five year transitional period of government in Somalia and was launched on 13th march 2004 at the IGAD council of Ministers meeting.

IGAD Conflict Early Warning and Response Mechanism (CEWARN)

IGAD has been successful in developing a number of projects to help build the capacity of member states in conflict prevention, management and resolution. The first step has been the through European Union Funding, the building of conflict and mediation capacities in the region.. At the 9th Summit of the IGAD Heads of state and Government in Khartoum in January 2002, a protocol was signed for the establishment of a conflict warning and response Mechanism (CEWARN)[145]

Cewarn was established in the first week of September in Addis Ababa. The Unit's staff component of three researchers underwent training in early warning data. The unit will work in cooperation with regional early warning units, or CEWARU's. Based in each IGAD member state. CEWARN office was officially opened on 30 June 2003. The CEWARN process is funded by the US and German governments to the amount of $700,000.

EAC and Conflict Resolution

The East African Community was established by a treaty signed by the Heads of State Kenya, Uganda and Tanzania in 1999 which entered into force in 2000. These three countries have a long history of regional cooperation dating back to the colonial period. Most significant among these organizations was the East African community, which collapsed in 1977. The new treaty of 2000 was driven largely by the economic imperative to 'improve the standard of living of the population by facilitating an adequate and economically, socially and ecologically sustainable development.

However the EAC also recognized that security and political stability are a prerequisite for sustainable development. Cooperation was partly conceived by EAC leaders as a strategy for conflict prevention. In their view, regional integration is a vehicle for regional peace.

---

145 CEWARN (Op cit)

The ultimate aim of the EAC cooperation is the establishment of a political federation to ensure 'a peaceful neighborhood'. Underpinning the EAC treaty is the notion that economic prosperity and regional integration will have the multiplier effect of reducing the possibility of conflict and enhancing security. Hence, a number of provisions in the treaty cast the EAC as an instrument of regional peace and security.

SECURITY COOPERATION IN THE EAC

A memorandum of Understanding on Common defense and Security issues was drafted by EAC leaders in April 1998[146]. At the time, it was thought that this memorandum could develop into a military pact. However, citing constraints relating to command structures and procedural irregularities, the Heads of State suggested that defense matters were best left for the last phase of cooperation.

Nonetheless, the EAC secretariat in Arusha, Tanzania has engaged in a range of confidence building measures in the Security sectors of its three members. While the heads of State were reluctant to undertake common defense initiatives, they allowed the creation of a defense liaison

---

146 The EAC has established a Sectoral Committee on Co-operation in Defence, as well as an Inter-State Security Committee. During 2003, these committees held meetings inter alia to exchange information on implementation of National Action Plans in line with the Nairobi Declaration on Small Arms and Light Weapons; to draft modalities for a common refugee registration mechanism; and a Defence Experts' Working Group on Operations and Training to discuss joint exercises on peacekeeping operations, counterterrorism and military level participation in disaster response.

unit within the secretariat manned by three military defence attaches from each country. In 2000, EAC leaders signed a memorandum of understanding on interstate security calling for the establishment of border committees between countries that experience cross- border clashes. EAC leaders have also called for harmonizing policies on the treatment of refugees.

The EAC, secretariat has facilitated regular visits by military personnel and has undertaken joint military training and exercises between its members. Together, these activities have introduced minimal elements of common procedure among armies with different histories. For instance a series of joint natural fires training sessions organized in 1999, 2000, and 2001 enhanced the sharing of experiences and generated case studies to guide responses to disasters and to improve civil military relation.

The Defense college in Karen, Kenya, which trains senior officers from a number countries in East, Central and Southern Africa has introduced Peace keeping into its curriculum for students from EAC countries, such training is useful for common operations and creates the possibility of the sub-region contributing a regional force for future peace keeping operations.

Chapter Five

ROOT CAUSES OF AFRICAN CONFLICTS: NOT CONSPIRACIES

"History is an account mostly false, of events mostly unimportant, which are brought about by rulers, mostly knaves, and soldiers, mostly fools."

Ambrose Gwinnett Bierce

Conflict analysis should aim at unearthing the ways by which existing social and political structures frustrate real needs. In Africa over the years, the prevalence of pseudo-analysis of the root causes of conflict has continued to prevent real solutions to the plethora of conflict in our societies.

Joseph (1999) contends that, in African conflicts where much is at stake and emotions run high, the temptation invariably exists among protagonists to resort to all manner of conspiracy theories to explain the causes of the conflict. Such conspiracy theories, which see the reason for the conflict primarily in the greed, malevolence or unreasonableness of the other party, are inspired by suspicion, distrust and ultimately, fear. By choosing to ignore the other party's underlying needs and interests, not only is adequate analysis denied, but so too is appropriate action.[147]

---

[147] In the case of Rwanda, which has become symbolic of the ultimate risk posed by heightened group conflict in Africa, Timothy Longman traces the course of the political opening in 1992 and the creation of a government of transition that heralded a shift from authoritarian rule to pluralist democracy. To foil these initiatives, the regime of Juvénal Habyarimana embarked on a campaign to neutralize the trans ethnic character of many civil society organizations by fomenting ethnic discord, which led inexorably to the genocide of 1994 and the country's continuing traumas. More generally, Marina Ottaway argues, "in much of Africa, ethnicity is not a problem until it is made a problem. " Competitive party politics invites divisive tactics by aspirant politicians as well as by incumbent regimes. One of the paradoxes unveiled by democratic openings after 1989 is that they disrupt the practices of group accommodation by which authoritarian regimes had long co- opted elites from various communities without providing appropriate transitional mechanisms.

It can be pointed that, governments suppress expressions of real needs of specific groups by labeling them conspiracies to grab power; disrespectful insurrections; manifestations of the 'false consciousness" of ethnic allegiance; rumblings of neo-colonialist puppets; and in the case of demands by women, an onslaught on the traditional values of Africa.

This compounds the truism of "wrong diagnosis, wrong treatment" which equally applies to medicine as in political conflict. The resolution of African conflicts have been more in the region of treating the symptoms which have brought temporary relief to the patient and satisfaction to the Doctor, while the basic ailment remains untreated. Informed by this injunction, what then may we consider as the principal sources of conflicts in Africa?

AFRICAN DIVERSITY

Africa is a vast and varied continent. African countries have different histories and geographical conditions, different sets of public policies and different patterns of internal and international interaction. The sources of conflict in Africa reflect this diversity and complexity. Some sources are purely internal, some reflect the dynamics of a particular sub-region, and some have important international dimensions. Despite these differences the sources of conflict in Africa are linked by a number of common themes and experiences.

HISTORICAL LEGACIES

At the congress of Berlin in 1885, the colonial powers partitioned Africa into territorial units, Kingdoms, states and communities in Africa were arbitrarily divided; unrelated areas and peoples were just arbitrarily joined together. In the 1960s, the newly independent African states inherited those colonial boundaries, together with the challenge that legacy posed to their territorial integrity and to their attempts to achieve national unity.

The challenge was compounded by the fact that the framework of colonial laws and institutions which some new states inherited had been designed to exploit local divisions, not overcome them.[148] Understandably therefore the simultaneous tasks of state building and nation building preoccupied many of the newly independent states and were given new momentum by the events that followed the outbreak of the secessionist fighting in the Congo.[149]

Too often, however, the necessary building of national unity was pursued through the heavy centralization of political and economic power and the suppression of political pluralism. Predictaly, political monopolies often led to corruption, nepotism, complacency and the abuse of power. The era of serious conflict over state boundaries in Africa has largely passed, aided by the 1963 decision of the Organization of African Unity (OAU) to accept the boundaries which African States inherited from colonial authorities. However, the challenge of forging a genuine national identity from among disparate and often competing communities has remained.

---

148 Christopher Clapham, in his 1996 book *Africa and the International System: The Politics of State Survival*, pulls together many of the factors relevant to an understanding of the new pattern of power relations in Africa. Clapham anchors his thesis to the distinction made by Robert Jackson and Carl Rosberg between empirical and juridical statehood in Africa, and to their discussion of the role of international society in sustaining states that lack most attribute of empirical statehood. He contends that
Post colonial African regimes have benefited greatly from the prevailing "international mythologies of statehood".

The character of the commercial relations instituted by colonialism also created long term distortions in the political economy of Africa. Transportation networks and related physical infrastructure were designed to satisfy the needs of trade with the metropolitan country, not to support the balanced growth of an indigenous economy. In addition to frequently imposing unfavorable terms of trade, economic activities that were strongly skewed towards extractive industries and primary commodities for export stimulated little demand for steady and widespread improvements in the skills and educational levels of the workforce.[150]

The consequences of this pattern of production and exchange spilled over into the post-independence state. As political competition was not rooted in viable national economic systems, in many instances the prevailing structure of incentives favored capturing the institutional remnants of the colonial economy for factional advantage.

During the cold war, the ideological confrontation between east and West placed a premium on maintaining order and stability among friendly states and allies., though super-Power rivalries in Angola and elsewhere also fuelled some of Africa's longest and deadly conflicts. Across Africa, undemocratic and oppressive regimes were supported and

---

[150] A few years after the end of the Cold War and the collapse of the Soviet Union, sub-Saharan Africa appeared to some observers to be a site of increasing anarchy and destitution. Not only writers for the popular media, but also academic scholars, expressed concern about the "sense of profound disorder on the continent. " A number of devastating conflicts contributed to these perceptions, notably, those in Liberia, Somalia, and Rwanda. At the same time, many African countries were experiencing the disruptions of the return to competitive party politics and the slow shift from statist to market-oriented economic systems.

sustained by the competing superpowers in the name of their broader goals but, when the cold war ended, Africa was suddenly left to fend for itself. Without external economic and political support, few African regimes could sustain the economic lifestyles they had become accustomed, or maintain the permanent hold on political power which they had come to expect.[151] As a growing number of states found themselves internally beset by unrest and violent conflict, the world searched for a new global security frame work.

For a brief period following the end of the cold war, the international community was eager to exercise its newly acquired capacity for collective decision making. Beginning in the early 1990s, the Security Council launched a series of ambitious peacekeeping initiatives in Africa and elsewhere. Despite a number of important successes, the inability of the United Nations to restore peace to Somalia soured international support for conflict intervention and precipitated a rapid retreat by the international community from peace keeping world wide.

An early and direct consequence of this retreat was the failure of the international community, including the United Nations to intervene to prevent the genocide in Rwanda.[152] That failure has had especially profound consequences

---

151 R, Joseph (Op cit)
152 Democratization provided a real opportunity to overcome the economic crisis, many observers felt, because the practices of the continent's authoritarian rulers during the first three decades of independence were largely to blame for the severity of the economic crisis. To be sure, the crisis has had multiple causes, including a number of external factors—most notably, the decline and instability of international commodity prices during the last several decades. Nonetheless, it was generally agreed

in Africa. Throughout the continent, the perception of near indifference on the part of the international community has left a poisonous legacy that continues to undermine confidence in the organization

INTERNAL FACTORS

More than three decades after African countries gained their independence, there is a growing recognition among Africans themselves that the continent must look beyond its colonial past for the causes of current conflicts. Today more then ever, Africa must look to itself. The nature of political power in many African states, together with the real and perceived consequences of capturing and maintaining power is a key source of conflict across the continent.

It is frequently the case that, political victory assumes a winner-takes-all form with respect to wealth and resources, patronage, closely linked to this phenomenon, which is heightened in many cases by reliance on centralized and highly personalized forms of governance. Where there is insufficient accountability of leaders, lack of transparency in regimes, inadequate checks and balances, non adherence to the rule of law, absence of peaceful means of change or replace leadership, or lack of respect for human rights, political control becomes excessively important, and the stakes become dangerously high.[153]

---

    that mismanagement by repressive and non accountable governments deserved a good deal of the blame. Thus, the emergence of a more participatory and competitive politics held the possibility of improved management of the economy.
153 When tyrannies collapse, the subsequent political transition can result in renewed authoritarianism; such was the case, for example, in Uganda, with the fall of Idi Amin. Alternatively, the transition can result in violence or chaos, as in Somalia. In some fortunate

This situation is exacerbated when, as is often the case in Africa, the state is the major provider of employment and political parties are largely either regionally or ethnically based. In such circumstances, the multiethnic character of most African states makes conflict even more likely, leading to an often violent politicization of ethnicity.

In extreme cases, rival communities may perceive that their security, perhaps their very survival, can be ensured only through control of state power. Conflict in such cases becomes virtually inevitable

EXTERNAL FACTORS

During the cold war, external factors to bolster or undermine African Governments were a familiar feature of superpower competition. With the end of the cold war, external intervention has diminished but has not disappeared. In the competition for oil and other precious resources in Africa, interest external to Africa continue to play a large and sometimes decisive role, both in suppressing conflict and in sustaining it.

Foreign interventions are not limited, however, to resources beyond Africa. Neighboring states, inevitably affected by conflicts taking place within other states, may also have other significant interests not all of them necessarily benign. While African peacekeeping and mediation efforts have become more prominent in recent years, the role that

---

cases, however, the collapse of tyranny results in the flowering of political liberty and the promotion of political restraint. This outcome characterizes southern Africa. A major reason for the relatively democratic outcome in that region is that the new regimes left the former repressors in possession of a political hostage: the private economy.

African Governments play in supporting, sometimes even instigating, conflicts in neighboring countries must be candidly acknowledged.[154]

Economic Motives

Despite the devastation that armed conflicts bring, there are many who profit from chaos and lack of accountability and who may have little or no interest in stopping a conflict and much interest in prolonging it. Very high on the list of those who profit from conflict in Africa are international arms merchants. Also high on the list, usually are the protagonists themselves.

In Liberia,[155] the control of diamonds, timber and other raw materials was one of the principal objectives of the warring

---

154 Despite these seemingly disparate processes, it has gradually become evident that a reconfiguration of power has been taking place. The term "reconfiguration" is used here to convey the tentative nature of these adjustments.

155 On December 24, 1989, a small band of Libyan-trained rebels led by Charles G. Taylor, invaded Liberia from the Ivory Coast. Taylor, Doe's former procurement chief, is an Americo-Liberia of both indigenous and Americo- Liberian ancestry. With explicit support from neighbouring African nations and a large section of Liberia's opposition, Taylor's National Patriotic Front rebels rapidly gained the support of Liberians because of the repressive nature of Samuel Doe and his government. Various unpredictable events, like the Gulf war and the consequent US disengagement from Liberia, coincided to turn this into a protracted civil war, with ultimately west African ECOMOG intervention. A final cease-fire and peace accord in 1996 was followed by the installation of a transitional government of all factional leaders. Liberian troops and provincial security forces were dispatched to Nimba County to counter the insurgency and indiscriminately killed Liberian civilians without regard to the distinction between combatants and noncombatants. In response

factions. Control over those resources financed the various factions and gave them the means to sustain the conflict. Clearly, many of the protagonists had a strong financial interest in seeing the conflict prolonged. The same can be said of Angola, where protracted difficulties in the peace process owed much to the importance of control over the exploitation of the country's lucrative diamond fields. In Sierra Leone, the chance to plunder natural resources and loot central Bank reserves was a key motivation for those who seized power from the government elected in may 1997.

SPECIFIC SITUATIONS

In addition to the broader sources of conflict in Africa that have been identified, a number of other factors are especially important in particular situations and sub regions. In Central Africa, They include the competition for scarce land and water resources in densely populated areas. In Rwanda, for example, multiple waves of displacement

---

to this insurgency, President Doe launched an unrelenting wave of violence against the inhabitants of Nimba County. Media reports and international human rights organizations estimated that at least 200 persons, primarily members of the Mano and Gio ethnic groups, were killed by troops of the Government of Liberia during the counterinsurgency campaign. When the cold war was over and Charles Taylor's band of rebels--some of them children--clashed with government forces and other ethnic militias in the streets, the resulting conflict was so frighteningly gruesome that for many it was almost impossible to understand. Between December 1989 and mid-1993, Charles Taylor's National Patriotic Front of Liberia (NPFL) is estimated to have been responsible for thousands of deliberate killings of civilians. As NPFL forces advanced towards Monrovia in 1990, they targeted people of the Krahn and Mandingo ethnic groups, both of which the NPFL considered supporters of President Doe's government

have resulted in situations where several families often claim rights to the same piece of land.

In African communities where oil is extracted, conflict has often arisen over local complaints that the community does not adequately reap the benefit of such resources, or suffers excessively from the degradation of the natural environment. In North Africa, the tensions between strongly opposing visions of society and the state are serious sources of actual and potential conflict in some states.

Chapter Six

THE BURUNDIAN CONFLICTS: SPECIFIC DYNAMICS

"Never in this world can hatred be stilled by hatred; it will be stilled only by non-hatred; this is the law eternal."

Gautama Siddhattha Buddha

At the center of the Burundi conflict is a wide range of issues which have influenced the people to rise up against each other. In a nutshell also, one can easily discern different periods of the entire ethnic set up in which one wonders how deep the fracas can be managed. The depth of the division and differences is legendary. The distortions in the history of such a small country of Lilliputian dimension makes it even more confusing. This therefore presents a special case study of what Azar calls protracted social conflict. A noticeable phenomenon of the Burundi conflict is that, the violence if ethnic based, but the sources of the tension which eventually leads to the violence is socio-economic. This chapter presents some of the interesting dynamics of the conflict as interpreted from the standpoint of ethnic groups.

HISTORY: THE MAIN PRETEXT[156]

History is a source of conflict and a pretext for impeding cooperation in the entire Burundi equation. Every historical account of the conflict has political connotations as the interpretation of history often serves to legitimize violence as 'retaliation' or 'pro-active'. At a general level, two different historical interpretations of events depending on whether the story is told by a Hutu or a Tutsi can be identified in the literature as well as the interviews with concerned actors of the Burundi conflict. The tables below explain the historical events and their dual interpretations by the protagonists.

---

156 Adebayo Adedeji, Comprehending and mastering African Conflicts: The Search for Sustainable Peace and Good governance (1999).

Table 5.1 Differences in perception and the interpretation of events

Theme/ Event	Hutu Interpretation	Tutsi Interpretation
Ethnicity – pre-colonial coexistence	There is an absence of secular symbiosis between the ethnic groups. The Hutus were exploited by the Tutsi particularly through the pastoral and land clientelism. There was a daily disgraceful discrimination of the Hutu by the Tutsi. The society was characterized by a humiliating stratification whereby the Hutu bought his promotion from a superior ethnic group- Tutsi through the kwibutura.	There was a strong cultural homogeneity and ethnic interpenetrations. There was no conflict based on ethnicity. The ubugabire and the ubugererwa were nothing but socio-economic exchanges between tutsi and tutsi, Hutu and hut and Tutsi and Hutu and Hutu and Tutsi.

As table 5.1[157] above indicates, Burundi's pre-colonial history bears no trace of ethnic conflict between Hutu, Tutsi and Twas from the 16th Century. Burundi had been under the leadership of the rural Kingdom. For example the Ganwa identity that represents the royal family contained both Bahutu and batutsi. The following five institutional foundations of Burundi Society helped create social cohesion;

---

157 Adedeji (op cit)

The *Nwami* (King)- Source of life and unity of the nation. He was directly connected with *Imana* and gave favors like cows, land, riches evenly to all his subjects for serving as official intermediaries to Imana

Imana – God Creator of all

Mupfumu and *Kiranga* – Intermediaries between Burundians and Imana

Mushingatahe – guardian and protector of peace and justice for Burundians, selected by the local population for his wisdom

Twiyungunya – Common faith and destiny. Communal work, collective needs, responding to one *Nwami* on earth while honoring one *Imana* in the heavens.

TABLE 5.2 –1965 Military Coup

The events of 1965	Hutu Interpretation	Tutsi Interpretation
An attempted coup by Hutu military officers directed at the Monarchy.	The events were preceded by acts of provocation and humiliation against the Hutu elites and the removal of the heads of the Hutu elite at the summit	This was the beginning of the tutsi genocide which started with the execution at the military camp known as base of the Tutsi soldiers: While Hutu soldiers were staging an up rising in Bujumbura, a Hutu militia systematically massacred Busangana Tutsi farmers in the province of Muramvya

As indicated in Table 5.2[158], the first attempted coup of 1965 by Hutu military officers had different interpretations. The assassination of the Hutu Prime Minister Pierre Ngendandumwe and the refusal by the King to appoint a Hutu as prime Minister despite the landslide victory by Hutu deputies in the May 1965 elections created political upheaval and poisoned the relations between the Hutu and Tutsi political elite on the one hand and between the King and the civilian elite on the other.

The events demonstrated that the monarch and the Tutsi elite were not ready to share power. Furthermore, the Tutsi elite were afraid of a possible repetition of the bloody overthrow of the King by the Hutu in neighboring Rwanda in 1959. The Hutu majority used the events in Rwanda to cultivate fear among the Tutsi of an impending danger of extermination in the event of control of power. The success of the coup was in the sense that it eroded whatever power was left for the monarchs. But contrary to the expectations of the coup leaders, It did not lead to Hutu rule but was in fact used as a political pretext to accelerate the system of Tutsi dominance.

TABLE 5.3 1969 Hutu Uprising

1969 EVENTS	Hutu Interpretation	Tutsi Interpretation
Violent uprising by Hutu soldiers against the Tutsi government as a result of the frustration	An attempt by Hutu Soldiers to regain their rights. This was followed by the summary execution of Hutu officers and soldiers	These were disturbances instigated by Hutu soldiers. Repetition of the 1965 events Crystallization of ethnic hatred by Hutu elite.

---

158 Adedeji (Op Cit)

In table 5.3,[159] these events led to reprisals from government against Hutu soldiers. The interpretation by Hutus and Tutsis to this event is as diverse and opposed as the table indicates.

TABLE 5.4 –1972 Hutu revolts[160]

The Events of 1972	Hutu Interpretation	Tutsi Interpretation
Uprising of Hutus	The large Scale genocide of Hutu following the Simbananyi plan;	Systematic and protracted preparation of the massacre whose password was to exterminate the entire Tutsi population presented as the enemy of the Hutu..
	The large scale massacre of Hutu up to the local level through out the country whereas the disturbances happened in a few regions of the South.	The execution of the Hutu following the so called Bubirize plan.
	The justification of the mono ethnic regime which spoke of legitimate defense in order to hide the ongoing genocide from the international community	Only the Hutu extremists were affected by the reprimand;
		The agitation of the extreme Hutu refugees destabilizing the country from outside.
	This led to More than 500.000 Hutu refugees	

The overthrow of the Monarchy by army officer Micombero in 1966 intensified and accentuated the tensions between

---

159 Adedeji (Op Cit)
160 Adedeji (Op cit)

the Tutsi from Muramvya (former royal head quarters) and those from Bururi. In 1971, rumors of a possible reestablishment of the Monarchy, the return of Prince Ndizeye and his assassination by the army deepened the tensions further. Alleged coup plot by the Hutu accelerated the descent into chaos.

The Southern Tutsi elite took advantage of this chaos to complete the ethnic cleansing of the Hutu from the military and the civil service that had started in 1965. The regime also took the opportunity to sideline the Tutsi from Muramvya and the rest of the country. This marked a serious turning point in the deterioration of the ethnic relations of the Hutus and Tutsis. It marked a point of no return and ushered in a period of ethnic hatred and barbarity. Burundi was thus put on the path of self destruction.

The 1972 events was indeed a distributional conflict in that the Southern Tutsi elite opted for the 'final solution' to consolidate their hold on power by eliminating the Hutu elite.

TABLE 5.5 The 1988 Provocations

1988 Ntega-Marangara Events	Hutu Interpretation	Tutsi Interpretation
	Theses events were a result of provocation by administrative authorities with a view to instigating a Hutu revolt; starting a blood bath and provoking a wave of refugees	The events were perpetrated by extreme Hutu within and outside the country who were afraid of political death because of the new direction of the third republic.

As indicated in Table 5.5[161] in 1988, Burundi experienced a civil war in the northern provinces of Ngozi and Kirundo following a long truce of 16 years. What makes the 1988 conflict a distributional conflict is the role played by state penetration and the resistance to it by the Hutu population. In the periods leading to the outbreak of the conflict, the government had been warned of tensions in the northern provinces between local administrators and the population.

One major area of contention was that these expatriate local administrators from the South were arrogant and insensitive to the needs of the local community. Moreover the wind from the east, that is the international drive for democratization energized by the fall of communism, also contributed to the intensification and mobilization by clandestine Hutu opposition movements.

Note worthy is the fact that, between 1972 – 1988, the country witnessed relative calm. While this allowed the military regimes to consolidate power, it also allowed the rebuilding of a sizeable Hutu intelligentsia abroad and at home. As the Hutu intelligentsia expanded, domestic demand for power sharing increased. This explains the increase in the intensity of the activities of the opposition groups but also the response from the Hutu to repression after the outbreak of the civil war in the north. Fearing a repetition of the 1972 massacre, the Hutu intelligentsia decided to challenge the government openly.

In a heroic move, Hutu intellectuals wrote a letter to the President to; Condemn the indiscriminate and arbitrary

---

161 Op cit

arrests and execution of Hutu intellectuals. Demand a national debate on ethnic discrimination and reform of the political system to achieve egalitarian representation. The open letter marked a turning point in the history of conflict in Burundi.

The intelligentsia had decided to no longer watch passively as the government security forces slaughter the people as in the past. They decided to not only confront the government but also to expose the tragedy to the international community. These reactions by the Hutu intelligentsia largely explain why repression was less widespread and shorter than in 1972.[162]

These reactions along with external pressure on the regime was instrumental in the initiation of the process of political opening, starting with the formation of an ethnically balanced 'government of unity' in 1989, the opening of a national debate on ethnic divisions and the ensuing opening of the political process that would eventually culminate into democratic elections in 1993.

---

[162] The reduced repression did not lead to peace. It was simply a period of calmness before the storm. Another cycle of violence was to later lead to more killing of Hutu intellectuals.

TABLE 5.6 1993 Democratic Elections[163]

FRODEBU victory – June 1993 election	Hutu Interpretation	Tutsi Interpretation
First multiparty elections which brought in a Hutu President for the first time in Burundi history	This was a victory for democracy based on popular wish It was a protest vote against 30 years of bad Tutsi management based on exclusion, injustice and genocide It ushered in a new perspective of democracy	It was an ethnic victory putting forward a numerical majority at the expense of a majority of ideas It was an endorsement of Hutu extremism Here was an absence of any political projects by the FRODEBU There was an absence of true leaders to ensure the survival of democracy

Following the adoption of a new constitution and the introduction of a multiparty system, the 1993 elections brought for the first time in the history of Burundi a Hutu President Melchoir Ndadaye who emerged the winner. Buyoya's eventual hand over of power to Ndadaye increased hope for long term stability and broader political participation, and Burundi was hailed internationally as a symbol of peaceful democratic transition.

President Ndadaye's assassination only four months after gaining power unleashed yet again years of accumulated fear, resentment and rage.

---

163 Op cit

TABLE 5.7 – Reactions to Tutsi Revolt[164]

1993 EVENTS	Hutu Interpretation	Tutsi Interpretation
The fall out of the assassination of the first democratically elected Hutu president	Tutsi refusal to accept democracy translated by the assassination of the first democratically elected president and his close collaborators The transformation of the acquisition by instigators of 21 October massacre of tutsi organized by FRODEBU Appeal of FRODEBU leaders for resistance to the disturbances and the general disobedience The showing of slight anger because of accumulated antecedents to avenge the death of the President and not previously programmed killings	The FRODEBU were accused of calling for the massacre of Tutsis immediately after President Ndadaye's death There was large scale killing of Tutsi and lynching of opposition Hutu following long term plan under FRODEBU leadership

The death of President Ndadaye led to massacres carried out in retribution and reprisals undertaken by the army to regain control of the country side. Tens of thousands of people were killed and hundreds of thousands fled to

---

164 Op cit

neighboring Tanzania and DRC. Those lucky enough to escape with their lives lost everything else including homes, land, livestock and their future.

These events led to a cycle of violence estimated at 300.000 lives, 600.000 to 800.000 regional refugees and between 280.000 to 380.000 internally displaced persons (Beuls, 2000). There are four key elements which place this conflict in the sphere of distributional conflict. Firstly, President Ndadaye wanted to build what he called a 'Burundi nouveau' (New Deal) by first of all reforming the military to make it representative of the ethnic and regional make up of the society.

But through out the transition period toward democracy which started in 1989, the military had systematically exhibited strong opposition to relinquish power.

Secondly, the Ndadaye regime quickly proceeded to replace former government officials in a drive to establish control of power but also to fulfill campaign promises. For the outgoing government officials and their allies in the private sector, these reforms meant the loss of means to extract rents, which explains the wide support that the military coup received among the Tutsi civilian elite.

Thirdly, the massive return of Hutu refugees and their demand for jobs and return of their land and other property constituted a major threat for members of the Tutsi ethnic group who had appropriated the property of the Hutu who fled the country. Reparation had never crossed the minds of the many Tutsi who had enriched themselves from looting the property of orphans and widows of their Hutu neighbors. Fourth, the Ndadaye government was also a threat to the Tutsi business community. Under the patrimonial regimes connections with the government was essential for success in the business sector. These advantages were to evaporate with the institution of a broad based government.

Table 5.8 – Government of National Unity[165]

The government convention	Tutsi Interpretation	Tutsi Interpretation
	That was a flagrant violation of people's sovereignty It marked a retrieval through blood spillage, of what political opposition (Tutsi) had lost democratically The convention was imposed by the mono ethnic army It was a distribution of portfolio without touching the army and the judiciary	It was an instrument brought at the instance of FRODEBU which should have been disqualified for committing genocide The convention should have dismissed FRODEBU from power Those who prepared it were sole concerned with the sharing of portfolios and not a return of peace.

---

165 Op cit

Conception of Democracy -+.	Democracy should be based on one man, one vote as well as the abolition of exclusion and privileges It should entail the respect of human rights and freedom	Democracy is not synonymous with ethnic-based numeric elections One man, one vote equals the dictatorship of the majority and not democracy. Democracy should promote the best and not the most numerous. There must be a democracy adapted to the realities of our country Pluralist elections are not appropriate for Burundi

Table 5.8 above indicates that, almost on every sphere ranging from the composition of government to the definition of democracy, the Hutus and the Tutsis differed in their perception. After the death of President Ndadaye. The country was ruled by a succession of weak and divided administrations and unrest continued. This led to another military coup by former President Buyoya which met international condemnation and sanctions which continued till 1999.

Table 5.9 – Institutional Differences

State Institutions	HUTU VERSION	TUTSI VERSION
The Army	The army is mono-ethnic It is responsible for all crimes of genocide It is a vehicle of Burundi malaise It is enemy number one of the Burundi people It is an instrument for usurping power They are mercenaries made up of one ethnic group which needs to be reformed It must be confined to the barracks	It is a peace purveyor The army is a stabilizing element Thanks to the army that Tutsis are alive A good army but maligned by the Hutu.
The judiciary	It is more than 90% Tutsi percent based An apparatus rendering expeditious judgment of the Hutu since 1965 Justice with system of double standards	The judicial apparatus which performs its tasks with few resources, but maligned by the Hutu Justice unable to try the FRODEBU perpetrators of genocide for lack of independence of the executive

As indicated in Table 5.9 above, the composition of state institutions and their functions was very contentious. There were serious disagreements regarding what state institutions stood for, as a consequence, the differing interpretations by Hutus and Tutsis was a factor.

SUMMING UP BURUNDI'S HISTORICAL CONFLICT DYNAMICS

Burundi's political history can be depicted as a series of provocations and reactions where opposing groups take turns in identifying the others as the primus motor in an endless historical regression to justify the next wave of violence. The most significant features of this deplorable dynamic are;

The erosion of the pre-colonial monarchical system by the German and later and more substantially the Belgian colonialists. The failure of the colonial state to create a functional state and the entrenchment of imagined ethnic identities.

The centralization of patronage resources in the state apparatus making the state the main instrument of group domination and an arena for competition between segments of the dominant group, but never anything that could be described as a legal-rational institution

The centralization of the state apparatus with all tax revenues being deported to Bujumbura and all public officials appointed from the capital. The failure to install majority rule with security guarantees for the Tutsi elite who use the national army for its protection. The systematic, violent and bloody system of minority rule by different constellations of elite networks centered around the Tutsi minority in general and the Hima from bururi in particular, making geography the second most salient line of political mobilization after ethnicity.

Chapter Seven

IMPLICATIONS AND DIMENSIONS FOR SUSTAINABLE PEACE

"If we do not end war - war will end us. Everybody says that, millions of people believe it, and nobody does anything".

H.G. Wells

The conflict configuration in Burundi is multidimensional and compounded by a number of different perspectives. The different factors contribute to the conflict complex in its own way. Additionally, conflict analysis in Burundi is intricately interwoven into the regional conflict configuration of the Great lakes region.

The sources of the conflict have a multi-country character and the consequences affect several countries. Consequently, the problems cannot be managed if the developments in the different states do not pull in the same direction. The following therefore are factors which impinge on the conflict as well as its final resolution.

SHIFTING ACTORS

The situation in Burundi has been one of variations in the level of direct violence in different parts of the country. On very few occasions has the conflict been homogenous throughout the country. Each stage of the conflict has been simultaneously pre-conflict, conflict and post conflict which makes awaiting a national ceasefire is an exercise in futility.

There is a very low level of institutionalization of actors and therefore there is surprisingly high level of flexibility in the patterns of alliances.[166] The absence of clearly manifested goals facilitates a pragmatic approach to the constellation and frequent change of actor alliances and networks of some

---

166 This state of affairs was recognized by Security Council Resolution 1653 (2006) Strongly condemned the activities of militias and armed groups operating in the Great Lakes region such as the Forces Démocratiques de Libération du Rwanda (FDLR), the Palipehutu-Forces Nationales de Libération (FNL) and the Lord's Resistance Army (LRA) which continue to attack civilians and United

groups with no long term military strategy. Reason why an observer said in an interview that 'their goal is on their nose, so they can't see it'.

A MILITARIZED REGIONAL SOCIETY

The long drawn-out conflicts have brought about a general militarization of all Burundi as well as the neighboring countries of Rwanda, Democratic Republic of the Congo and Uganda. These countries spend much of their budget allocation in the purchase of arms and ammunitions. The lifestyle is so militarized so much so that, security is measured by both ethnic origin and the possession of a weapon which has rendered the security situation absolutely insecure.

Interlinked to the militarization of society is a staggering level of criminalization of every day lives of millions of people which amount to a generally very high state of insecurity. Criminals have taken advantage of the high level of insecurity and the availability of arms and ammunitions to ply their trade. The proliferation of armed groups of different character and extent is a major challenge both for conflict prevention, post-conflict rehabilitation and peace building.

Nations and humanitarian personnel and commit human rights abuses against local populations and threaten the stability of individual States and the region as a whole and *reiterates* its demand that all such armed groups lay down their arms and engage voluntarily and without any delay or preconditions in their disarmament and in their repatriation and resettlement.

ARMS AND AMMUNITIONS TRADE

The almost unlimited access to weapons in the area is an important source and amplifier of conflict. Control of the trade and distribution of arms is a pre-requisite for stability in Burundi and the region. The difficulties in addressing the arms trade stems from the strong economic and political interests involved, and the fact that the trade is typically conducted in an informal manner.

The question has often been asked. Who provides these arms? In the case of Rwanda, the machetes used for the genocide were alleged to have been imported from China. The arms trade in the Great lakes region involves countries, smugglers, drug cartels and a whole host of other organizations. This has created a multidimensional interest in the conduct of the war.[167] These powerful interests would definitely not want to see the war come to an end as it would affect their business.

SCARCE RESOURCES AND DEMOGRAPHIC STRESS

As already stated, Rwanda and Burundi are very small nations with huge populations. They are the most densely populated countries in Africa. The birth rates of these countries are also very high. These rapid population

---

167 In their work Jeffrey Boutwell and Michael Klare 'Light weapons and civil conflict: controlling the tools of violence' they indicate that the conflicts in the great lakes have generated an insatiable demand for weapons through out the region on the part of both governments and sub state actors. They add that, historically, weaponry and military training have been obtained by governments in the great lakes region through military assistance agreements with the major powers.

growth and the high population density in Burundi as well as in different areas in the region (Rwanda and Uganda), creates increased demands for land, firewood and economic resources and social services. Considering that these countries are poor and have been involved in conflict for much their time after independence, the governments have been unable to provide these social services [168] The warring factions such as the FNL and FDD are known to recruit from social groups under stress.

REGIONAL DEMOGRAPHIC FLUIDITY

The Great Lakes region has been embroiled in conflict for such a long time. There's been conflict in Rwanda, Uganda, Burundi, Democratic Republic of the Congo and far off Somalia. The border area between Rwanda, DRC and Burundi is covered with thick rainforest where borders are not discernible. Therefore movement between these countries is easy because of the porosity of the borders. Burundi is the largest net contributor to the refugee

---

168 The recent United Nations Environment Programme (UNEP) publication, From Conflict to Peace building, the Role of Natural Resources and the Environment provides some arguments for giving this area greater attention: The UNEP reports find that:

a) 40 % of all intrastate conflicts since 1960 have a link to natural resources b)less than a quarter of peace agreements for conflicts with links to natural resources address the management and governance of natural resources c) intrastate conflicts linked to natural resources are twice as likely to relapse within five years. These findings provoke questions about the links between natural resources and conflict, the apparent reluctance of mediators to engage with the issue and the potential risks of ignoring it

problem in the Great Lakes Region.[169] Adding to the magnitude of demographic fluidity are the vast numbers of internally displaced persons which call into question these categorizations.

THE CONSTRUCTION OF KNOWLEDGE AND IDENTITIES

An extremely significant source of the Burundi conflagration is based on the cognitive process wherein the history, identity and interpretations of today's situation are constructed. A key process is the systematic manipulation by elites of the uneducated and marginalized masses, selling off self-sustaining processes of the construction of identities built on fear and stereotypes of the other. Perhaps the most complex knowledge construction in Burundi is ethnicity which of course is also a major source of mobilization and violence.[170]

---

169 Kurt Mills confirms this when he states that 'The presence of the refugees itself had significant effects on the entire region. It brought increased crime, and, in some regions added increased economic and environmental stress. Whole forests were decimated as refugees searched for firewood and building materials. Refugees received resources from humanitarian actors, whereas local residents frequently did not. Incidents of both petty and more major crimes increased in many areas. All of this created resentment on the part of some local residents and officials. This, combined with a perceived lack of attention and resources from the international community led to increased pressure to expel the refugees, particularly in western Tanzania.

170 Jean Berchmans Ndayizigiye indicates that 'The events, which may have triggered the actual crisis in Burundi can be located in the brutal political and social changes introduced by the 1991 democratic process, which include the contradiction in leadership vision: the Tutsi fight to maintain the status quo while the Hutu increasingly demand for democratic elections;

A prime conflict generator in the region and Burundi in particular is the interpretations of historical atrocities by constructed collectives, legitimizing retaliation. In all cases reports about the reality are never neutral.

VIOLENT PSYCHOLOGY

The historical and cultural proximity between Burundi and the regional conflict configuration creates what could be called a regional conflict psychology. Events every where in the world are interpreted in light of this psychology and add to the narrations in which different groups are stigmatized or portrayed as martyrs.[171] The regions cycle of violence has also served to legitimize violence through the establishment of a culture of impunity for politically sanctioned violence.

---

a precipitated and ill prepared democratic process (the former unique Uprona party manages the process, drafts the new constitution and the electoral law, has the power to admit or refuse other emerging political parties); a very short campaign period (two weeks) and the victory of the opposition; the assassination of the democratically elected President and his cabinet; the anarchy characterized by the absence of authority and the lack of a strong government for decision making

171 According to Kimmel, shorter historical events allow deeply seated structural forces to emerge as politically potent and begin to mobilize potential discontents (Kimmel, 1990,p. 9). In the case of Burundi, these structural forces include the assassination of Hutu political leaders (1962 up 1965), the different (real or prefabricated) military coups d'etat (1965, 1966, 1969, 1971, 1976, 1987, 1993), the different Hutu rebellions followed by brutal repression of the civilian population (1965, 1972, 1988, 1990) and most of all, the fear generated by many refugees in the neighboring countries.

DEFICIENT INSTITUTIONS

Burundi faces a situation of lack of democracy, good governance and a legitimate political order based on a social contract between the rulers and the ruled providing a foundation for citizenship. The structures, institutions, regulatory frameworks and the culture of democracy and good governance are weak. A number of more or less elaborate democratic institutions existed in the traditional society, but most of these have been destroyed or hollowed out during the colonial era.[172] Based on the reasons above, one can safely conclude that, the Burundi conflict is multi-dimensional. The various dimensions of the conflict are socio-political, anthropological, socio-cultural, psychological and economic.

THE SOCIO-POLITICAL DIMENSION

According to Gahama, colonization has been seen to have largely contributed to the ethnic crystallization by favoring the 'Ganwa' and some Tutsi's over the Hutu on the political, cultural and social levels. The catastrophic management of the postcolonial era by the Burundi elite worsened an already compromised situation, to the extent that they had resorted to their identity references (ethnicity, regionalism, clanism) in order to accede to power. Violence and authoritarian regimes have characterized the politics of the country.

---

[172] Burundians are disputing over access to and control of territory and economic and natural resources. There are wide structural inequalities between the "Haves" and the "Haves not", including the unequal distribution of land, income, housing, employment, public health, and political rights and representation. The increase of the population and the environmental degradation and exiguity of the land further perpetuates this inequality of resources

Note worthy is the fact that, the first constitution, which was promulgated on 16 October 1962, provided for a parliamentary type of constitutional monarchy along similar lines to that of the then Belgian constitution. The "Mwami" or Monarch, the government, the parliament and the judiciary at the central level, and the communes at the local level constituted the main institutions of the Monarchy. Much emphasis was placed on the central level where the various conflicts were hatched, even though sometimes executed at the local level. The Mwami, who prior to independence embodied all legislative, executive and judiciary powers, lost all powers of responsibility under the first constitution. He reigned but did not govern; he was reduced at best to an arbitrator, in spite of the legitimacy of his hereditary powers. This concept of a reigning but not a governing Monarch was totally alien to Burundi tradition. Ethnicity gradually emerged within the ruling class and contaminated the lower strata of the society.

According to Guichaoua (1995), another horrendous error that was made came when, on the eve of independence, the supervising authority, considered it necessary to dismiss the rest of the traditional authorities, introduce a multiparty system and organize elections.

At that time, political formations were advocating what was legally termed the emancipation of the Hutu in the style of neighbouring Rwanda.

Divisions then tore the various governments apart, and following the various censure motions and misunderstanding among members of the government political instability became the order of the day. Instead of governing, the ministers became involved in permanent quarrel and intrigues. That marked the irreversible onslaught of political violence.

It can perhaps be argued that, it is not the institutional machinery that was directly responsible for the chaotic exercise of power.[173] The institutions were after all, seemingly modern, democratic and of good quality. It could be the poor management that led to tensions and indeed trouble. This view is exemplified by the 1965 coup, which was blamed on the tribal rivalries inherent in the institutions of government. The coup d'etat had the simple effect of consummating the irreversible cycle of political violence.

THE ANTHROPOLOGICAL, SOCIOCULTURAL AND PSYCHOLOGICAL DIMENSION

According to Chretien, (1997), the deformation of the sociological reality of Burundi vis-à-vis ethnicity and the consequent deterioration of sociocultural values is a major cause of the Burundi conflict. When the colonizer arrived Burundi, he found a culturally homogenous society with a

---

173 Mahmoud says: "Before the slavery and colonialist period, Tutsi was an identity of wealth and power. Hutu signified a lack of both. A Hutu with means could go through a social ritual called Kwihutura. It was a ritual by which a Hutu shed his Hutuness. Your children could now marry Tutsi and their children would be considered Tutsi. Likewise, a Tutsi family without means may find it difficult to find a Tutsi spouse for their off-spring. These children would then have no choice but marry Hutu. While the social space between Hutu and Tutsi was vast, with Tutsi as power and Hutu as subject, it was a space that some could and did negotiate, either through opportunity that came with enrich mentor through compulsion that was a consequence of impoverishment..

strong solidarity prevailing in daily activities. Armed with different theories on race inequality, fashionable at that time in Europe, the colonizer deliberately falsified the sociological reality of Burundi by affirming that the ethnic components were fundamentally different.

On this basis was manufactured the hermitic myth where by the Tutsi was superior, came from 'outside', proud, arrogant ... in short a 'black European' made to govern and lord over all others. On the other hand, Young (1986) states that, the colonizer deemed that, the Hutu was Negroid and like all other Negroes, a big child and all children are superficial, being light, and impulsive. The Bantu farmer with his stocky build was naturally created to serve blindly and obey the 'Tutsi lord'.

To further break the Burundi identity, a system of ethnic identification was established based on the 'baganwa', who got assimilated by the 'Batutsi' for governance and the making of chiefs and sub chiefs as auxiliaries of administration, since they were the only ones likely to govern, their children were given education.[174] This racist vision of Burundi culminated

---

174 During many occasions throughout Burundi history, the Hutu denounced injustices committed against other human beings. They got organized into social movements to claim the respect of human rights dignity (Ubuntu). Some movements were non violent (revolt of Inanmujandi, 1933 refusal of ethnic identity cards, 1960 political parties, 1988 open letter to president Buyoya) while others were violent (1965, 1972, 1990), but they all were bloodily repressed. The summit of the repression was in 1972 where almost 300,000 Hutu were killed within three months. As the democratic recourse to redress the situation seemed impossible, the only ways the Hutu opposition could oblige the Tutsi to bring about social change in Burundi was to organize themselves into violent social protest movements with the formation of an armed rebel group in 1994. Despite repression

historically in the 1925-1930 administrative reform aimed at dismissing all Hutu chiefs and only a handful of Tutsi chiefs. By 1945 there were no Hutu chiefs in Burundi. This destruction of the socio-political fabric of the society and alienation of the traditional authority ran down the chief and psychologically reduced him to an inferior being.

Further more Bayard (1995) explains that the colonizer divided the Burundi society on the basis of ethno sociological cliché into distinct ethnic groups based on physical differences and differentiation in the public service, economic and religious activities. Unfortunately, both national and international opinion clung to this cliché and the myth became a reality, with each person identifying with the colonizers fantasy.

The impact of this was the transmission of a cultural heritage based on physical, intellectual and psychological traits of the Hut/Tutsi/Twa of Burundi. Consequently, each ethnic group developed a stereotype and passed Judgement on one another based on mutual preconceptions. The breakdown of Burundi society into distinct ethnic groups has led to each group taking a stand as a separate entity but developing a negative image and demonizing the other group, and thus generating reciprocal fears. The former United Nations Secretary General Boutros Ghali[175] confirmed this during his

---

and alienation, the Hutu had managed to develop some area of competence and new forms of expertise. Unfortunately, the social structure did not change to integrate them. A perceived discrepancy between the Hutu expectation and the Tutsi society values has persisted up today. In his book, Gurr states that when the perceived difference between what the people expect of society and what it appears, society will be able to provide generates revolution (Kimbell, 1990, p.77).

175 Mr. Boutros Boutros-Ghali became the sixth Secretary-General of the United Nations on 1 January 1992, when he began a five-year

visit to Bujumbura when he said 'The enemy number one of Burundi is fear'.

As a result of this scenario, Chretien, (1997) submits that, in self-defence, both the Hutu and the Tutsi have developed protection mechanisms. For instance whenever a Hutu commits a crime or a Tutsi, the Tutsi or the Hutu will excuse, understand, explain away and almost approve the criminal behaviour of his fellow Hutu or Tutsi. Consequently, an anomic society has emerged which no longer has consensual values, thus dangerously compromising the moral system of the country. The door was opened to the settling of accounts in an arbitrary fashion, thus increasing the conflict.

In the same light, there has also been a massive deterioration of socio-cultural values. Burundian social identity is generally recognized by language, beliefs and their attendant practices (ideological, religious and popular), social and family organization, production techniques and occupation, mode of life, artistic expression and perception and daily activities constituting the essence of its culture.

The erosion of values has led to negative consequences. First of all there is a crisis of authority, be it parental, educational, administrative or even religious. Authority has been discredited during the successive crises, which have shaken

---

term. At the time of his appointment by the General Assembly on 3 December 1991, Mr. Boutros-Ghali had been Deputy Prime Minister for Foreign Affairs of Egypt since May 1991 and had served as Minister of State for Foreign Affairs from October 1977 until 1991. Mr. Boutros-Ghali has had a long association with international affairs as a diplomat, jurist, scholar and widely published author.

the nation.[176] Regarding political administrative authority, it is widely known that, a large number of leaders were directly implicated in the massacres that took place either by master minding and spearheading the killings, training the killers, supplying the killers with killing instruments and by taking over administrative space and turning them into killing grounds.

As for religious authority, the impression is that religion has not had any positive influence in the practical life of the people because the religious authorities have not always practiced what they preach. The crisis therefore is the result of a long process of society's ethnic division by internal and external factors. Internally by the double standards of the leaders and externally by the crisis of social values which has derailed the population.

THE ECONOMIC DIMENSION

At the core of the Burundi conflict is the underdevelopment of the economy. While some analysts have perceived the conflict as basically political or ethnic, others have persistently linked it to socio-economic dimensions. The following economic indicators can best explain the relationship between the economy and the exacerbation of the conflict;

In 1994 the per capita GDP was US$160 and has continuously been falling. Between 1985 and 1994 the average growth of the GDP was 1.32 per cent, a sign of relative deterioration in

---

176 Secretary General Boutros Boutros-Ghali has urged the U.N. Security Council to consider creating a standby multinational force of up to 25,000 troops ready to intervene in the small African country of Burundi to prevent ethnic violence from becoming a slaughter like the one that caused approximately 500,000 deaths in neighboring Rwanda.

the standard of living. Regarding macro-economic indicators, the country recorded a budgetary deficit of 1.9 per cent of GDP and an annual average inflation of 5.4 percent in the period 1984-1994. Official development assistance, which was 12.8 percent in 1980 rose to 32.2 percent in 1994. The situation of budgetary deficit and therefore recourse to debt or external aid has been with the Burundi economy since independence.

The Burundi economy with a dual structure of traditional and modern sectors where the former evolves outside the world capitalist economy is heavily dependent on the agricultural sector, which today represents more than half of GDP. The secondary and tertiary sectors are not yet sufficiently developed and they represent 18 per cent of GDP.

It is an economy largely dependent on the outside world; financially dependent because of its weak domestic savings which cause it to seek external capital to finance its development; and economically dependent for external trade purposes. This dependency is heightened by its lack of diversified sources of foreign exchange. The main export is coffee, generating more than 80% of its export earnings.

The modern sector of the Burundi economy[177] was a state monopoly extensively dominated by government directly

---

[177] Olivier Basdevant on an IMF working paper indicates that '**One of the main issues facing Burundi is how to move toward a market-friendly economy and tightly limit direct intervention by the state. Burundi has significant growth potential in agriculture, notably coffee, tea, and sugar**. This potential will depend on the country's capacity to produce high-quality products and enter niche markets. State intervention has failed to accomplish this in recent years. Privatizing these sectors could raise economic efficiency and pave the way for entering

and through some public and para-public enterprises. The private sector was virtually non-existent. The state was therefore the main, if not the sole employer, while national wealth was concentrated in state coffers. Hence the state was perceived by many, particularly the elite, as the milking cow and the battleground for the survival of the fittest. Power or the need to govern, and naturally to attendant material advantages, was nurtured by the two phenomena of exclusion and clientelism.

The politics of exclusion became a mode of governance applied against anyone who did not think like the leaders and who refused to be their yes-men. Appointment to a post was centered on personal rapport and resulted in inefficiency and poor management of the public service. It is important to also note that, the issue of modern state-traditional sector relations arises. While there was no seemingly obvious sign of the exclusion/clientelism phenomenon in the management of the traditional sector, there were conflicts between the sectors. There is an overgrowing deterioration in state farmer relations because of the state's omnipresent attitude which created a scenario of obedience without complaint.

For instance one cannot but observe that the technologies are not sufficiently credible to farmers to adopt them and that the unilateral and authoritarian extension system did lead the traditional sector to reject the new techniques.

> niche markets. Over the medium to long run, Burundi could also exploit its mineral resources (nickel, vanadium and rare-earth elements), which have not even been fully assessed yet. Developing these sectors will require not only reforms like privatization and a better business climate, but also investment in infrastructure so as to reduce transport costs and eliminate bottlenecks like those created by the lack of reliable electrical power.

From the economic standpoint education has been valuable to Burundi. In as much as the educated Burundians are better off, regarding the accumulation of wealth, unfortunately education infrastructure in the country is not equitably distributed and the system fosters general training rather than professional training, thus creating a lot of frustration. This has created a class of frustrated youths ready for any kind of adventure in the absence of the prospect of a viable profession.

On the land issue, suffice it to state that the agrarian question[178] in Burundi is 'a question of life and death for the rural population of Burundi who have no their salvation but their land'. There exists strong competition for access to cultivable land. This sometimes degenerates into social tension, and has also been the reason for violence within families and among neighbors wishing to expand their land in Burundi.

---

178 A study conducted by the ACTS show that more than half the refugees feel that land shortage was either crucial or important obstacle to their returning. Following the August 2000 signing of a peace agreement in Arusha, Tanzania and the enhanced regional stability brought about by the peace process in neighbouring DR Congo, there is now an opportunity for peace, a mass return of refugees and development. Article IV of the Arusha Accord provides that all returning refugees will be able to access their property, including their land or receive adequate compensation and recognizes the need for the equitable apportionment and redistribution of national resources throughout the country. According to Huggins, the current situation of mass refugee return is not lacking a historical precedent. He says that in 1993, land disputes related to the return of refugees significantly contributed to the deterioration of the political situation that culminated in a coup d'etat and the assassination of President Ndadaye.

Chapter Eight

THE VERDICT

"When the music changes, so does the dance"

African proverb

The Burundi situation which is a reflection of Africa's conflict resolution strategy leave open a lot of questions. They include:

1. Did the peace process adequately take into consideration the root causes of the conflict?

2. Is the Burundi Conflict merely an ethnic conflict?

3. Where there some red flags in the Burundi peace trajectory.

Safe for the last question, we believe that the responses to the first two questions are debatably in the negative. In consideration of the first question, history tells us that, Burundians (Hutu, Tutsi and Twa) had coexisted for many decades without problems. The question then arises as to the source of this sudden hatred amongst the ethnic groups. This could be unearthed through an incisive look at how colonialism disfigured the psyches of the Burundians. The only way to deal with this colonial creation is to go back to how it was done and see how it can be reversed. Even if it can be done through the use of force, then that should be it.

But instead of doing that, an ethnic solution of power sharing was prescribed and implemented through the Arusha Agreement. This has dealt a serious blow to long term coexistence and perpetuated an eternally ethnic mentality in the populace. One major consequence of this prescription is that ethnicity becomes a qualification to attain whatever objective one needs to attain in Burundi. In the era of globalization and ethnic coexistence it is grossly criminal for anyone to implement solutions to African conflicts which prescribe long term conflict in those areas for short term peace. We argue that, peace should be a process not an event. The manner in which the Arusha agreement was rushed speaks for itself and therefore we conclude that the first question was not dealt with.

With regards to the second question, we assert that, the Burundi conflict is not merely an ethnic conflict. History also shows that, the Hutu-Tutsi classification in Burundi was some point an occupational description. The occupation of a person could determine whether you were Hutu or Tutsi. Therefore, a Hutu could be Tutsi while a Tutsi could be a Hutu depending on your occupation and wealth. Peace studies theory explains that, when people are poor, landless, and without access to social, economic, religious and political rights, it creates a situation of stress, strain and tension which eventually degenerates either in the long run or short run. A case in point, taking the issue of land, Burundi is a very small and densely populated country. The Arusha agreement which is the road map to peace in Burundi provides the right to return. Considering that, the conflict has been for a very long time, involving huge numbers of population displacement, the question then arises as to where these refugees would return to? The land law in Burundi restores ownership to anyone who has resided on land over a period of ten years. If the land issue is not properly addressed, then the long term solution to the crisis is in jeopardy.

In conclusion we are of the view that, Arusha brought some semblance of peace in Burundi and in its implementation we have seen the constant progress in bringing in the last rebel groups which did not sign the agreement. But we assert that, this is a negative peace because of the long term consequences of what has been created in the name of a peaceful country. A nation of ethnic inclusion has been created not one of ethnic coexistence and intercourse. A nation of ethnicity as a qualification has been created rather than a meritocracy. A hugely social and economically challenged nation has been created rather than a long term peace which addresses those problems has been created. This explains the title of Burundi's Negative Peace and we believe that is the shadow in which African conflicts are being resolved. A relapse by post conflict countries in Africa cannot be totally ruled out.

Warning: The history of African conflict resolution has shown that, when conflicts are resolved peripherally for the purposes of obtaining a peace prize, this does not translate to peace on the ground. The cost of relapse or ignoring conflict is usually huge than the conflict which engendered the resolution. We dare to say that when one visits, Nigeria, Sierra Leone, Liberia, DRC, Burundi, Rwanda, Uganda, Sudan, Cote D'Ivoire, Zimbabwe, Algeria, Western Sahara, Somalia, Eritrea, Cameroon, he/she would better appreciate what we are saying because there is no peace in any of those countries because what exist is a temporal negative peace. What Africa needs is a permanent positive peace. But this can only be achieved, if the peace negotiators are bold enough to speak out for the cause of peace.

Annexure

POST SCRIPT BURUNDI

The Republic of Burundi is located in East Central Africa. It consist of an area of 10.740 square miles (27,816 sq km) The July 2009 population estimate puts the population at 8,988,091. The capital is Bujumbura. The population is approximately four-fifths who are Hutu and the approximately one-fifth who are Tutsi. The first inhabitants, the Twa Pygmies make up about 1% of the population.

The languages are Rundi (Kirundi), French (both official), Swahili. The religions are Christianity (mostly Roman Catholic, also Protestant, and Other Christians).Also traditional beliefs. The currency: Burundi franc. Burundi occupies a high plateau straddling the divide of the Nile and Congo watersheds. The divide runs north to south, rising to about 8,500 Ft (2,600 m). The plateau contains the Ruvubu River basin, the southernmost extension of the Nile basin. In the west, the Rusizi River connects Lake Kivu in the north with Lake Tanganyika to the south. (Britannica Concise Encyclopedia, 2006).

Government

Republic with two legislative bodies (Senate (49): National Assembly (100). Head of state and government: President

Pierre Nkurunziza (Since 2005), assisted by Vice President Yves Savinguvu (since, 2007).

Demography

Population density 837.4 per square km. Urban population density 323.4 persons per square km. Sex distribution: Male 48.82 %, Female 51.18 %. Age breakdown, under 15= 45.1%, 15-29= 29%, 30-44= 13.7 %, 45-59=8.2%.60-74 =3.2%. 75-84=0.7%. 85 and over =1.05.

Ethnic composition: Hutu 80.9%, Tutsi15.6%, Lingala 1.6%; Twa Pygmy 1.0%

Religious affiliation: Christian 67% of which Roman catholic 62%, Protestant 5%; traditional beliefs 23%, Muslim 10%.

Vital Statistics

Birth rate: 45.6 per 1000. (World average 20.3) **Death rate:** 16.1 per 1000. (World average 8.6). Natural increase rate per 29.5 per 1000 (World average 11.7). **Total fertility rate:** 6.80. **Life Expectancy:** Male 47 years , female, 49.5 years.

National Economic Overview

Burundi is a landlocked, resource-poor country with an underdeveloped manufacturing sector. The economy is predominantly agricultural with more than 90% of the population dependent on subsistence agriculture. Economic growth depends on coffee and tea exports, which account for 90% of foreign exchange earnings. The ability to pay for imports rests primarily on weather conditions and international coffee and tea prices. The Tutsi minority, 14% of the population, dominates the coffee trade. An ethnic-based war that lasted for over a decade resulted in more than 200,000 deaths, forced more than 48,000 refugees into Tanzania, and displaced 140,000 others internally. Only one in two children go to school, and approximately one in 15 adults have HIV/AIDS. Food, medicine, and electricity remain in short supply. Burundi's GDP grew around 4% annually in 2006-08. Political stability and the end of the civil war have improved aid flows and economic activity has increased, but underlying weaknesses - a high poverty rate, poor education rates, a weak legal system, and low administrative capacity - risk undermining planned economic reforms. Burundi will continue to remain heavily dependent on aid from bilateral and multilateral donors; the delay of funds after a corruption scandal cut off bilateral aid in 2007 reduced government's revenues and its ability to pay salaries.

Military:

National Defense Force (Forces de Defense National, FDN): Army (includes naval detachment and Air Wing), Gendarmerie (2009)

Military service age and obligation

Military service is voluntary; the armed forces law of 31 December 2004 did not specify a minimum age for enlistment, but the government had previously specified that each recruit would need to have a primary school leaving certificate (2009)

Manpower available for military service

Males age 16-49: 1,878,544

Females age 16-49: 1,851,676 (2008 est.)

Manpower fit for military service

Males age 16-49: 1,124,072

Females age 16-49: 1,102,729 (2009 est.)

Manpower reaching militarily significant age annually
Male: 101,402

Female: 101,897 (2009 est.)

Military expenditures

5.9% of GDP (2006 est.)

country comparison to the world: 11

TRANSNATIONAL ISSUES

Burundi and Rwanda dispute sections of border on the Akanyaru/Kanyaru and the Kagera/Nyabarongo rivers, which have changed course since the 1960s, when the boundary was delimited; cross-border conflicts among Tutsi, Hutu, other ethnic groups, associated political rebels, armed gangs, and various government forces persist in the Great Lakes region

Refugees and internally displaced persons:

Refugees (country of origin): 9,849 (Democratic Republic of the Congo)

IDPs: 100,000 (armed conflict between government and rebels; most IDPs in northern and western Burundi) (2007)

Trafficking in persons:

Current Situation: Burundi is a source country for children trafficked for the purposes of child soldiering, domestic servitude, and commercial sexual exploitation; a small number of Burundian children may be trafficked internally for domestic servitude or commercial sexual exploitation; in early 2008, Burundian children were allegedly trafficked to Uganda, via Rwanda, for agricultural labor and commercial sexual exploitation

tier rating: Tier 2 Watch List - Burundi is on the Tier 2 Watch List for the second consecutive year for its failure to provide sufficient evidence of increasing efforts to combat trafficking in persons in 2007; the government's inability to provide adequate protective services to children accused of association with armed groups and to conduct anti-trafficking law enforcement activities continue to be causes for concern; Burundi has not ratified the 2000 UN TIP Protocol (2008)

ARUSHA PEACE AND RECONCILIATION AGREEMENT FOR BURUNDI

We, the representatives of:

- The Government of the Republic of Burundi,

- The National Assembly,

- The *Alliance Burundo-Africaine pour le Salut* (ABASA),

- The *Alliance Nationale pour le Droit et le Développement* (ANADDE),

- The *Alliance des Vaillants* (AV-INTWARI),

- The *Conseil National pour la Défense de la Démocratie* (CNDD),

- The *Front pour la Démocratie au Burundi* (FRODEBU),

- The *Front pour la Libération Nationale* (FROLINA),

- The *Parti Socialiste et Panafricaniste* (INKINZO),

- The *Parti pour la Libération du Peuple Hutu* (PALIPEHUTU),

- The *Parti pour le Redressement National* (PARENA),

- The *Parti Indépendant des Travailleurs* (PIT),

- The *Parti Libéral* (PL),

- The *Parti du Peuple* (PP),

- The *Parti pour la Réconciliation du Peuple* (PRP),

- The *Parti Social-Démocrate* (PSD),

- The *Ralliement pour la Démocratie et le Développement Economique et Social* (RADDES),

- The *Rassemblement du Peuple Burundais* (RPB) and

- The *Union pour le Progrès National* (UPRONA),

Hereinafter referred to as "the Parties",

Considering the rounds of talks held in Mwanza in 1996, Having participated in the negotiations held in Arusha pursuant to the Declaration by the Participants in the Burundi Peace Negotiations involving all the Parties of the Burundi Conflict signed at Arusha on 21 June 1998 ("the Declaration of 21 June 1998") under the facilitation of the late Mwalimu Julius Kambarage Nyerere, and subsequently of Mr. Nelson Rolihlahla Mandela, on behalf of the States of the Great Lakes region and the international community, Expressing our deep appreciation for the persistent efforts of the Facilitators, the late Mwalimu Julius Kambarage Nyerere and Mr. Nelson Rolihlahla Mandela, the States of the Great Lakes region and the international community with a view to assisting the people of Burundi to return to peace and stability, Determined to put aside our differences in all their manifestations in order to promote the factors that are common to us and which unite us, and to work together for the realization of the higher interests of the people of Burundi, Aware of the fact that peace, stability, justice, the rule of law, national reconciliation, unity and development are the major aspirations of the people of Burundi, Reaffirming our unwavering determination to put an end to the root causes underlying the recurrent state of violence, bloodshed, insecurity, political instability, genocide and exclusion which is inflicting severe hardships and suffering on the people of Burundi, and seriously hampers the prospects for economic development and the attainment of equality and social justice in our country, Reaffirming our commitment to shape a political order and a system of government inspired by the realities of our country and founded on the values of justice, democracy, good governance, pluralism, respect for the fundamental rights and freedoms of the individual, unity, solidarity, mutual understanding, tolerance and cooperation among the different ethnic groups within our society, In the presence of:

- Jean-Baptiste Bagaza and Sylvestre Ntibantunganya, former Presidents of Burundi,

- The representatives of Burundian civil society and women's organizations and Burundian religious leaders,

- H. E. Mr. Nelson Rolihlahla Mandela, Facilitator,

- H. E. General Gnassingbé Eyadéma, President of the Republic of Togo and current Chairman of the Organization of African Unity,

- H. E. Yoweri Kaguta Museveni, President of the Republic of Uganda,

- H. E. Daniel T. arap Moi, President of the Republic of Kenya,

- H. E. Benjamin William Mkapa, President of the United Republic of Tanzania,

- H. E. Frederick J. T. Chiluba, President of the Republic of Zambia,

- H. E. Major-General Paul Kagame, President of the Republic of Rwanda,

- H. E. Laurent Désiré Kabila, President of the Democratic Republic of the Congo,

- H. E. Meles Zenawi, Prime Minister of the Republic of Ethiopia,

- H. E. Mr. Kofi Annan, Secretary-General of the United Nations,

- H. E. Dr. Salim Ahmed Salim, Secretary-General of the Organization of African Unity,

- Hon. Charles Josselin, Minister of Cooperation of the French Republic, representing the European Union,

- H. E. Dr. Boutros Boutros Ghali, Secretary-General of the International Organization of la Francophonie, and

- Mr. Joseph Waryoba Butiku, Executive Director of the Mwalimu Nyerere

Foundation,

Do hereby resolve and commit ourselves to be bound by the provisions of the Arusha

Peace and Reconciliation Agreement for Burundi, hereinafter referred to as "the

Agreement".

Article 1

The Parties accept as binding the following Protocols and Annexes thereto, which form an integral part of the Arusha Peace and Reconciliation Agreement for Burundi:

Protocol I: Nature of the conflict, problems of genocide

and exclusion and their solutions;

Protocol II: Democracy and good governance;

Protocol III: Peace and security for all;

Protocol IV: Reconstruction and development;

Protocol V: Guarantees on the implementation of the Agreement.

ANNEXES

Annex I: Pledge by participating parties;

Annex II: Structure of the National Police Force;

Annex III: Ceasefire agreement;

Annex IV: Report of Committee IV;

Annex V: Implementation timetable.

2. The Parties, recognizing the need to provide in the Agreement for contingencies unforeseen at the time that the protocols were finalized, agree that the provisions of the Agreement over-ride any contrary provisions within the protocols, and further agree as follows.

(a) Where the Protocols of the Agreement contemplates that decision was to be taken by the Parties at the time of signature of the Agreement, and such matters or decisions have not been so taken at the date of signature of the Agreement, they shall be taken by the signatory parties, with or without the assistance of the Facilitator, within 30 days of signature.

(b) Any provision of the Agreement or the protocols may be amended as provided for in article 20 of Protocol II or, pending the establishment of the Transitional National Assembly, with the consent of nine-tenths of the Parties;

(c) Pending the negotiation and agreement of a comprehensive cease-fire agreement with the armed wings of non-signatory parties, Chapter III of Protocol III to the Agreement shall not come into effect; following the conclusion of the ceasefire agreement, it shall be deemed to be amended so as to be consistent with the provisions thereof. Members of the parties to the Burundi Peace Negotiations in Arusha which do not sign the Agreement shall not be entitled to participate or hold office in the transitional Government or the transitional Legislature unless such parties are admitted as participating parties in accordance with article 14 of Protocol II to the Agreement with the consent of four-fifths of the Parties.

Article 2

1. The Parties acknowledge the need for the Agreement to be accompanied by and to be a condition for lasting peace and a cessation of violence in Burundi.

2. The Parties accordingly call upon armed wings of non-signatory parties to suspend hostilities and violent actions immediately, and invite such non-signatory parties to participate in or engage in serious negotiations towards a cease- fire. The Parties agree that in addition to this public invitation included herein, they will as a priority take all reasonable and necessary steps to invite such Parties to participate in cease-fire negotiations.

3. The Parties pledge that in the event of belligerent parties spurning or refusing such an invitation and continuing their belligerent activities against the people of Burundi, or any section of them, the violent acts of such parties will be deemed to be constitute an attack on all the Parties comprising this national platform of the Burundian people, as well as on this endeavour to establish an inclusive democratic Burundian state. In such an event the Parties agree to call collectively, through the appropriate agencies including the Implementation Monitoring Committee, upon the Governments of neighbouring States, the international agencies which are guarantors of the Agreement and other appropriate national and international bodies to take the necessary steps to prohibit, demobilize, disarm, and if necessary arrest, detain and repatriate, members of such armed groups, and further to take such steps as are appropriate against any Party which encourages or supports such activities.

Article 3

The Parties commit themselves to refrain from any act or behaviour contrary to the provisions of the Agreement, and to spare no effort to ensure that the said provisions are respected and implemented in their letter and spirit in order to ensure the attainment of genuine unity, reconciliation, lasting peace, security for all, solid democracy and on equitable sharing of resources in Burundi.

Article 4

The Agreement shall be signed by the Parties. The Facilitator, the President of the Republic of Uganda as the Chairman of the Regional Peace Initiative on Burundi, the President of the Republic of Kenya as the region's elder statesman and the President of the United Republic of Tanzania as the host, and the representatives of the United Nations, the Organization of African Unity, the European Union and the Mwalimu Nyerere Foundation shall also affix their signatures hereto as witnesses and as an expression of their moral support for the peace process.

Article 5

The Agreement shall enter into force on the date of its signature.

Article 6

All of the final documents shall be drawn up in English, French and Kirundi. The English and French texts be equally authentic. The French text, being the original, shall be deposited with the Secretary-General of the United Nations, the Secretary General of the Organization of African Unity and the Government of

Burundi, and certified true copies thereof shall be transmitted by the Government to all Parties. Signed in Arusha on the 28th day of the month of August 2000.

SIGNATORY PARTIES

For the **Government of Burundi**

Name of Representative: Mr. Ambroise NIYONSABA
Title: Minister for the Peace Process
* * * *

For the **National Assembly**

Name of Representative: Hon. Léonce NGENDAKUMANA
Title: Speaker of the National Assembly
* * * *

For **ABASA**

Name of the Party's representative: Amb. Térence NSANZE
Title: Chairman
* * * *

For **ANADDE**

Name of the Party's representative: Prof. Patrice NSABABAGANWA
Title: Chairman

For **AV-INTWARI**

Name of the Party's representative: Prof. André NKUNDIKIJE
Title: Chairman
* * * *

For **CNDD**

Name of the Party's representative: Mr. Léonard NYANGOMA
Title: Chairman
* * * *

For **FRODEBU**

Name of the Party's representative: Dr. Jean MINANI
Title: Chairman
* * * *

For **FROLINA**

Name of the Party's representative: Mr. Joseph KARUMBA
Title: Chairman
* * * *

For **INKINZO**

Name of the Party's representative: Dr. Alphose RUGAMBARARA
Title: Chairman

* * * *

For **PALIPEHUTU**

Name of the Party's representative: Dr. Etiénne KARATASI
Title: Chairman
* * * *

For **PARENA**

Name of the Party's representative: H. E. Jean-Baptiste BAGAZA
Title: Chairman
* * * *

For **PIT**

Name of the Party's representative: Prof. Nicéphore NDIMURUKUNDO
Title: Chairman
* * * *

For **PL**

Name of the Party's representative: Mr. Gaëtan NIKOBAMYE
Title: Chairman
* * * *

For **PP**

Name of the Party's representative: Mr. Shadrack NIYONKURU
Title: Chairman

* * * *

For **PRP**

Name of the Party's representative: Mr. Mathias HITIMANA
Title: Chairman

* * * *

For **PSD**

Name of the Party's representative: Mr. Godefroy HAKIZIMANA
Title: Chairman

* * * *

For **RADDES**

Name of the Party's representative: Mr. Joseph NZEYIMANA
Title: Chairman

* * * *

For **RPB**

_____

Name of the Party's representative: Mr. Balthazar BIGIRIMANA
Title: Chairman
* * * *

For **UPRONA**

_____

Name of the Party's representative: Mr. Libère BARARUNYERETSE
Title: Chairman
* * * *

COSIGNATORIES
H. E. Mr. Nelson Rolilhalha Mandela, Facilitator;

_____

* * * *

H. E. Yoweri Kaguta Museveni, President of the Republic of Uganda,

_____

* * * *

H. E. Daniel T. arap Moi, President of the Republic of Kenya,

_____

* * * *

H. E. Benjamin William Mkapa, President of the United Republic of Tanzania

───────────────────────────

* * * *

H. E. Mr. Kofi Annan, Secretary-General of the United Nations,

───────────────────────────

* * * *

H. E. Dr. Salim Ahmed Salim, Secretary-General of the Organization of African Unity,

───────────────────────────

* * * *

Hon.Charles Josselin, Minister of Cooperation of the French Republic, representing

the European Union,

───────────────────────────

* * * *

Mr. Joseph Waryoba Butiku, Executive Director of the Mwalimu Nyerere Foundation

───────────────────────────

* * *

PROTOCOL I

NATURE OF THE BURUNDI CONFLICT, PROBLEMS OF GENOCIDE AND EXCLUSION AND THEIR SOLUTIONS

PREAMBLE

We, the Parties,

Having analyzed the historical causes of the conflict in Burundi during the precolonial, colonial and post-colonial periods,

Having engaged in a lengthy, exhaustive, introspective and frank debate on the perceptions, root causes, practice and ideology of genocide, war crimes and other crimes against humanity, the role of the national political class and institutions in this regard, the regional and international context in which they occur and their manifestation in Burundi,

Having also discussed the origins and evolution, causes and manifestations of exclusion in Burundi,

Resolved to eradicate genocide and to reject all forms of division, discrimination and exclusion,

Motivated by the concern to work towards national reconciliation,

Have agreed as follows:

CHAPTER I
NATURE AND HISTORICAL CAUSES OF THE CONFLICT

Article 1

Pre-colonial period

1. During the pre-colonial period, all the ethnic groups inhabiting Burundi owed allegiance to the same monarch, *Umwami*, believed in the same god, *Imana*, had the same culture and the same language, Kirundi, and lived together in the same territory. Notwithstanding the migratory movements that accompanied the settlement of the various groups in Burundi, everyone recognized themselves as Barundi.

2. The existence of *Bashingantahe* who came from among the Baganwa, the Bahutu and the Batutsi and were judges and advisors at all levels of power was, *inter alia*, a factor in promoting cohesion.

3. As a result of the mode of management of national affairs, there were no known ethnic conflicts between the various groups during this period.

4. Nevertheless, certain traditional practices such as *Ukunena, Ukwihutura, Ubugeregwa, Ubugabire, Ukunyaga, Ukwangaza, Ugutanga ikimazi-muntu, Ugushorerwako inka* and others could, depending on the circumstances, constitute sources of injustice and of frustration both among the Bahutu and the Batutsi and among the Batwa.

Article 2

Colonial period

1. The colonial administration, first German and then Belgian under a League of Nations mandate and United Nations trusteeship, played a decisive role in the heightening of frustrations among the Bahutu, the Batutsi and the Batwa, and in the divisions which led to ethnic tensions.

2. In the context of a strategy of "divide and rule", the colonial administration injected and imposed a caricatured, racist vision of Burundian society, accompanied by prejudices and clichés relating to morphological considerations designed to set the different components of Burundi's population against one another on the basis of physical characteristics and character traits.

3. It also introduced an identity card which indicated ethnic origin, thus reinforcing ethnic awareness to the detriment of national awareness. This also enabled the colonizer to accord specific treatment to each ethnic group in accordance with its theories.

4. It manipulated the existing system to its advantage by resorting to discriminatory practices.

5. Moreover, it undertook to destroy certain cultural values that until then had constituted a factor for national unity and cohesion.

6. On the eve of independence the colonizer, sensing that its power was threatened, intensified divisionist tactics and orchestrated socio-political struggles. However, the charismatic leadership of Prince Louis Rwagasore and his

colleagues made it possible for Burundi to avoid political confrontation based on ethnic considerations and enabled it to attain independence in peace and national harmony.

Article 3

Post-colonial period

1. Since independence, and throughout the different regimes, there have been a number of constant phenomena which have given rise to the conflict that has persisted up to the present time: massive and deliberate killings, widespread violence and exclusion have taken place during this period.

2. Views differ as to the interpretation of these phenomena and their influence on the current political, economic and socio-cultural situation in Burundi, as well as of their impact on the conflict.

3. Nevertheless, without prejudice to the results and conclusions of the International Judicial Commission of Inquiry and National Truth and Reconciliation Commission to be established pursuant to Chapter II of the present Protocol in order to shed light on these phenomena, the Parties recognize that acts of genocide, war crimes and other crimes against humanity have been perpetrated since independence against Tutsi and Hutu ethnic communities in Burundi.

Article 4

Nature of the Burundi conflict

With regard to the nature of the Burundi conflict, the Parties recognize that:

(a) The conflict is fundamentally political, with extremely important ethnic dimensions;

(b) It stems from a struggle by the political class to accede to and/or remain in power.

In the light of the foregoing, the Parties undertake to abide by the principles and implement the measures set forth in Chapter II of the present Protocol.

CHAPTER II: SOLUTIONS

Article 5

General political measures

1. Institution of a new political, economic, social and judicial order in Burundi, in the context of a new constitution inspired by Burundian realities and founded on he values of justice, the rule of law, democracy, good governance, pluralism, respect for the fundamental rights and freedoms of the individual, unity, solidarity, equality between women and men, mutual understanding and tolerance among the various political and ethnic components of the Burundian people.

2. A reorganization of the State institutions to make them capable of integrating and reassuring all the ethnic components of Burundian society.

3. Speedy establishment of the transitional institutions pursuant to the provisions of Protocol II to the Agreement.

4. Orientation of political parties' programmes towards the ideals of unity and national reconciliation and of socio-

economic development rather than the protection of a specific component of the Burundian people.

5. Adoption of constitutional provisions embodying the principle of separation of powers (executive, legislative and judicial), pursuant to the provisions of Protocol II to the Agreement.

6. Enactment of an electoral law that takes into account the concerns and interests of all components of the nation on the basis of the provisions of Protocol II to the Agreement.

7. Prevention of *coups d'état.*

Article 6

Principles and measures relating to genocide, war crimes and other crimes against humanity

Political principles and measures

1. Combating the impunity of crimes.

2. Prevention, suppression and eradication of acts of genocide, war crimes and other crimes against humanity, as well as violations of human rights, including those which are gender-based.

3. Implementation of a vast awareness and educational programme for national peace, unity and reconciliation.

4. Establishment of a national observatory for the prevention and eradication of genocide, war crimes and other crimes against humanity.

5. Promotion of regional cooperation to establish a regional observatory for the prevention and eradication of genocide, war crimes and other crimes against humanity.

6. Promotion of a national inter-ethnic resistance front to combat genocide, war crimes and other crimes against humanity, as well as generalization and collective attribution of guilt.

7. Erection of a national monument in memory of all victims of genocide, war crimes and other crimes against humanity, bearing the words "NEVER AGAIN".

8. Institution of a national day of remembrance for victims of genocide, war crimes and other crimes against humanity, and taking of measures that would facilitate the identification of mass graves and ensure a dignified burial for the victims.

Principles and measures in the area of justice

9. Enactment of legislation to counter genocide, war crimes and other crimes against humanity, as well as human rights violations.

10. Request by the transitional Government for the establishment by the United Nations Security Council of an International Judicial Commission of Inquiry on genocide, war crimes and other crimes against humanity responsible for:

(a) Investigating and establishing the facts relating to the period from independence to the date of signature of the Agreement;

(b) Classifying them;

(c) Determining those responsible;

(d) Submitting its report to the United Nations Security Council;

(e) The Commission shall make use of all the reports that already exist on this subject, including the 1985 Whitaker report, the 1994 nongovernmental organizations' report, the 1994-1994 report by ambassadors and the 1996 report of the United Nations International

Commission of Inquiry.

11. Request by the Government of Burundi for the establishment by the United Nations Security Council of an international criminal tribunal to try and punish those responsible should the findings of the report point to the existence of acts of genocide, war crimes and other crimes against humanity.

Article 7

Principles and measures relating to exclusion

1. Constitutional guarantees of the principle of the equality of rights and duties for all citizens, men and women, and all the ethnic, political, regional and social components of Burundian society.

2. Combating conflict-generating injustices of all kinds.

3. Banning of all political or other associations advocating ethnic, regional, religious or gender discrimination or ideas contrary to national unity.

4. Deliberate promotion of disadvantaged groups, particularly the Batwa, to correct the existing imbalances in all sectors. This exercise shall be conducted, while maintaining professionalism and avoiding the quota system, in accordance with a timetable starting at the same time as the transition period.

Principles and measures relating to public administration

5. A qualified, efficient and responsible administration that shall work in the general interest and promote balance, including gender balance.

6. A transparent administration committed to the sound management of public affairs.

7. Training, in such a way as to include all the components of Burundian society, of civil servants, particularly for regional and local government, by establishing a national school of administration.

8. Equal opportunities of access to this sector for all men and women through strict respect for, or the introduction of, laws and regulations governing the recruitment of State personnel and the staff of public and parastatal enterprises, as well as through transparency of competitive entrance examinations.

9. Depoliticization of the public administration to ensure its stability; in this respect, there is a need for legislation that will distinguish between political and technical functions; staff in the first category may change with the Government, whereas the technical staff must be guaranteed continuity.

10. Reinstatement of former refugees, taking into account experience gained before and during their exile.

Principles and measures relating to education

11. Equitable regional distribution of school buildings, equipment and textbooks throughout the national territory, in such a way as to benefit girls and boys equally.

12. Deliberate promotion of compulsory primary education that ensures gender parity through joint financial support from the State and the communes.

13. Transparency and fairness in non-competitive and competitive examinations.

14. Restoration of the rights of girls and boys whose education has been interrupted as a result of the Burundi conflict or of exclusion, by effectively reintegrating them into the school system and later into working life.

Principles and measures relating to the defence and security forces

15. Clear definition of the roles of the defence and security forces.

16. Organization of the defence and security forces as a voluntary and professional entity, and their modernization.

17. Relevant reforms to correct the ethnic, gender and regional imbalances within these forces pursuant to the relevant provisions of Protocol III to the Agreement.

Principles and measures relating to justice

18. Pursuant to the relevant provisions of Protocol II to the Agreement:

(a) Promotion of impartial and independent justice. In this respect, all petitions and appeals relating to assassinations and political trials shall be made through the National Truth and Reconciliation Commission established pursuant to the provisions of article 8 of the present Protocol;

(b) Reform of the judicial machinery at all levels, *inter alia* with a view to correcting ethnic and gender imbalances where they exist;

(c) Amendment of laws where necessary (Criminal Code, Code of Criminal Procedure, Civil Code, Nationality Act, etc.);

(d) Reform of the Judicial Service Commission so as to ensure its independence and that of the judicial system;

(e) Organization of a judicial training programme, *inter alia* through the establishment of a National School for the Magistracy;

(f) Provision of adequate human and material resources for the courts;

(g) Establishment of the post of Ombudsperson.

Principles and measures relating to the economy

19. Equitable apportionment and redistribution of national resources throughout the country.

20. Urgent implementation of an economic recovery programme with a view to combating poverty and raising the income of the people and of a programme for the reconstruction of destroyed economic infrastructures.

21. Legislation and structures for combating financial crime and corruption (tax legislation, customs legislation, legislation on public markets, etc.).

22. Recovery of State property plundered by some citizens.

23. Introduction of incentives for economic development in the context of fairness and harmony.

24. Development of the private sector by means of incentives with a view to creating new jobs and reducing the burden and pressures on the public sector.

Principles and measures relating to social services

25. Pursuant to the relevant provisions of Protocol IV to the Agreement:

(a) Equitable distribution of and access to social infrastructures, particularly schools and hospitals;

(b) Promotion of a policy of assumption by the communes of responsibility for their own affairs, in the context of decentralization;

(c) Definitive resolution of the issues relating to refugees, displaced persons, regrouped persons, dispersed persons and other *sinistrés*: rehabilitation, resettlement, reintegration and compensation for plundered property;

(d) Return to the rightful successors of the victims of the various crises of property confiscated by certain bodies or by the State or stolen by third parties: movable and immovable property, bank and Savings Bank (CADBU) assets, contributions to the Social Security Fund (INSS);

(e) Establishment of a National Commission for the Rehabilitation of *Sinistrés* to benefit the victims of the various crises;

(f) Establishment by the State of mechanisms to facilitate the recovery and repatriation of refugees' assets abroad.

Cultural principles and measures

26. Education of the population, particularly of youth, in positive traditional cultural values such as solidarity, social cooperation, forgiveness and mutual tolerance, *Ibanga* (discretion and sense of responsibility), *Ubupfasoni* (respect for others and for oneself) and *Ubuntu* (humanism and character).

27. Rehabilitation of the institution of *Ubushingantahe*.

Article 8

Principles and measures relating to national reconciliation

1. A national commission known as the National Truth and Reconciliation

Commission shall be established. This Commission shall have the following functions:

(a) Investigation

The Commission shall bring to light and establish the truth regarding the serious acts of violence committed during the cyclical conflicts which cast a tragic shadow over Burundi from independence (1 July 1962) to the date of signature of the Agreement, classify the crimes and establish the responsibilities, as well as the identity of the perpetrators and the victims. However, the Commission shall not be competent to classify acts of genocide, crimes against humanity and war crimes;

(b) Arbitration and reconciliation

The Burundian crisis is a profound one: the task of reconciliation will be long and exacting. There are still gaping wounds which will need to be healed. To this end the Commission shall, upon completion of its investigations, propose to the competent institutions or adopt measures likely to promote reconciliation and forgiveness, order indemnification or restoration of disputed property, or propose any political, social or other measures it deems appropriate. In this context, the transitional National Assembly may pass a law or laws providing a framework for granting an amnesty consistent with international law for such political crimes as it or the National Truth and Reconciliation Commission may find appropriate;

(c) Clarification of history

The Commission shall also be responsible for clarifying the entire history of Burundi, going as far back as possible in order to inform Burundians about their past. The purpose of this clarification exercise shall be to rewrite Burundi's history so that all Burundians can interpret it in the same way.

2. Membership of the commission

(a) Source

Candidates for membership of the Commission shall be put forward by civil society associations, political parties, religious denominations or women's organizations, or may stand as individual candidates.

(b) Appointing body

Members of the Commission shall be appointed by the transitional Government in consultation with the Bureau of the transitional National Assembly.

(c) Profile and selection of candidates

Members of the Commission must show probity, integrity and ability to rise above divisions of all kinds. In the selection of candidates, balance must be taken into account, and the following criteria shall apply:

(i) Age of members: at least 35 years;

(ii) Level of education: at least a full secondary education certificate or equivalent.

3. Functioning of the Commission

The Commission must have the leeway to work independently, *inter alia* through autonomy in managing the material and financial resources to be allocated to it. The Commission shall, whenever necessary, propose additional reconciliation mechanisms, and shall be free to set up sub-commissions as appropriate. The public authorities shall have the obligation to do their utmost to enable the Commission to accomplish its mission without hindrance, by providing it with sufficient material, technical and financial resources.

4. Duration

The Commission shall conduct its work over a two-year period. At the end of two years, the appropriate transitional institutions shall assess the work done, and may decide on an extension for one year.

Late Tanzanian President Julius Kambarage Nyerere:
First Mediator of the Burundi Conflict

Former South African President Nelson Rolihlahla Mandela:
The Second Mediator of the Burundi Conflict

Former Deputy South African President, now President:
Jacob Gedleyihlekisa Zuma
Third Mediator of the Burundi Conflict

Former South African Minister of Safety and Security
Charles Nqaqula:
Fourth Mediator of the Burundi Conflict

Burundian President, Pierre Nkurunziza (right) and FNL leader, Agathon Rwasa, hug after the signing of the September 2006 peace accord.

Burundian refugees returning home

Brick making in Northern Burundi

Burundi: Hilly country

Burundian Shores of Lake Tangayika

HEADS OF STATE OF BURUNDI SINCE INDEPENDENCE

General Michel Micombero: 1966-1976

Lt Gen Jean Baptiste Bagaza:
1976-1984 and 1984-1987

PROTOCOL II

DEMOCRACY AND GOOD GOVERNANCE

PREAMBLE

We, the Parties,

- Aware of the vital need to promote lasting peace in Burundi and to put an end to the conflict, division and suffering inflicted on the Burundian people,

- Reaffirming our commitment to a democratic system of government, inspired by the realities of our country, that guarantees security and justice for all, and is founded on the values of unity without exclusion,

Have agreed:

1. To ensure that a constitutional text for the people of Burundi is drafted during the transition period that is in conformity with the principles set forth in

Chapter I of the present Protocol, and to ensure that such a text is adopted and brought into force in accordance with the time-frames and procedures herein, in conformity with a vision of democracy and good governance and the principles listed hereunder.

2. To provide for a transition period that is in conformity with the transitional arrangements set forth in Chapter II of the present Protocol.

3. To give effect, within the designated time limits, to the obligations set forth in this and other protocols with regard to the establishment of the transitional institutions.

CHAPTER I

CONSTITUTIONAL PRINCIPLES OF THE POST-TRANSITION CONSTITUTION

Article 1

Fundamental values

1. All Burundians are equal in value and dignity. All citizens are entitled to equal rights and to equal protection of the law. No Burundian shall be excluded from the social, economic or political life of the nation on account of her/his race, language, religion, gender, or ethnic origin.

2. All Burundians are entitled to live in Burundi in security and peace, and must live in harmony with one another while respecting one another's dignity and tolerating one another's differences.

3. Government shall be based on the will of the Burundian people, shall be accountable to them, and shall respect their fundamental rights and freedoms.

4. The Government of Burundi shall be so structured as to ensure that all Burundians are represented in and by it; that there is equal opportunity to serve in it; that all citizens have access to government services; and that the decisions and actions of government enjoy the widest possible level of support.

5. The task of government shall be to realize the aspirations of the Burundian people, and in particular to heal the divisions of the past, to improve the quality of life of all Burundians, and to ensure that all Burundians are able to live in Burundi free from fear, discrimination, disease and hunger.

6. The function of the political system shall be to unite, reassure and reconcile all Burundians while ensuring that the Government is able to serve the people of Burundi, who are its source of power and authority. In its functioning the Government shall respect the separation of powers, the rule of law, and the principles of good governance and transparency in the management of public affairs.

Article 2

General principles

1. Burundi shall be a sovereign independent nation, united but respecting its ethnic and religious diversity and recognizing the Bahutu, the Batutsi and the Batwa, who make up the one nation of Burundi.

2. The national territory of Burundi shall be inalienable and indivisible subject to the provisions of the Constitution. Its frontiers shall be those recognized by international law.

3. Burundi shall be divided into provinces, communes and *collines* or zones, and such other subdivisions as are provided for by law. Their organization and operation shall be determined by the Constitution and by law.

4. The National Assembly shall take a decision regarding the status and revival of the monarchy, and any party

peacefully promoting the restoration of the monarchy shall be allowed to function.

5. The national language of Burundi shall be Kirundi. The official languages shall be Kirundi and any other languages decided upon by the National Assembly.

Article 3

Charter of Fundamental Rights

1. The rights and duties proclaimed and guaranteed *inter alia* by the Universal Declaration of Human Rights, the International Covenants on Human Rights, the African Charter on Human and Peoples' Rights, the Convention on the Elimination of All Forms of Discrimination against Women and the Convention on the Rights of the Child shall form an integral part of the Constitution of the Republic of Burundi. These fundamental rights shall not be limited or derogated from, except in justifiable circumstances acceptable in international law and set forth in the Constitution.

2. All citizens shall have rights and obligations.

3. Human dignity shall be respected and protected.

4. All women and men shall be equal. No one may be discriminated against, *inter alia*, on grounds of origin, race, ethnicity, gender, colour, language, social situation, or religious, philosophical or political convictions, or by reason of a physical or mental handicap. All citizens shall enjoy equal protection of the law, as well as equal treatment under the law.

5. No person shall be arbitrarily dealt with by the State or its organs.

6. All women and men shall have the right to life.

7. All women and men shall have the right to personal freedom, including to physical and mental integrity, and to freedom of movement. Torture and any other kind of cruel, inhuman, degrading treatment or punishment shall be prohibited. Everyone shall have the right to be free from violence from either public or private sources.

8. No one shall be held in slavery or servitude. Slavery and the slave trade shall be prohibited in all their forms.

9. The State shall to the extent possible ensure that all citizens have the means to lead an existence consistent with human dignity.

10. All women and men shall have the right to respect for their private and family life, residence and personal communications.

11. There shall be freedom of marriage, including the right to choose one's partner. Marriage shall be entered into only with the free and full consent of the intending spouses.

12. The family, as the fundamental unit of society, shall be entitled to protection by society and the State.

13. Freedom of expression and of the media shall be guaranteed. The State shall respect freedom of religion, belief, conscience and opinion.

14. Freedom of assembly and association shall be guaranteed, as shall freedom to form non-profit- making associations or organizations in conformity with the law.

15. All Burundian citizens shall have the right to move and settle freely anywhere in the national territory, as well as to leave it and return to it.

16. No one shall be arbitrarily deprived of her/his nationality or denied the right to change it.

17. No one may be denied access to basic education. The State shall organize public education, and shall develop and promote access to secondary and post-secondary education.

18. The State shall ensure the good management and utilization of the nation's natural resources on a sustainable basis, conserving such resources for future generations.

19. Property rights shall be guaranteed for all women and me n. Compensation that is fair and equitable under the circumstances shall be payable in case of expropriation, which shall be allowed only in the public interest and in accordance with a law which shall also set forth the basis of compensation.

20. The right to form and join trade unions and to strike shall be recognized. The law may regulate the exercise of these rights and prohibit certain categories of persons from going on strike.

21. Everyone shall have the right, in judicial or administrative proceedings, for her/his case to be dealt with equitably and

decided within a reasonable time limit. Everyone shall have the right to due process and a fair trial.

22. No one may be deprived of her/his liberty other than in conformity with the law.

23. The State shall be under an obligation to promote the development of the country, especially rural development.

24. Each individual shall have the duty to respect and show consideration for her/his fellow citizens without any discrimination.

25. All citizens shall be required to discharge their civic obligations, and to defend their homeland.

26. Every child shall have the right to special measures to protect or promote her/his care, welfare, health and physical security, and to be protected from maltreatment, abuse or exploitation.

27. No child shall be used directly in armed conflict, and children shall be protected in times of armed conflict.

28. No child shall be detained except as a measure of last resort, in which case the child may be detained only for the shortest appropriate period of time and shall have the right to be kept separately from detained persons over the age of 16 years and to be treated in a manner, and kept in conditions, that take account of her/his age.

29. Any restriction of a fundamental right must have a legal basis; it must be justified by the public interest or by the protection of another person's fundamental right; it must be proportional to the objective pursued.

30. Fundamental rights must be respected throughout the legal, administrative and institutional order. The Constitution shall be the supreme law and must be upheld by the Legislature, the Executive and the Judiciary. Any law that is not in conformity with the Constitution shall be invalid.

Article 4

Political parties

1. The multiparty system shall be recognized in the Republic of Burundi.

2. Political parties may be formed freely in conformity with the law.

3. A political party shall be a non-profit association uniting citizens around a democratic blueprint for society founded on national unity, and having a political programme with precise objectives dictated by the desire to serve the public interest and ensure the development of all citizens.

4. Political parties must comply with democratic principles in their organization and functioning, be open to all Burundians and be national in character and leadership, and shall not promote ethnic, regional or religious violence and hatred.

5. Political parties - and coalitions of political parties - shall promote the free expression of suffrage and shall participate in political life by peaceful means.

6. For the purposes of promoting democracy, a national law may authorize the financing of political parties on

an equitable basis in proportion to the number of seats they hold in the National Assembly. Such financing may apply both to the functioning of the political parties and to electoral campaigns, and shall be transparent. The law shall define the types of subsidies, benefits and facilities that the State may grant political parties.

7. Registration of political parties shall fall within the competence of the Ministry of the Interior.

8. The law shall guarantee non- interference by the public authorities in the internal functioning of political parties, save for such restrictions as may be necessary for the prevention of ethnic hatred and the maintenance of public order.

9. Political parties may form coalitions during elections in accordance with the electoral law.

Article 5

Elections

1. The right to vote shall be guaranteed.

2. Elections shall be free, fair and regular in accordance with the electoral law and the law governing political parties.

3. Elections shall be organized impartially at the national, commune and *colline* levels and at other levels prescribed by the Constitution or by law.

4. Until amended in accordance with the post-transition Constitution, the rules relating to the electoral system shall be the same as those governing the elections for institutions

at the national, commune and *colline* levels to be held during the transition period.

5. An Independent National Electoral Commission constituted in conformity with the provisions of article 20 of the present Protocol shall guarantee the freedom, impartiality and independence of the electoral process.

Article 6

The Legislature

1. Legislative power shall be exercised by the National Assembly and, where specified herein, by the National Assembly and the Senate. A law adopted by a legislative body or bodies may only be amended by the same body or bodies.

2. The number of members of the National Assembly shall be specified in the Constitution, and in the first instance shall be 100. The Constitution may allow for the number of members to be determined in accordance with a designated ratio per number of inhabitants or by setting an absolute number.

3. The National Assembly shall pass legislation, oversee the actions of the Government and exercise all other functions assigned to it by the Constitution. The National Assembly shall be responsible for approving the national budget. This provision shall not preclude the submission of matters for popular approval by way of referendum.

4. A Court of Audit responsible for examining and certifying the accounts of all public services shall be established and organized by law. Its composition shall be specified in the

post-transition Constitution. It shall be given the resources required for the performance of its duties. Administrative departments shall not withhold their co-operation from the Court of Audit. The Court of Audit shall submit to the National Assembly a report on the regularity of the general account of the State, and shall also ascertain whether public funds have been spent in accordance with the proper procedures and in accordance with the budget approved by the National Assembly.

5. The Constitution may not be amended except with the support of a **four-fifths** majority in the National Assembly and a **two-thirds** majority in the Senate.

6. Organic laws may not be amended except by a **three-fifths** majority in the National Assembly and with the approval of the Senate.

7. Members of the National Assembly and the Senate may not be prosecuted, made the subject of a warrant, arrested, detained or subjected to a penalty for acts performed as a member of the National Assembly or of the Senate.

8. Any criminal case involving a person holding political office shall be referred to a Chamber of the Supreme Court, and in the event of conviction, any appeal shall be receivable by the Chambers of the Supreme Court sitting together.

9. During sessions, a member of the National Assembly or the Senate may be prosecuted in respect of acts other than those referred to in paragraph 7 above only with the authorization of the National Assembly or the Senate, as the case may be.

10. The mechanisms for replacing members of the National Assembly or the Senate in the event of the vacancy of a seat shall be determined by law.

11. The National Assembly and the Senate shall adopt the rules of procedure governing their respective organization and functioning and the election of their bureaux. The post-transition Constitution must specify the duties of the bureaux, when the National Assembly shall convene for the first time and who shall preside at the initial meeting. The National Assembly's Bureau shall have a multiparty character, while the Senate's Bureau shall be of a multi-ethnic character.

12. The compensation and benefits regime, as well as the incompatibility regime, for members of the National Assembly and of the Senate shall be established by law.

13. The opposition parties within the National Assembly shall participate by right in parliamentary commissions, whether sectoral or of inquiry.

14. There shall be a Senate having the functions set forth herein, and such other functions as are allocated to it in the Constitution or in any law. The Senate shall comprise two delegates from each province. They shall be elected by an Electoral College comprising members of the commune councils in the province in question, shall be from different ethnic communities and shall be elected in separate ballots.

15. A former president shall be entitled to sit in the Senate. The Senate may co-opt up to three members of the Batwa group so as to ensure representation of this community.

16. The Senate shall have the following functions:

(a) To approve constitutional amendments and organic laws, including laws governing the electoral process;

(b) To receive the report of the Ombudsperson on any aspect of the public administration;

(c) To conduct inquiries into the public administration and where necessary recommend action, to ensure that no region or group is excluded from the delivery of public services;

(d) To monitor compliance with those prescripts of the Constitution requiring representativeness or balance in the composition of any part of the public service, including the defence and security forces;

(e) To advise the President and the National Assembly on any matter, including legislation;

(f) To monitor compliance with the present Protocol;

(g) To comment on or suggest amendments to legislation adopted by the National Assembly, as well as to initiate and introduce bills for consideration by the National Assembly;

(h) To approve laws dealing with the boundaries, functions and powers of Provinces, communes and *collines*.

17. The Senate shall approve solely the following appointments:

(a) The heads of the defence forces, the police and the intelligence service;

(b) The provincial governors appointed by the President of the Republic;

(c) The Ombudsperson;

(d) The members of the Judicial Service Commission;

(e) The members of the Supreme Court;

(f) The members of the Constitutional Court;

(g) The Principal State Prosecutor and members of the National Department of Public Prosecutions;

(h) The presidents of the Court of Appeal and the Administrative Court;

(i) The principal State Prosecutor in the Court of Appeal;

(j) The presidents of the Court of First Instance, the Commercial Court and the Labour Court;

(k) The State Prosecutors.

18. The Senate shall ensure that commune councils in general reflect the ethnic diversity of their constituencies; if the composition of any Commune Council does not do so, it may order the co-optation of persons by the Commune Council from an underrepresented ethnic group to that Council, provided that no more than **one-fifth** of the Council may consist of such co-opted persons. The persons to be co-opted shall be identified by the Senate from a list of names supplied to it by the Commune Council or by any *colline* chief within the commune.

19. Where the Senate proposes amendments to laws other than those in respect of which its consent is necessary, the National Assembly must consider those proposed amendments, and may if it so chooses give effect to them, before referring the bill to the President for his formal assent.

20. Members of the National Assembly and of the Senate shall have the right to debate the Government's actions and policies.

21. The Constitution shall grant the Senate the powers and resources necessary to perform its functions.

Article 7

The Executive

(a) The Constitution shall provide that, save for the very first election of a President, the President of the Republic shall be elected by direct universal suffrage in which each elector may vote for only one candidate. The President of the Republic shall be elected by an absolute majority of the votes cast. If this majority is not obtained in the first round, a second round shall follow within 15 days.

(b) Only the two candidates who have received the greatest number of votes during the first round may stand in the second round. The candidate who receives the majority of votes cast in the second round shall be declared the President of the Republic.

(c) For the first election, to be held during the transition period, the President shall be indirectly elected as specified in article 20, paragraph 10 below.

2. The President of the Republic shall exercise regulatory power and shall ensure the proper enforcement and administration of legislation. She/he shall exercise her/his powers by decrees, countersigned, where required, by a Vice-President or a minister concerned.

3. She/he shall be elected for a term of five years, renewable only once. No one may serve more than two presidential terms.

4. In the exercise of her/his functions, the President of the Republic shall be assisted by two Vice-Presidents. They shall be appointed by the President of the Republic, who shall previously have submitted their candidacy for approval by the National Assembly and the Senate, voting separately, by a majority of their members. The President of the Republic may dismiss the Vice-Presidents. They shall belong to different ethnic groups and political parties.

5. The President of the Republic, after consultation with the two Vice-Presidents, shall appoint the members of the Government and terminate their appointments.

6. Parties or coalitions thereof shall be invited, but not obliged, to submit to the President a list of persons to serve as ministers if such parties or coalitions have received more than **one-twentieth** of the vote. They shall be entitled to at least the same proportion, rounded off downwards, of the total number of ministers as their proportion of members in the National Assembly. If the President dismisses a minister, she/he must choose a replacement from a list submitted by the party or coalition of the minister in question.

7. The President of the Republic shall be the Head of State and Commander- in- Chief of the defence and security

forces. She/he shall declare war and sign armistices following consultation with the Government and the bureaux of the National Assembly and of the Senate.

8. The President of the Republic may be impeached for serious misconduct, impropriety or corruption by resolution of **two -thirds** of the members of the National Assembly and the Senate sitting together.

9. The President of the Republic may be charged only with the crime of high treason. The case shall be heard by the Supreme Court and the Constitutional Court sitting together and presided over by the President of the Supreme Court.

10. The Supreme Court shall receive a written statement of the assets and property of the President, the Vice-Presidents and members of the Government when they assume and relinquish office.

Article 8

Local government

1. The provinces shall be administered by civilian governors appointed by the President of the Republic and confirmed by the Senate.

2. Communes shall be decentralized administrative entities. They sha ll be the basis of economic and social development, and shall be divided into *collines* or zones and such other subdivisions as are provided for by law.

3. The law shall make provision for the circumstances under which a commune administrator may be dismissed or

suspended, by the central authorities or by the Commune Council, for good cause including incompetence, corruption, gross misconduct or embezzlement.

Article 9

The Judiciary

1. The judicial authority of the Republic of Burundi shall be vested in the courts.

2. The Judiciary shall be impartial and independent and shall be governed solely by the Constitution and the law. No person may interfere with the Judiciary in the performance of its judicial functions.

3. The Judiciary shall be so structured as to promote the ideal that its composition should reflect that of the population as a whole.

4. The courts and tribunals shall operate in Kirundi and the other official languages. Laws shall be enacted and published in Kirundi and the other official languages.

5. The Constitution shall provide for a Supreme Court of Burundi. Its Rules of Procedure, composition and chambers, and the organization of its chambers, shall be determined by an organic law.

6. The judges of the Supreme Court shall be appointed by the President from a list of candidates nominated by the Judicial Service Commission and approved by the National Assembly and the Senate.

7. There shall be a National Department of Public Prosecutions attached to the Supreme Court; its members

shall be appointed in the same manner as the judges of the Supreme Court.

8. The other courts and tribunals recognized in the Republic of Burundi shall be the Court of Appeal, the High Courts, the Resident Magistrates' Courts and such other courts and tribunals as are provided for by law. The *Ubushingantahe* Council shall sit at the level of the *colline*. It shall administer justice in a conciliatory spirit.

9. The President of the Court of Appeal, the presidents of the High Courts, the public prosecutors and the state counsels shall be appointed by the President of the Republic following nomination by the Judicial Service Commission and confirmation by the Senate.

10. The Government, within the limits of its resources, shall ensure that magistrates possess the desired qualifications and necessary training for the performance of their duties, and that the resources needed by the Judiciary are made available to it.

11. No one shall be denied a post in the magistracy on grounds of ethnic origin or gender.

12. A Judicial Service Commission with an ethnically balanced composition shall be established. It shall be made up of five members nominated by the Executive, three judges of the Supreme Court, two magistrates from the National Department of Public Prosecutions, two judges from the resident magistrates' courts and three members of the legal profession in private practice. The judges, magistrates and members of the legal profession shall be chosen by their peers. All members of the Commission shall be approved by the Senate.

13. The Commission shall have a secretariat. It shall be chaired by the President of the Republic, assisted by the Minister of Justice. It shall meet on an *ad hoc* basis. Its members who are not members of the Judiciary shall not be construed as members of the Judiciary solely because they are members of this oversight commission.

14. The Judicial Service Commission shall be the highest disciplinary body of the magistracy. It shall hear complaints by individuals, or by the Ombudsperson, against the professional conduct of magistrates, as well as appeals against disciplinary measures and grievances concerning the career of magistrates. No magistrate may be dismissed other than for professional misconduct or incompetence, and solely on the basis of a finding by the Judicial Service Commission.

15. Trials shall be public except where the interests of justice or a compelling public interest require otherwise. Judgments shall be reasoned and shall be handed down in public.

16. Magistrates shall be appointed by decree of the President on the proposal of the Judicial Service Commission. The presidents of resident magistrates' courts shall be appointed in the same manner except that the nominees shall be proposed to the President after obtaining the approval of the Senate.

17. The Constitutional Court shall be the highest court for constitutional matters. Its jurisdictions shall be those set forth in the 1992 Constitution. The organization of the Court shall be laid down in an organic law. Reference is made for this purpose to the elements contained in Chapter II of the present Protocol.

18. The members of the Constitutional Court, seven in number, shall be appointed by the President of the Republic and confirmed by the Senate by a **two-thirds** majority. They shall have a term of office of six years non-renewable. The first Constitutional Court shall be that established under Chapter II of the present Protocol for the transition period. The members shall have the qualifications set forth in Chapter II of the present Protocol.

19. Matters shall be referred to the Constitutional Court by the President of the Republic, the President of the National Assembly or the President of the Senate, by petition by **one quarter** of the Members of the National Assembly or **one quarter** of the Members of the Senate, or by the Ombudsperson. In addition, every natural person with a direct interest in the matter, as well as the Public Prosecutor, may request the Constitutional Court to rule on the constitutionality of laws, either directly by means of an action or by an exceptional procedure for claiming unconstitutionality raised in a matter which concerns that person before an authority.

20. The Constitutional Court may sit validly only if at least five of its members are present.

21. Decisions of the Constitutional Court shall be taken by an absolute majority of its members, except that the President of the Court shall have a casting vote if the Court is evenly split on any matter.

22. The Constitutional Court shall be competent to:

(a) Rule on the constitutionality of adopted laws and regulatory acts;

(b) Rule on the constitutionality of executive action;

(c) Interpret the Constitution and rule on vacancies in the posts of President of the Republic and President of the National Assembly if a dispute arises in regard thereto;

(d) Rule on the regularity of president ial and legislative elections;

(e) Administer the oath to the President of the Republic before she/he assumes office;

(f) Verify the constitutionality of organic laws before their promulgation,

and of the Rules of Procedure of the National Assembly before their application;

(g) Rule on any other matters expressly provided for in the Constitution.

Article 10

The administration

1. The administration shall function in accordance with the democratic values and principles enshrined in the Constitution, and with the law.

2. The administration shall be so structured, and all civil servants shall so perform their duties, as to serve all users of public services with efficiency, courtesy, impartiality and equity. Embezzlement, corruption, extortion and misappropriation of all kinds shall be punishable in accordance with the law. Any state employee convicted

of corruption shall be dismissed from the public administration following a disciplinary inquiry.

3. The administration shall be organized in ministries, and every minister in charge of a ministry shall report to the President of the Republic and to the National Assembly on the manner in which the ministry performs its functions and utilizes the funds allocated to it.

4. The administration shall be broadly representative and reflect the diversity of the components of the Burundian nation. The practices with respect to employment shall be based on objective and equitable criteria of aptitude and on the need to correct the imbalances and achieve broad representation.

5. A law shall specify the distinction between posts that are career or technical posts and those that are political posts.

6. No civil servant or member of the Judiciary may be accorded favorable or unfavorable treatment solely on grounds of her/his gender, ethnicity or political affiliation.

7. An independent Ombudsperson shall be created by the Constitution. The organization and functioning of her/his service shall be determined by law.

8. The Ombudsperson shall hear complaints and conduct inquiries relating to mismanagement and infringements of citizens' rights committed by members of the public administration and the judiciary, and shall make recommendations thereon to the appropriate authorities. She/he shall also mediate between the administration and citizens and between administrative departments, and

shall act as an observer of the functioning of the public administration.

9. The Ombudsperson shall possess the powers and resources required to perform her/his duty. She/he shall report annually to the National Assembly and the Senate. Her/his report shall be published in the Official Gazette of Burundi.

10. The Ombudsperson shall be appointed by the National Assembly by a three quarters majority. The appointment shall be subject to confirmation by the Senate.

Article 11

Defence and security forces

1. The post-transition Constitution shall contain in full the principles relating to the defence and security forces and principles of organization of those forces set forth respectively in articles 10 and 11 of Protocol III to the Agreement.

2. An organic law shall determine the organization and functioning of the defence and security forces.

3. The military head of the defence force shall be appointed by the President, subject to confirmation by the Senate.

(a) The defence and security forces shall be subordinate to the civil authority of the State, and shall uphold the Constitution and the law.

(b) The defence and security forces shall be professional and non-partisan, and shall not promote or disadvantage any political party or ethnic group.

(c) The defence and security forces shall be trained at all levels to respect international humanitarian law and the supremacy of the Constitution.

(d) For a period to be determined by the Senate, not more than 50% of the national defence force shall be drawn from any one ethnic group, in view of the need to achieve ethnic balance and to prevent acts of genocide and *coups d'état*.

(e) No civilian shall be subject to a military code of justice or tried by a military court.

5. Only the President may authorize the employment of the defence and security forces:

(a) In defence of the State;

(b) In the restoration of order and public safety;

(c) In the discharge of international obligations and commitments.

If the defence and security forces are employed in any of the capacities set forth above, the President shall promptly inform the National Assembly and the Senate of the nature, extent and reasons for this employment. If the National Assembly is not in session it shall be convened within seven days for the consideration of such matter, as specified in Protocol III to the Agreement.

CHAPTER II
TRANSITIONAL ARRANGEMENTS

Article 12

Objectives

1. Exceptional and special arrangements concerning the government of Burundi shall be made pending the adoption and entry into force of a Constitution that is in conformity with the constitutional principles set forth in Chapter I of the present Protocol.

2. The objectives of the transitional arrangements shall be:

(a) To ensure the adoption of a post-transition Constitution that is in conformity with the constitutional principles;

(b) To reconcile and unite Burundians and lay the foundations for a democratic and united Burundi, *inter alia* by promoting a broad programme of education in peace, democracy and ethnic tolerance;

(c) To ensure the repatriation, resettlement and reintegration of Burundians living outside the national territory and the rehabilitation of the *sinistrés*;

(d) To apply the measures and arrangements relating to the restoration of peace, the cessation of hostilities and the building of a professional army loyal to Burundi;

(e) To ensure the adoption of agreed measures to confront the consequences of the past and avoid any recurrence of genocide, exclusion and impunity;

(f) To implement the measures and carry out the reforms relating to the Judiciary, the administration and the defence and security forces in accordance with the Agreement;

(g) To adopt an electoral law, establish an independent electoral commission and ensure the holding during the transition period of elections at the local and national levels as provided for in article 20 below;

(h) To adopt laws on political parties, local administration, the press and other matters as required by the present Protocol and by the needs of the transitional institutions;

(i) To implement the Agreement in accordance with the implementation timetable in Annex V to the Agreement.

Article 13

Duration of the transition

1. The transition period shall commence from the time that the conditions necessary for installing the transitional Government in accordance with the applicable instruments have been met, which shall be as soon as possible after three months, and in any event not later than six months, from the date of signature of the Agreement. The Implementation Monitoring Committee alone shall determine this date, and may bring it forward if it decides that the necessary conditions exist. Until the transition period commences, all parties shall meet their obligations under the Agreement to establish or co-operate in establishing the agreed legal and institutional framework. The Implementation Monitoring Committee, established as set forth in Protocol V, shall be the mechanism for guaranteeing compliance with the Agreement.

2. The transition period shall culminate upon the election of the new President. The presidential election shall take place after the first democratic election of the National Assembly. Both elections shall take place within 30 months of the commencement of the transition period.

Article 14

Political parties during the transition

1. The transitional National Assembly shall within twelve months of its installation adopt a law setting forth the qualifications and procedure for registration of political parties.

2. The said law shall specify a judicial authority which shall receive and adjudicate on applications by political parties for registration. Decision of the authority shall be posted in public places and published in the official Gazette of Burundi.

3. Pending the adoption of such a law, all political parties shall be entitled to function in accordance with the 1993 law on political parties.

4. The political parties shall commit themselves in writing to oppose any political ideology and any action that has at its purpose the promotion of violence, hatred or unlawful discrimination.

5. In order to promote national renewal, reconciliation and unity, no party shall be registered if it is established on the basis of ethnic or regional exclusivity. This sub-clause shall take effect nine months after the commencement of the transition period, in order to enable parties whose names or

constitution do not satisfy this requirement to duly amend them so as to comply.

6. No political party may participate in the transitional arrangements, including those relating to the integration of the defence and security forces, if they do not respect the commitments embodied in the Agreement. Each such "participating party" must sign the pledge annexed hereto confirming its intention to participate in the transitional arrangements and its commitment to peace, reconciliation and democracy.

7. If political parties represented within the transitional National Assembly decide to merge, the merging parties shall retain the number of seats they had acquired initially.

8. Subject to the provisions of paragraphs 6 and 9 of this article, all Parties shall be entitled, but not obliged, to become participating parties.

9. The Government and National Assembly that are signatories to the Agreement shall not be participating parties unless specifically so provided in the Agreement.

10. A non-signatory party may become a participating party subsequent to the date of signature of the Agreement if **four-fifths** of the Parties represented in the Implementation Monitoring Committee so agree.

11. If a non-signatory party is admitted as a participating party in accordance with the present Protocol, it shall be accorded the same entitlement to participate in the transitional institutions and the Implementation Monitoring Committee as the other participating parties.

Article 15

Transitional institutions

1. There shall be a transitional Legislature made up of a National Assembly and a Senate, a transitional Executive, a Judiciary and other transitional institutions as set forth in the present Protocol.

2. The constitutional provisions governing the powers, duties and functioning of the transitional Executive, the transitional Legislature and the Judiciary, as well as the rights and duties of citizens and of political parties and associations, shall be as set forth hereunder and, where this text is silent, in the Constitution of the Republic of Burundi of 13 March 1992. When there is any conflict between that Constitution and the Agreement, the provisions of the Agreement shall prevail. To give legal effect to this provision, the terms of the Agreement shall be appropriately adopted and promulgated within Burundi within four weeks of its signature.

3. The composition of the transitional National Assembly shall be as follows: The National Assembly

(a) The Members of the National Assembly elected in 1993 shall retain or resume their seats. Where vacancies have occurred, the parties whose members occupied the vacant seats before the vacancy occurred shall fill them or allow those who have already filled them to remain;

(b) The transitional National Assembly shall be augmented so that each of the participating parties which are not represented under (a) will be entitled to at least three seats so as to be represented within the transitional National Assembly;

(c) It shall thereafter be augmented by the 28 members representing civil society currently sitting in the National Assembly;

(d) The appointed members of the National Assembly shall retain their seats in the transitional National Assembly regardless of the return from exile of the members of the National Assembly elected in 1993. The Senate

(a) The Senate shall be put in place by the President of the Republic and the Bureau of the National Assembly, while ensuring respect for the political, regional and ethnic balances;

(b) It shall include *inter alia* former heads of State, three individuals from the Twa ethnic group and members of the transitional National Assembly coopted by the President of the Republic and the Bureau of the transitional National Assembly;

(c) No provision shall be made for replacement of the members of the transitional National Assembly coopted to sit in the transitional Senate;

(d) The transitional Senate shall perform the functions provided for *inter alia* in article 6 paragraph 16, and all such other functions and are expressly provided for in the constitutional principles embodied in the Agreement;

(e) The Senate shall draw up its rules of procedure, which shall go into effect following verification by the Constitutional Court of their conformity with the transitional arrangements. Its first session shall be devoted to drawing up its rules of procedure and establishing its bureau. This session shall be presided over by the oldest Senator;

(f) Its Bureau shall consist of a Speaker, and a Deputy Speaker, a Secretary- General and a Deputy Secretary-General.

4. The transitional National Assembly and the traditional Senate shall within 18 months adopt in the same terms, by a **two -thirds** majority, a post-transition Constitution in conformity with the principles set forth in Chapter I of the present Protocol.

5. After such adoption, the text in question shall be submitted to the Constitutional Court for verification of its compliance with the principles set forth in Chapter I. If the text does not so comply, the Court shall indicate which provisions must be amended. If and whenever the Court declines to certify a text submitted to it pursuant to this provision, the transitional National Assembly and the transitional Senate shall within 30 days amend the text and resubmit it to the Court.

6. A text referred to above shall, if certified, be submitted for popular approval by way of referendum. A text which is so approved shall be the post-transition Constitution and shall come into force upon the termination of the transition period.

7. If no duly adopted text has been certified and approved by referendum within 23 months of the commencement of the transition, the Implementation Monitoring Committee may instruct experts - either national or international - to

prepare a text in conformity with Chapter I of the present Protocol. The experts shall have regard to any judgments of the Constitutional Court and to any constitutional texts not certified by it. The text prepared by the experts shall be submitted for direct approval by way of referendum. If approved, it shall become the post transition Constitution. If not approved, it shall serve provisionally as the Constitution for purposes of the Legislature and Executive elected during the transition period under the provisions of article 20 of the present Protocol. Such first elected Legislature shall draft a post-transition Constitution and adopt it in conformity with the procedure for amending the post-transition Constitution set forth in Chapter I of the present Protocol.

(a) The rules of procedure of the transitional National Assembly shall be those of the National Assembly elected in 1993 until they are duly amended.

(b) The President and the Vice-President of the transitional National Assembly shall come from two different political families.

9. During the transition period, the National Assembly shall not pass a vote of no confidence and may not be dissolved.

10. A **two-thirds** majority shall be required for the adoption of legislation.

11. Any commission required under the present Protocol to be established by the transitional National Assembly shall be established by the Bureau of the transitional National Assembly unless otherwise indicated in the present Protocol.

12. The first transitional President and Vice-President of the Republic shall come from different ethnic groups and political parties. In the event of the death or incapacity of either of them, the new transitional President or Vice-President of the Republic shall be elected by the transitional National Assembly by a resolution which receives the support of **two-thirds** of the members. Pending the election of a new President, the President of the transitional National Assembly, assisted by the Vice-President of the Republic, shall act as President. The term of the transitional President and Vice-President shall terminate upon the election of the first President under the provisions of this Protocol.

13. During the transition period, there shall be a broad-based transitional Government of national unity. The Government shall include representatives of different parties in a proportion whereby more than **half** and less than **three-fifths** of the portfolios are allocated amongst the G-7 group of parties.

14. The precise identity of the members of the transitional Executive shall be decided by the transitional President and Vice-President after consultations with the heads of the parties participating in the transitional National Assembly.

(a) There shall be between 24 and 26 members of the transitional Executive, in addition to the transitional President and Vice-President.

(b) The transitional President and Vice-President shall determine the initial function of each Minister when allocating the ministries to parties. The transitional President and Vice-President shall ensure that the minister in charge of the defence force belongs to a different family of parties from the minister responsible for the police.

16. The transitional Executive shall take its decisions and otherwise function in accordance with the spirit embodied in the concept of a Government of national unity, and shall make or propose appointments to the public administration and to diplomatic positions in the same spirit. It shall strive to take its decisions by consensus. It shall also take into account the need to reflect ethnic, religious, political, and gender balance in its decisions and appointments.

17. Any decision to be taken, by law or in accordance with the present Protocol, by the transitional President shall be taken only after consultation with the transitional Vice-President or the transitional Executive.

18. The transitional Executive shall confirm the appointment of the heads of the police and the defence force.

19. The transitional President, after consultation with the transitional Executive, shall within 30 days prepare for submission to the transitional Senate in accordance with the present Protocol a list of appointments for a period or periods specified by her/him to the offices listed below:

(a) Provincial governors;

(b) Judges of the Constitutional Court;

(c) Commune administrators.

(a) The transitional Government shall within 30 days of the commencement of the transition establish a commission under the chairmanship of a judge to investigate, as a matter of urgency, and to make recommendations on:

(i) The conditions in jails, the treatment of prisoners and the training and conditions of service of warders;

(ii) The release of prisoners awaiting trial in respect of whom there has been an undue delay in the prosecution of their cases;

(iii) The existence of and release of any political prisoners.

(b) The establishment of this commission shall not preclude the transitional Government or the transitional National Assembly dealing with the above matters.

21. The transitional National Assembly and the transitional Executive may establish commissions with or without expert participation to assist in preparing texts or for any other purpose which is part of their respective missions during the transition.

Article 16

Legal and administrative continuity

1. For purposes of continuity, all laws in force prior to the commencement of the transition shall remain in force until amended or repealed.

2. The transitional National Assembly shall as a priority review all legislation in force with a view to amending or repealing legislation incompatible with the objectives of the transitional arrangements and the provisions of the present Protocol.

3. The transitional National Assembly may pass laws with retrospective effect. However, no law may impose a penalty for conduct or action for which there was no penalty at the

time it was committed, or provide for retrospective increase in a penalty.

Article 17

Judicial and administrative reforms

1. Within 30 days of the commencement of the transition period, a commission of the transitional National Assembly in which all the parties are represented shall be established to monitor the reforms of the public administration and of the administration of justice and to submit recommendations thereon to the transitional National Assembly and the transitional Executive.

2. The transitional National Assembly may for purposes of reforming the judicial sector amend by **two-thirds** majority any existing law, including the provisions of the 1992 Constitution, dealing with the structure and functioning of the SupremeCourt.

3. For purposes of improving the judicial services in Burundi, the transitional Government shall implement the following reforms:

(a) The promotion of gender and ethnic balances in the Burundian judicial sector shall be undertaken, *inter alia* through recruitment and appointment;

(b) So as to correct the ethnic and gender imbalances in the Burundian judicial sector during and after the transition period, training colleges for employees of the judicial system shall be created, accelerated training shall be promoted, and the status and the internal promotion of magistrates shall be improved;

(c) Existing legislation relating to the organization of the Judiciary, the codes of criminal and civil procedure and the map of judicial jurisdiction shall be reviewed;

(d) All legislation shall be made available in Kirundi;

(e) Respect for the law shall be promoted;

(f) Steps shall be taken to discourage corruption, to denounce officials guilty of corruption, to enforce all legislation related to corruption, to establish effective oversight bodies, to improve working conditions in the judicial sector and to take necessary measures to require civil servants to report instances of corruption;

(g) The necessary measures shall be taken, including those specified in Protocol I to the Agreement, to deal with the problem of impunity and take any other steps required to ensure that any travesties of justice are dealt with or re-opened;

(h) The judicial sector shall be given the necessary resources so as to discharge its responsibilities impartially and independently.

4. Any appointment to the Judiciary required by Chapter I of the present Protocol to be made by the President shall, during the transition, be made by the transitional President and Vice-President in consultation with the Minister of Justice.

5. Any appointment to the Judiciary required by Chapter I of the present Protocol to be submitted for approval or confirmation to the National Assembly or the Senate shall, during the transition period, be required to be approved or

confirmed by the transitional National Assembly by **two-thirds** majority.

6. There shall be a Constitutional Court possessing the jurisdiction and functions set forth in the 1992 Constitution of the Republic of Burundi.

7. The Constitutional Court shall be made up of seven members, two of whom shall be permanent (the President and Vice-President). They shall be appointed by the President of the Republic, subject to confirmation by the transitional National Assembly by a majority of **two -thirds** . Three of these judges shall be appointed for a period of three years only, and shall be replaced in the manner provided for in the post-transition Constitution. The remaining four shall be appointed for six years beginning at the commencement of the transition. The appointments shall be made within one month of the commencement of the transition. Judges of the Constitutional Court shall be persons of moral integrity and shall have legal training or experience. A member of a standing court must be amongst the nominees.

8. The Constitutional Court may sit validly only if at least five of its members, including its President or Vice-President, are present.

9. Decisions of the Constitutional Court shall be taken by an absolute majority of its members, except that the President of the Court shall have a casting vote if the Court is evenly split on any matter.

10. International co-operation and legal assistance will be required by the transitional Government to assist it in improving and reforming the legal system. Foreign jurists,

including former Burundian nationals living outside the country, shall be requested to assist in the reform of the judicial system. The transitional Government may appoint any such persons to judicial positions so as to promote confidence in the Judiciary.

11. Members of the public administration, including local government and the diplomatic corps, shall be so appointed by the transitional Executive as to ensure that imbalances observed in these sectors are corrected. The Government may appoint a commission with expert participation to assist it in making appointments.

12. Provincial governors and commune administrators shall be appointed by the President, subject to confirmation by the transitional National Assembly. They shall be natives of the territorial entity placed under their authority. They shall be civilians.

Article 18

Combating impunity during the transition

1. In accordance with Protocol I to the Agreement, the transitional Government shall request the establishment of an International Judicial Commission of Inquiry which will investigate acts of genocide, war crimes and other crimes against humanity and report thereon to the Security Council of the United Nations.

2. In accordance with Protocol I to the Agreement, a National Truth and Reconciliation Commission shall be established to investigate human rights abuses, promote reconciliation and deal with claims arising out of past practices relating to the conflict in Burundi.

3. The transitional Government shall scrupulously fulfill the commitments contained in Protocol IV to the Agreement concerning the repatriation and resettlement of refugees and *sinistrés* as well as the restitution of property, including land, belonging to such persons.

Article 19

Defence and security forces

1. Associations having the character of militias shall be prohibited.

2. The transitional arrangements regarding the defence and security forces, including the constitutional and legal framework governing such forces, shall be those set forth in Protocol III to the Agreement. Where that Protocol is silent, the provisions of the 1992 Constitution of the Republic of Burundi shall apply.

Article 20

Elections

1. Elections at the commune level and at the national level shall be held during the transition period in accordance with the provisions and within the time-frames set forth in the present Protocol.

2. An Independent National Electoral Commission shall be established by the transitional Government as set forth hereunder.

3. The Commission shall be made up of five independent personalities and shall solicit advice from a multiparty commission of the transitional National Assembly. Its

members shall be approved by a **three-fourths** majority of the transitional National Assembly, and may include non-Burundians who have expertise and integrity.

4. The Commission shall have as its functions:

(a) To organize elections at the national, commune and *colline* levels;

(b) To ensure that these elections are free, fair and transparent;

(c) To proclaim the results of the elections within a period determined by law, which shall be as short as possible;

(d) To promulgate the arrangements, the code of conduct, and the technical details, including the location of voting stations and times of voting;

(e) To hear and adjudicate on complaints regarding observance of the rules of the elections. The decisions of the commission shall be final;

(f) To ensure through appropriate rules that parties do not operate in a manner that incites ethnic violence or is otherwise not in conformity with the present Protocol;

(g) To ensure, and hear disputes regarding, compliance with the multiethnic requirements set forth in the present Protocol.

5. The transitional National Assembly shall within 12 months and by a **two-thirds** majority adopt a law regarding electoral rules.

6. The revised electoral code may set a threshold - up to 2% - below which no political party may be allocated seats if it has not won that percentage of the votes cast at the national level.

7. There shall be elections for the National Assembly, which shall take place after the commune elections and before the election of the President. The National Assembly shall have 100 directly elected members. As an exceptional measure and for the purpose of the first election only, and only if one party has received more than **three-fifths** of the directly elected seats, an additional 18 to 21 members in total shall be co-opted in equal numbers from the lists of all the parties that have obtained more than the threshold vote, or two persons per party if more than seven parties qualify.

8. The electoral system for the National Assembly shall be the system of blocked lists with proportional representation. The revised electoral code shall prescribe that lists be multi-ethnic in character and reflect gender representation. For each three names in sequence on a list, only two may belong to the same ethnic group, and for each five names at least one shall be a woman.

9. The election of the President of the Republic shall take place after the National Assembly elections and before the end of the transition period.

10. The first post-transition President shall be elected by the National Assembly and Senate sitting together by a majority of **two-thirds** of the votes.

11. Any person who has served as President during the transition period shall be ineligible to stand for President

in the first election. Candidates for the presidency must be Burundian citizens and over 35 years of age.

12. Elections at the commune level shall be held, in accordance with the procedures listed below, within eighteen months of the commencement of the transition period.

13.

(a) The *collines* shall be administered by *colline* councils of five members elected by direct universal suffrage. The councillor with the greatest number of votes shall become the chief of the *colline*. Elections for the *colline* chiefs shall, for the first elections, not be based on party political lists and all candidates shall stand as independents.

(b) The communes shall be administered by commune councils, which shall be elected by direct universal suffrage.

(c) For purposes of the first election, each Commune Council shall appoint a Commune Administrator and may dismiss her/him for good cause, including incompetence, corruption, misconduct or embezzlement. For subsequent elections, the National Assembly and the Senate may, after evaluation, legislate for the administrators to be elected by direct universal suffrage.

(d) At the national level, not more than 67% of commune administrators shall be from either of the two main ethnic components. The Senate shall ensure respect for this principle.

Article 21

Amendment of the transitional arrangements

Changes may be made to the transitional arrangements and the text of the Agreement with the consent of **nine-tenths** of the members of the transitional National Assembly.

Article 22

Interim period

1. The Parties agree to comply during the period between the signature of the Agreement and the installation of the transitional National Assembly with the obligations, arrangements and commitments set forth in Chapter II of the present Protocol.

2. By its signature the National Assembly agrees, within four weeks, to:

(a) Adopt the present Protocol as the supreme law without any amendments to the substance of the Agreement;

(b) Repeal the provisions of any legislation which prevent free political activity, or which would hinder the implementation of the present Protocol;

(c) Pending the installation of a transitional Government adopt such legislation as is necessary for the granting of temporary immunity against prosecution for politically motivated crimes committed prior to the signature of the Agreement.

3. The parties wishing to participate in the transitional arrangements (the"participating parties") agree to file with the Implementation Monitoring Committee the following:

(a) Within seven days of the signature of the Agreement, a pledge, which appears as Annex I to the Agreement, committing the participating party to observe its commitments to democracy, peace and reconciliation, to reject all forms of violence and to participate in a public programme on peace and reconciliation;

(b) Within 60 days of signature, a document nominating the members representing the participating party in the transitional National Assembly.

4. The transitional President and Vice-President shall within 60 days of the signature of the Agreement submit to the Implementation Monitoring Committee a list identifying the members of the Cabinet.

5. Starting one month after the signature of the Agreement, the Implementation Monitoring Committee shall continuously review whether the conditions for the installation of a transitional Government have been met, and may direct the Government or any Party or participating party to undertake any steps which would enable those conditions to be met. It alone shall fix the date on which the transitional National Assembly and transitional Government shall be installed, and may postpone such date, provided the final date is not later than six months after the signature of the Agreement.

6. Between the date of signature of the Agreement and the installation of the transitional Government, the Government shall:

(a) Provide all necessary assistance and cooperation to international agencies, the political parties and the Implementation Monitoring Committee in regard to establishing structures and facilities and issuing the necessary documentation, including travel documents for all returning exiles, refugees and members of the armed groups as provided for in this and other protocols, as required by the international agencies or as directed by the Implementation Monitoring Committee;

(b) Compile, within 30 days of the signature of the Agreement, an inventory co-signed by the Minister of each ministry listing each of the assets owned by the State exceeding the value of US$ 250 in the possession of such ministry, and lodge a copy of such inventory with the Implementation Monitoring Committee;

(c) Not destroy or allow the destruction of any record, file, or information or of any building or other property held by it during this period;

(d) Take the necessary steps, including the signing of international agreements, to facilitate the entry and deployment of observers and members of forces or security personnel as agreed in Protocol III to the Agreement.

7. The Minister and the chief career public servant in each ministry shall be jointly liable in law for any damage or destruction of any government property, including any record, file or any other document, held by it, for any misrepresentation in the asset inventory filed with the Implementation Monitoring Committee, or for any wasteful use of the ministry's financial resources.

8. The Government shall be responsible for the day-to-day government of Burundi during the interim period. If during that period the Government should, without the approval of the Implementation Monitoring Committee, take any of the actions indicated in subparagraphs (a) – (d) below, such action may subsequently be reviewed by the transitional Government and, if found not to have been in the interests of good governance, summarily cancelled or reversed:

(a) Alter the conditions of service or levels of remuneration of public servants;

(b) Make any appointment to or promotion within the public administration;

(c) Sell State-owned immovable property;

(d) Enter into any contract for the supply of goods or services or the construction of any building, or for the erection or maintenance of any Government infrastructure, which will have the effect of incurring financial obligations on the part of the transitional Government. Any such contract concluded without the approval of the Implementation Monitoring Committee may be annulled by the transitional Government.

9. During the interim period there shall be no deployment of the defence force or of any armed wing of a Party outside the framework of Protocol III.

10. No arrest of a returnee or refugee shall be permitted without notification and justification to the Implementation Monitoring Committee or a sub-committee or agency designated by it, and in any event no arrest or charging of a refugee or returnee or holder of political public office

for a crime committed for a political purpose prior to the signature of the Agreement shall be permitted until the installation of the transitional Government.

11. The Implementation Monitoring Committee may request and shall receive from the transitional Government any information relating to governmental activities, any relevant data regarding governance or any information relating to or required for the monitoring, supervision or implementation of the Agreement, including information relating to any international financial assistance.

12. The Implementation Monitoring Committee shall assist in soliciting or obtaining any international or foreign aid or assistance contemplated by the Agreement. It may generally advise any donor and suggest conditionalities in regard to any aid or assistance to be granted to, or agreements to be concluded with, the Government of Burundi. For this purpose it shall be informed of the details of any international agreements to be concluded with, or foreign aid to be donated to, the Burundian Government.

13. The Implementation Monitoring Committee may, at its discretion and for purposes of supervising, monitoring or ensuring the implementation of the Agreement, issue directives to any Party or participating party. All parties shall comply with such directives within the period specified in the directive.

14. In the event that a Party or participating party fails to comply with a directive of the Implementation Monitoring Committee, the Committee may:

(a) Place the party on terms to comply;

(b) Failing compliance with such warning, and after offering the party an opportunity to explain its non-compliance, suspend such party from participating in the transitional arrangements;

(c) Request the appropriate assistance of any international body or State or Party in enforcing compliance.

15. The participating parties shall do all in their power to ensure that their members observe the provisions of the Agreement, including, but not limited to, the prompt full and wide dissemination of the provisions of the Agreement relating to the ceasefire, disarmament, and reporting to quartering locations.

16. The participating Parties shall assist the Implementation Monitoring Committee and the Facilitator in an intensive public campaign to win support for the Agreement and to promote peace and reconciliation.

17. They shall take disciplinary measures, including expulsion, against any member who contrary to the spirit and letter of the Agreement and the pledge annexed hereto commits an act of violence or destroys or damages public or private property.

PROTOCOL III

PEACE AND SECURITY FOR ALL

PREAMBLE

We, the Parties,

Recalling the commitments entered into in the Declaration of 21 June 1998 with a view to resolving the Burundi conflict through peaceful means and putting an end to all forms of violence, Aware of the necessity to promote lasting peace and having analyzed the questions relating to the principles of peace and security for all, to the defence and security forces and to the cessation of hostilities, and the arrangements with a view to achieving a permanent ceasefire,

Have agreed as follows:

CHAPTER I
PEACE AND SECURITY FOR ALL

Article 1

Principles of peace and security for all

1. All Burundian citizens have the right to live in peace and security without any discrimination whatsoever.

2. The sovereignty of the people through the Constitution and the laws that stem from it shall be respected by all.

3. The institutions have the primary duty to guarantee:

(a) The security of all citizens;

(b) The protection of the inalienable rights of the human person, starting with the right to life, and the rights embodied *inter alia* in the Universal Declaration of Human Rights and in the international conventions to which Burundi is a party;

(c) The protection of all the ethnic communities of the population through specific mechanisms for the prevention of *coups d'état*, segregation and genocide;

(d) Respect for the law and combating of impunity;

(e) Good governance;

(f) Sovereignty of the State and integrity of the national territory.

4. Any foreign intervention other than under international conventions shall be prohibited. All recourse to foreign forces shall be prohibited, except when authorized by the institutions empowered to do so.

5. All Burundian citizens shall be under an obligation to respect the right of their fellow citizens to peace and security, as well as to respect public order.

6. The prerequisites for the establishment and maintenance of peace and security are:

(a) Unity within the defence and security forces;

(b) Political neutrality of the defence and security forces;

(c) The professional, civic and moral qualities of the defence and security forces;

(d) Neutrality and independence of the magistracy;

(e) Control of illegal possession and use of weapons.

7. The use of force as a means of access to and retention of power shall be rejected.

8. The defence and security forces belong to all the people of Burundi. They shall be an instrument for the protection of all the people, and all the people must identify with them.

9. The establishment of militias and terrorist and genocidal organizations, the practice of terrorism and genocide and incitement to those practices shall be prohibited.

10. Political organizations shall promote inclusion; exclusion on ethnic, sexual, regional and religious grounds shall be prohibited.

11. The ideals of peace and national unity shall be promoted and developed within the political parties, and propagation of the ideologies of exclusion, racism and genocide shall be prohibited.

12. The principle of participation of all components of society in the management of all the organs of the State, as well as equality of opportunity for citizens in all sectors of national life, shall be respected.

13. An economic and social policy that ensures the harmonious and balanced development of the people and the nation, as well as a policy of harmonious resolution of social problems, shall be pursued.

14. A culture of peace and tolerance shall be promoted through the development of a sense of patriotism among citizens and of mutual solidarity in the event of a threat, as well as through education and training of all political and technical officials.

15. Provisions for penalizing the violation of these principles shall be adopted.

Article 2 Causes of the violence and insecurity in Burundi

The causes of the violence and security in Burundi are:

The colonial period

1. The breaking apart of the pre-colonial political and administrative equilibrium

among the Baganwa, the Batutsi and the Bahutu triggered off by the implementation of the administrative reforms of the 1930s which resulted in the dismissal from their administrative positions of most of the Hutu chiefs and some of the Tutsi chiefs.

2. A discriminatory system which did not offer equal educational access to all Burundian youths from all ethnic groups.

3. The erosion of some basic traditions, cultural norms and values that had hitherto been the foundations of the unity, solidarity and cohesion of the fabric of Burundian society and of Burundians.

4. The disruption of the traditional socio-political system in effect under the monarchy, which led to erosion of the

bonds that provided the foundations of Burundi's political stability.

The post-colonial period

5. Political instability consequent upon the undermining of the legitimacy of the post-colonial institutions, accentuated by:

(a) The poor conception of power; lack of good leadership, lack of respect for the law and demonization of political opponents;

(b) The assassination of great Burundian leaders (Rwagasore, Ngendandumwe, Ndadaye);

(c) Impunity of those committing political crimes and human rights violations and practicing regionalism, patronage, cronyism and corruption;

(d) The struggle for influence by the great powers, foreign interference in Burundi's internal affairs and the proliferation of arms in the region;

(e) Failure to satisfy the basic needs of the citizens as a result of economic underdevelopment and lack of a sound economic policy that led to disillusionment and an erosion of support for the political system;

(f) The distortion of Burundi's history;

(g) The ideology and practice of genocide and exclusion.

6. The aftermath of the colonial system, the inadequacy of the basic reforms of the institutional arrangements inherited from colonization for governance, administration and the maintenance of order and security for all.

7. The unbridled struggle for power which, following the principle that "the end justifies the means", resulted in recourse to violence and the deliberate manipulation of ethnic sentiments as legitimate methods of access to and retention of power.

8. Lack of respect by certain political actors for the basic normative rules and principles of good governance, particularly those concerning separation of the legislature, the executive and the judiciary, independence of the magistracy, satisfaction of basic human needs and the maintenance of order and security for all.

9. Lack of respect for the traditions, norms and cardinal principles of the democratic system, including tolerance and respect for the inalienable rights of the human person, especially the right to life.

10. Non-acceptance of peaceful co-existence, diversity and pluralism as guiding principles of life and the basis of national cohesion, unity and solidarity.

11. Lack of appropriate action by the United Nations to rule on the acts of genocideperpetrated in Burundi since independence.

Article 3

Persons responsible for and agents of the insecurity and violence

The following were identified as responsible for and agents of the insecurity and violence:

(a) Some foreign countries, foreign organizations, political or otherwise, and certain foreign lobbies;

(b) National and foreign individuals and groups, as well as organizations, institutions, parties and movements, which conceived, abetted, condoned, encouraged, incited and practiced divisions, violence and violent methods of access to and retention of power;

(c) Political, administrative and religious leaders, as well as technical staff, who contributed to perpetrating the genocide;

(d) Persons responsible for the violence perpetrated during the crises of 1965-1969, 1972, 1988, 1991 and 1993 to date;

(e) The members of the judicial system who have promoted and continue to promote impunity and partiality through corruption, intimidation and manipulation;

(f) Those instruments of State power responsible for protecting the population which failed in their mission, particularly those elements of the defence and security forces guilty of excesses and violence against the innocent population;

(g) Those elements who practice genocide and their allies.

Article 4

Nature of the insecurity and violence

The violence is political, economic and social in nature and is expressed in genocidal, criminal and terrorist form.

Article 5

Manifestations of the insecurity and violence

The insecurity and violence are manifested in:

(a) Civil war; the destruction of public and private property; genocide, massacres, *coups d'état*, extra-judicial executions, premeditated murders, torture, rape, arbitrary arrests and imprisonment and other inhuman and degrading forms of treatment;

(b) Massive forcible displacements of individuals, families and groups who as a result leave their customary places of residence and become refugees outside the country or remain inside the country as displaced and regrouped persons in camps, tents, shacks and other makeshift arrangements;

(c) Destruction of national and socio-economic infrastructures, as well as of public and private property.

Article 6

Consequences of the insecurity and violence

The most serious consequences of the insecurity and violence are:

(a) Increase in crime, in the number of disabled persons, orphans, widows and widowers, impoverishment of the people, and all kinds of social deviation;

(b) Lack of respect for authority and the law giving rise to anarchy, mistrust and lack of civic spirit, which lead to civil unrest and rebellion;

(c) The spread of the culture of violence, leading to a general disdain for the sanctity of human life;

(d) Arbitrary practices, widespread abuse of power, corruption and the plundering of national resources.

Article 7

Victims of the insecurity and violence

The main victims of the insecurity and violence are:

(a) The nation, some political officials, and individuals forced to flee from their original places of residence into exile, settlements and camps;

(b) Individuals, groups, and categories of the population, both Hutu and Tutsi, targeted on account of their beliefs or political affiliation and on the basis of their ethnic origin.

Article 8

Protection of the inalienable rights of the human person

It is the duty of the State:

(a) To protect the inalienable rights of the human person, starting with the right to life and including the rights to freedom, security, work, education and freedom of expression, and all other rights embodied *inter alia* in the Universal Declaration of Human Rights and in the international conventions to which Burundi is a party;

(b) To prohibit and punish violations of the inalienable rights of the human person;

(c) To institute a proactive policy aimed at promoting human rights through education and training of the population, including all political and technical officials.

Article 9

Security-related regional and international issues

The three most pertinent security-related regional and international issues are:

(a) The close relationship of Burundi's internal security to security in Great Lakes region and to external factors such as insecurity in the neighbouring countries, hegemonist and/or genocidal ideologies in the Great Lakes region, the arms trade and the presence of mercenaries;

(b) The need to create conditions that encourage peaceful co-existence, foster a culture of peace and tolerance and cultivate a hospitable environment that encourages people to remain in their places of residence within their country rather than flee as refugees;

(c) The need to promote participation in and respect for the international conventions on refugees.

CHAPTER II
THE DEFENCE AND SECURITY FORCES

Article 10

Principles relating to the defence and security forces

1. The defence and security forces shall reflect the firm resolve of Burundians, as individuals and as a nation, to

live as equals, in peace and harmony, and to be free from fear.

2. The defence and security forces shall be established in accordance with the Constitution. Apart from the defence and security forces so established, no other armed organization may be created or raised.

3. The defence and security forces shall teach and require their members to abide by the Constitution and the laws in force and by the international conventions and agreements to which Burundi is a party.

4. The maintenance of national security and of national defence shall be subject to Government authority and parliamentary oversight.

5. The defence and security forces shall be accountable for their actions and work in all transparency. Parliamentary committees shall be set up to supervise the work of the defence and security forces in accordance with the legislation in force and the parliamentary rules and regulations.

6. Neither the defence and security forces nor any of their members shall, in the performance of their duties:

(a) Injure the interests of a political party which is legitimate under the Constitution;

(b) Manifest their political preferences;

(c) Favour in any manner the interests of a political party;

(d) Be a member of a political party or an association of a political nature;

(e) Take part in political activities or demonstrations.

Article 11

Principles of organization of the defence and security forces

1. The defence and security forces shall consist of a national defence force, a national police and an intelligence service, all established in conformity with the Constitution.

2. The defence and security forces shall be subordinate to civilian authority in respect for the Constitution, the law and the regulations.

3. The defence and security forces shall be open to all Burundian citizens without discrimination.

4. The defence and security forces shall promote within their services a nondiscriminatory, non-ethnicist and non-sexist culture.

5. Organic laws shall determine the creation, organization, training, conditions of service and functioning of the defence and security forces.

6. Within the limits determined by the Constitution and the laws, only the President may authorize the use of armed military force:

(a) In defence of the State;

(b) In the restoration of order and public safety;

(c) In the discharge of international obligations and commitments.

7. When the national defence force is utilized in one of the cases referred to in paragraph 6 above, the President shall officially consult the authorized competent bodies and shall promptly inform the Legislature, in detail, of:

(a) The reason or reasons for the use of the national defence force;

(b) Any location where that force is deployed;

(c) The period for which that force is deployed.

8. If the Legislature is not in session, the President shall convene it in special session within seven days from the use of the national defence force.

9. The defence and security forces shall respect the rights and dignity of their members in the context of the normal constraints of discipline and training.

10. The members of the defence and security forces shall have the right to be informed of the socio-political life of the country and to receive civic education.

Article 12

Missions of the defence and security forces

1. Missions of the national defence force

The missions of the national defence force shall be:

(a) To ensure the integrity of the national territory and the sovereignty of the country;

(b) To combat any armed aggression against the institutions of the Republic;

(c) To intervene exceptionally in the maintenance of public order at the formal request of the authorized civilian authority;

(d) To participate in assistance activities in case of natural disasters;

(e) To contribute to the development of the country through major works, production and training;

(f) To defend the vital points.

2. Missions of the national police The missions of the national police shall be:

(a) To maintain and restore public order;

(b) To prevent offences provided for by law, investigate and prosecute their perpetrators and make arrests in accordance with the law;

(c) To ensure respect for the laws and other regulations for whose enforcement they are directly responsible;

(d) To ensure the physical protection of persons and their property;

(e) To ensure the protection of infrastructures and public property;

(f) To relieve and assist persons in danger or in distress;

(g) To intervene in case of catastrophe or disaster;

(h) To develop various civil defence scenarios;

(i) To ensure road safety throughout the national territory;

(j) To ensure protection of public gatherings at the request of those involved, on orders from the administrative authorities, or on their own initiative;

(k) To ensure the missions of the judicial and administrative police;

(l) To ensure protection of the courts and tribunals;

(m) To deal with criminal cases of major importance, such as economic crimes and cases attributable to roving delinquents or groups organized at the national or international level;

(n) To produce and make use of crime statistics;

(o) To deal with the policing of immigration and emigration and the status of aliens;

(p) To monitor the movements of aliens throughout the national territory;

(q) To keep watch on the land, lake and air borders;

(r) To issue travel documents and residence permits;

(s) To ensure protection of the institutions.

3. Missions of the intelligence service. The missions of the intelligence service shall be:

(a) To seek out, centralize and make use of all information likely to contribute to the protection of the State, its institutions and its interests at the international level, as well as to the prosperity of its economy;

(b) To detect as early as possible activities aimed at creating insecurity and violence or at changing the institutions of the State by unlawful means;

(c) To detect as early as possible recourse to the manipulation of ethnic or regionalist feelings as means of access to or retention of power;

(d) To detect as early as possible any threat to the constitutional order, public safety, territorial integrity or national sovereignty;

(e) To detect as early as possible any threat to the country's ecological environment;

(f) To detect as early as possible terrorist intrigues, illicit drug trafficking and the formation of criminal organizations;

(g) To detect malfunctions and cases of misappropriation of funds within the State services.

Article 13

Structure of the defence and security forces

1. Structure of the national defence force

The transitional Government shall be responsible for deciding upon the structure of the national defence force.

2. Structure of the national police

(a) The national police shall be coordinated within one Ministry, i.e., the one responsible for public security.

(b) Its structure shall be:

(i) First level: Since the Ministry is responsible for public security, the head shall be a member of the Government;

(ii) Second level: A national police headquarters responsible for coordinating all the police forces. It shall be headed by a director general with administrative skills and knowledge of police techniques;

(iii) Third level: Departments: each department shall represent a specialized area of police work. This structure is illustrated in Annex II to the Agreement.

3. Structure of the intelligence service. The structure of the intelligence service shall be such as to enable the service, given its special nature, to preserve the secrecy of its operations while allowing for control by the National Assembly, especially with regard to the budget. The intelligence service shall be placed under the responsibility of a member of government.

4. Command of the defence and security forces. Command posts shall be distributed on the basis of competence and merit while ensuring the necessary ethnic balances.

Article 14

Composition of the defence and security forces

1. Composition of the national defence force

(a) There shall be a single defence force composed of all components of the Burundian nation irrespective of ethnic, regional, gender and/or social status.

(b) The national defence force shall include members of the Burundian armed forces and combatants of the political parties and movements in existence at the time of restructuring of the army, as well as other citizens who wish to enlist.

(c) After the signature of the Agreement, the combatants of the political parties and movements, as well as the existing national defence force, shall be placed under the authority of the transitional Government.

(d) A technical committee consisting of representatives of the Burundian armed forces and combatants of the political parties and movements, as well as of an external military advisory and training group, shall be established by decision of the transitional Government to implement the procedures for the establishment of the national defence force.

(e) Members of the Burundian armed forces found guilty of acts of genocide, *coups d'état*, violation of the Constitution and human rights and war crimes shall be excluded from the national defence force. Combatants of the political parties and movements found guilty of the same offences shall also not be accepted into the national defence force.

(f) Recruitment into the national defence force shall be conducted in a transparent manner, individually, voluntarily and on the basis of personal merit, physical fitness, moral and professional qualifications and potential.

(g) For a period to be determined by the Senate, not more than 50% of the national defence force shall be drawn from any one ethnic group, in view of the need to achieve ethnic balance and to prevent acts of genocide and *coups d'état*.

2. Composition of the national police

(a) There shall be a single national police composed of all citizens of the Burundian nation wishing to form part of it, irrespective of ethnic, regional, gender and social status.

(b) The national police shall include members of the current national police, combatants of the political parties and movements and other citizens who meet the requirements.

(c) A technical committee comprising representatives of the existing police force and the political parties and movements and of external advisors and instructors on police issues shall be established by decision of the transitional Government to implement the procedures for the establishment of the national police.

(d) All persons, including current members of the police force and combatants of the political parties and movements, found guilty of genocide, the *coup d'état* of 21 October 1993, human rights violations or war crimes shall be excluded from the national police.

(e) Not more than 50% of the members of the national police shall be drawn from any one particular ethnic group, with a view to achieving the necessary balances and preventing acts of genocide or of *coup d'état*.

3. Composition of the intelligence service. The composition of the intelligence service shall be such as to enable the

service, given its special nature, to preserve the secrecy of its operations while allowing for control by the National Assembly.

Article 15

Size of the defence and security forces

1. Size of the national defence force

(a) The following criteria shall be used to determine the strength of the national defence force:

(i) Potential internal and external threats;

(ii) The economic and financial resources of the country;

(iii) The budget allocated to the defence and security forces;

(iv) The defence policy of the country.

(b) The transitional Government, in consultation with the technical committee, shall determine the size of the national defence force.

2. Size of the national police

(a) The following criteria shall be used to determine the strength of the national police:

(i) Surface area of the country;

(ii) Population;

(iii) Population density;

(iv) Urbanization level;

(v) Economic resources;

(vi) Crime level;

(vii) Budgetary allocation.

(b) The transitional Government, in consultation with the technical committee, shall determine the size of the national police.

3. Size of the intelligence service. The size of the intelligence service shall be such as to enable the service, given its special nature, to preserve the secrecy of its operations while allowing for control by the National Assembly.

Article 16

Balances within the defence and security forces

1. The following criteria shall be used to determine the imbalances in the defence and security forces:

(a) Political;

(b) Ethnic;

(c) Regional;

(d) Gender.

2. Correction of the imbalances in the defence and security forces shall be approached progressively in the spirit of reconciliation and trust in order to reassure all Burundians.

3. Correction of the imbalances shall be achieved during the transition period through the integration into the current defence and security forces of the combatants of the political parties and movements and through the recruitment of other Burundian citizens.

4. For purposes of rapid reduction of the command-level imbalances, accelerated training of commissioned and non-commissioned officers from among the combatants of the political parties and movements shall be conducted in Burundi and abroad as soon as the transition period commences.

Article 17

Recruitment

1. Recruitment shall be conducted in accordance with the following criteria:

(a) Transparency;

(b) Voluntary service;

(c) Age;

(d) Personal record and level of training;

(e) Medical tests of physical and intellectual aptitude.

2. Recruitment criteria based on educational level shall be determined by the transitional Government.

3. A national commission shall be assigned responsibility for selecting candidates for all levels of the national

defence force and national police, taking care to ensure the necessary ethnic balance.

Article 18

Training

1. The defence and security forces shall have technical, moral and civic training. This training shall include the culture of peace, aspects of conduct relating to the democratic multi-party political system, human rights and humanitarian law.

2. Decentralization of the centres for training police constables, rank and file troops and non-commissioned officers shall be undertaken.

Article 19

Organic laws, regulatory texts and disciplinary system

For the defence and security forces, organic laws, regulatory texts and disciplinary rules in conformity with the relevant provisions of the Agreement shall be adopted.

Article 20

Names of the defence and security forces

1. The name of the defence force shall be decided upon by the transitional Government.

2. The name of the police shall be "National Police of Burundi".

3. The name of the intelligence service shall be "General Intelligence Service".

Article 21

Demobilization

1. Demobilization shall begin after the signature of the Agreement in accordance with the implementation timetable (see Annex V).

2. To move from war to peace requires demobilization within the defence and security forces as well as for the combatants of the political parties and movements.

3. Demobilization shall involve both the members of the Burundian armed forces and the combatants of the political parties and movements.

4. Lists of people to be demobilized shall be compiled.

5. Members to be demobilized shall be provided with some form of appropriate identification.

6. Demobilization criteria and a demobilization package shall be drawn up.

7. The categories of people to be demobilized shall be:

(a) Volunteers;

(b) Those members who are handicapped or disabled;

(c) Those who do not meet the age criteria;

(d) Those whose discipline is such that they cannot be retained within the new defence and security forces;

(e) Individuals whose educational level is such that they would not be able to undergo military or police training;

(f) Members of the Burundian armed forces and combatants of the political parties and movements who will be rationalized to yield efficient and affordable defence and security forces.

8. An organ to deal with the socio-professional reintegration of demobilized troops shall be established.

9. A technical committee to work out the programme and modalities of demobilization shall be set up.

10. The international community shall be requested to assist in the process of demobilization.

11. Following the demobilization process, a certificate shall be issued to demobilized troops.

12. Each demobilized person shall receive a demobilization allowance.

Article 22

Military or compulsory civic service

The future institutions of the country shall examine the issue in the light of the needs of the time.

Article 23

National, regional, and international environment

1. Peace in Burundi requires a favorable national, regional and international environment.

2. Burundian politicians shall undertake to respect the political neutrality of the defence and security forces.

3. After the signature of the Agreement, the armed signatories to the Agreement, politicians and political leaders, religious organizations and civil society shall be called upon to address to the Burundian population signals and messages of peace, reconciliation and national unity.

4. National observatories shall be established on genocide, ethnic hegemony and domination, oppression and exclusion, *coups d'état*, political assassinations, arms trafficking and human rights violations in the Great Lakes region. The establishment of similar observatories at the regional and international levels shall be promoted.

5. The Parties undertake to contribute to the restoration of peace in the Great Lakes region.

Article 24

Security partners

The security partners are:

1. The Government and the defence and security forces;

2. State institutions including local authorities;

3. The population, particularly through their support and cooperation in enforcing the laws;

4. The countries in the region;

5. The international community.

CHAPTER III
PERMANENT CEASEFIRE AND CESSATION OF HOSTILITIES

Definitions and general principles

Article 25

Definitions

1. Ceasefire means the cessation of:

(a) All attacks by air, land and lake, as well as all acts of sabotage;

(b) Attempts to occupy new ground positions and movements of troops and resources from one location to another;

(c) All acts of violence against the civilian population – summary executions, torture, harassment, detention and persecution of civilians on the basis of ethnic origin, religious, beliefs and political affiliations, incitement of ethnic hatred, arming of civilians, use of child soldiers, sexual violence, training of terrorists, genocide and bombing of the civilian population;

(d) Supply of ammunitions and weaponry and other war-related stores to the field;

(e) All hostile propaganda between the Parties, both within and outside the country;

(f) Any other actions that may impede the normal evolution of the ceasefire process.

2. The cessation of hostilities shall involve:

(a) Announcement of a cessation of hostilities 48 hours after the signing of the ceasefire agreement, through command channels and print and electronic media;

(b) Cessation of hostilities shall be regulated and monitored through the committee to follow up, supervise, monitor and implement the Agreement (Implementation Monitoring Committee);

(c) Release of all the political prisoners, closure of all the forced regroupment camps and respect for civil and political rights and freedoms shall take place from the date of signature of the Agreement;

(d) Cessation of hostilities brought about by emergency laws, political imprisonment and arbitrary arrests shall take effect from the date of signature of the Agreement;

(e) Cessation of defamatory, untruthful or ethnicist statements by the media and publications shall take place from the date of signature of the Agreement.

3. The different types of hostilities are:

(a) Political hostilities:

(i) Verbal aggression and denigration;

(ii) Political imprisonment;

(iii) Forced regroupment camps;

(iv) Violation of political rights and freedoms;

(b) Military hostilities:

(i) Armed clashes between the belligerents;

(ii) Infiltration of armed groups from neighbouring countries;

(iii) Attacks on the population by the belligerents.

4. The belligerents are:

(a) The Government forces;

(b) The combatants of the political parties and movements which signed the

Declaration of 21 June 1998;

(c) The combatants of political parties and movements operating within the country which did not sign the Declaration of 21 June 1998;

(d) The political and ethnic militias operating within the country.

Article 26

General principles

1. The following principles are agreed upon:

(a) The provisions of article 25.1 (d) above shall not preclude the supply of food, clothing and medical support to forces in the field;

(b) Freedom of movement of persons and goods throughout the country shall be guaranteed;

(c) All persons detained or taken hostage on account of political belief or activities shall be released and given the latitude to relocate to anywhere within the country;

(d) Humanitarian assistance shall be facilitated through humanitarian corridors in order to render assistance to displaced persons, refugees and other *sinistrés*;

(e) The parties shall establish a Joint Commission for Peace and Security, hereinafter referred to as the Ceasefire Commission, which shall be responsible for peace and security functions and shall work in close conjunction with a peacekeeping force following the entry into force of the Agreement;

(f) The laying of mines of any type shall be prohibited, and all parties shall be required to undertake to mark and signpost any danger areas to be identified to peacekeeping forces;

(g) The forces in areas of direct contact shall proceed to an immediate disengagement;

(h) Illicit trafficking of arms and the infiltration of armed groups shall be controlled with the collaboration of neighbouring countries;

(i) The parties shall undertake to locate, identify, disarm, and assemble all armed groups in the country;

(j) The parties shall ensure that armed groups operating under their command comply with the process;

(k) Mechanisms for dismantling and disarming all militias and disarming civilians holding arms illegally shall be established;

(l) Amnesty shall be granted to all combatants of the political parties and movements for crimes committed as a result of their involvement in the conflict, but not for acts of genocide, crimes against humanity or war crimes, or for their participation in *coups d'état*.

2. Disengagement

(a) Disengagement shall mean the immediate breaking of contact between the opposing military forces of the Parties to the Agreement at places where they are in direct contact by the effective date and time of the ceasefire.

(b) Immediate disengagement at the initiative of all military units shall be limited to the effective range of all weapons. Disengagement to put all weapons out of range shall be conducted under the guidance of the Ceasefire Commission established pursuant to article 27 below.

(c) Where disengagement by a party is impossible or impractical, the Ceasefire Commission shall find an alternative solution to render the weapons safe.

Article 27

Verification and supervision

1. Ceasefire Commission

(a) The Ceasefire Commission shall consist of representatives of the Government, the combatants of the political parties and movements, the United Nations, the Organization of African Unity and the Regional Peace Initiative for Burundi.

(b) The Ceasefire Commission shall be a decision-making body.

(c) The Ceasefire Commission shall take its decisions by consensus.

(d) The Ceasefire Commission shall be responsible, among other things, for:

(i) Establishing the location of units at the time of the ceasefire;

(ii) Establishing liaison between the parties for the purpose of the ceasefire;

(iii) Finding appropriate solutions in the event of difficulty in disengagement;

(iv) Conducting investigations of any ceasefire violations;

(v) Verifying all information, data and activities relating to military forces of the parties;

(vi) Verifying the disengagement of the military forces of the Parties where they are in direct contact;

(vii) Monitoring the storage of arms, munitions equipment;

(viii) Monitoring the quartering of troops and police;

(ix) Undertaking the disarmament of all illegally armed civilians;

(x) Undertaking mine clearance throughout the country.

(e) The parties undertake to provide the Ceasefire Commission immediately with all relevant information on the organization, equipment and positions of their forces, on the understanding that such information shall be held in strict confidence.

2. Re-deployment of all troops to quartering centres

(a) Following disengagement, all troops shall be re-deployed to quartering locations.

(b) A map identifying the military quartering locations shall be made available to the Implementation Monitoring Committee.

(c) Upon re-deployment, all forces shall provide relevant information to the Ceasefire Commission on troop strength, movements and weapons they hold at each location.

(d) All facilities customarily made available to soldiers, but which cannot be provided at the quartering locations, such as hospitals, logistics units and training facilities, shall be supervised by the Ceasefire Commission.

(e) The Ceasefire Commission shall verify the reported data and information. All forces shall be restricted to the declared and recorded centres and all movements shall be subject to authorization by the Ceasefire Commission. All forces shall remain in the declared and Recorded centers until the integration and demobilization process is completed.

(f) Quartering shall be conducted in two stages:

(i) The first stage shall cover the quartering of the current Government's troops in their barracks;

(ii) The second stage shall cover the quartering of the other negotiating armed parties' troops at sites previously identified and prepared.

3. Maintenance of peace and security

(a) In the context of the Agreement, the Ceasefire Commission shall be responsible for the maintenance of peace and security.

(b) Upon the entry into force of the Agreement, each Party shall agree with the Ceasefire Commission appropriate security measures for:

(i) Its leading members;

(ii) The free movement of its members in Burundi;

(c) All embassies of Burundi in neighbouring and other countries providing shelter for Burundian refugees and residents shall provide them with passports, identity papers and any other requisite documents to which all Burundian citizens are entitled;

(d) Entry into Burundi through border posts shall be facilitated for the civilian and combatant members of the political parties and movements Peace and security functions

(a) The peace and security functions of the Ceasefire Commission shall be:

(i) To guarantee respect by all the parties for the definitive cessation of hostilities;

(ii) To guarantee the peace and security of the people;

(iii) To ensure the search for and recovery of all arms, the neutralization of militias throughout the country and the disarming of the civilian population;

(iv) To ensure the security of institutions and high-ranking political figures;

(v) To ensure the security of senior foreign personnel and experts;

(vi) To ensure the demining of the whole country;

(vii) To ensure the effective quartering of the defence and security forces, arms control, and respect for disciplinary rules within and outside the camps;

(viii) To supervise the operations for resupplying the troops.

(b) The expert functions shall be:

(i) To assign the defence and security forces to their stations;

(ii) To conduct the identification of sites for military camps in military zones located outside the towns;

(iii) To supervise the operation for the demobilization of troops and police not retained within the new defence and security forces.

International peacekeeping force

The mandate of the peacekeeping force referred to in article 8 of Protocol V to the Agreement shall be to verify implementation of the provisions contained in this Chapter. In addition to its verification function, the force may be requested by the Ceasefire Commission to provide assistance and support to the implementation process, as appropriate.

Article 28

Ceasefire implementation timetable

The ceasefire implementation timetable shall be determined by the Ceasefire Commission.

PROTOCOL IV

RECONSTRUCTION AND DEVELOPMENT

PREAMBLE

We, the Parties,

Having considered the issues relating to the overall problem of reconstruction and development, including those associated with rehabilitation and resettlement of the refugees and *sinistrés*, with physical and political reconstruction and with economic and social development, Having identified the principles, guidelines and activities for the transitional institutions in dealing with these issues, Having incorporated the essentials of our work, including the analysis of the origin of the specific problems and the principles, guidelines and activities required to remedy this problem, in a report of Committee IV which serves as a reference document for the present Protocol and is reproduced as Annex IV to the Agreement,

Have agreed:

1. To support the rehabilitation and resettlement of the refugees and *sinistrés* by complying with the provisions of Chapter I of the present Protocol;

2. To work towards the country's physical and political reconstruction in conformity with the principles and measures set out in Chapter II of the present Protocol;

3. To strive towards the economic and social development of Burundi by following the guidelines defined in Chapter III of the present Protocol.

CHAPTER I
REHABILITATION AND RESETTLEMENT OF REFUGEES AND *SINISTRES*

Article 1

Definitions

1. For the definition of the term "refugee", reference is made to international conventions, including the 1951 Geneva Convention Relative to the Status of Refugees, the 1966 Protocol Relative to the Status of Refugees and the 1969 Organization of African Unity Convention Governing the Specific Aspects of Refugee Problems in Africa.

2. The term *"sinistrés"* designates all displaced, regrouped and dispersed persons and returnees.

Article 2

Principles governing return, resettlement and reintegration

1. The Government of Burundi shall encourage the return of refugees and *sinistrés* and resettle and reintegrate them. It shall seek the support of other countries and international and non-governmental organizations in carrying out this responsibility.

2. It shall respect the following principles:

(a) All Burundian refugees must be able to return to their country;

(b) Refugees no longer in their first country of asylum are entitled to the same treatment as other returning Burundian refugees;

(c) Return must be voluntary and must take place in dignity with guaranteed security, and taking into account the particular vulnerability of women and children;

(d) The reception mechanisms must be put in place in advance of the return;

(e) Returnees must have their rights as citizens and their property restored to them in accordance with the laws and regulations in force in Burundi after the entry into force of the Agreement;

(f) All *sinistrés* wishing to do so must be able to return to their homes;

(g) Specific conditions must be provided for *sinistrés* who believe that they can no longer return to their property, so as to enable them to return to normal socio-professional life;

(h) In the return of the refugees and the resettlement and reintegration of the returnees and displaced and regrouped persons, the principle of equity, including gender equity, must be strictly applied in order to avoid any measure or treatment that discriminates against or favours any one among these categories.

Article 3

Preparatory activities

The Government shall undertake the following preparatory activities:

(a) Establishing and constituting a National Commission for the Rehabilitation of *Sinistrés* (CNRS), which shall have the mandate of organizing and coordinating, together with international organizations and countries of asylum, the return of refugees and *sinistrés*, assisting in their resettlement and reintegration, and dealing with all the other issues listed in the report of Committee IV. To this end, it shall draw up a plan of priorities. The members of the CNRS shall be drawn *inter alia* from the participating parties and the Government of Burundi, and shall elect the Commission's chairperson;

(b) Establishing and constituting a Sub-Commission of the CNRS with the specific mandate of dealing with issues related to land as set out in article

(j) of the present Protocol;

(c) Convening, in collaboration with the countries of asylum and the Office of the United Nations High Commissioner for Refugees, the Tripartite Commissioner, involving in it representatives of the refugees and international observers;

(d) Requesting international organizations and the host countries concerned to conduct a gender and age disaggregated census of the refugees, including the old caseload refugees (1972);

(e) Conducting a multi-dimensional census of the *sinistrés*;

(f) Organizing information and awareness campaigns for refugees and *sinistrés* as well as visits to their places of origin;

(g) Undertaking information and awareness campaigns on the mechanisms for peaceful coexistence and return to *collines* of origin;

(h) Setting up reception committees where they do not yet exist. The role of these committees shall be to receive and provide support services for all the *sinistrés* returning to their homes, ensure their security and assist them in organizing their socio-economic reintegration.

Article 4

Guidelines governing resettlement and integration

The CNRS shall decide on the activities for the resettlement and integration of refugees and *sinistrés* in accordance with the priority plan taking into account the availability of resources, in order to achieve the following aims and objectives:

(a) To ensure the socio-economic and administrative reintegration of the *sinistrés*;

(b) To give all returning families, including female- and child- headed families, food aid, material support and assistance with health, education, agriculture and reconstruction until they become self-sufficient;

(c) To provide communes, villages and *collines* with assistance in the reconstruction of community infrastructures and with support for income generating activities, paying special attention to women and enhancing their roles in building and sustaining families and communities;

(d) To settle all those who believe that they cannot yet return on sites close to home, in order to enable them to go and till their fields initially and return to their land later on;

(e) To encourage, to the extent possible, grouped housing in the reconstruction policy in order to free cultivable land;

(f) To ensure equity in the distribution of resources between the ethnic groups on the one hand and the provinces on the other, and to avoid overlap between the various parties involved;

(g) To promote the participation of the population in the resettlement activities;

(h) To help returnees to recover the property and bank accounts left in Burundi before their exile and whose existence has been duly proven;

(i) To offer intensive language courses for returnees to mitigate the language problems;

(j) To assist returnees in other areas such as medical services, psycho-social support, social security and retirement, education of children and the equivalency of diplomas awarded outside Burundi.

Article 5

Actions with regard to returnees in their country of asylum

The Government shall undertake the following actions with regard to returnees in their country of asylum:

(a) Helping returnees settle their disputes in their country of asylum relating notably to immovable property, bank accounts, social security, etc;

(b) In the context of agreements between countries or social security institutions, helping those who were employed in the country of asylum receive social security benefits to which they are entitled in respect of such employment;

(c) Studying ways of indemnifying and compensating returnees for property in the country of asylum they are unable to take with them profit from or sell;

(d) Assisting pupils and students in their two final years of study in primary, secondary and higher education wishing to complete their studies in the country of asylum.

Article 6

Other actions

Any other action decided upon by the CNRS in accordance with the priority plan and in the light of available resources may be taken.

Article 7

Access and safety of international personnel

The Government shall allow international organizations and international and local non-governmental organizations unrestricted access to returnees and other *sinistrés* for purposes of the delivery of humanitarian assistance. It must guarantee the safety of the staff of such organizations and must also facilitate the provision of short-term aid for repatriation, appropriately supervised and without discrimination.

Article 8

Issues relating to land and other property

To resolve all issues relating to land and other property, the following principles and mechanisms shall be applied:

(a) Property rights shall be guaranteed for all men, women and children. Compensation which is fair and equitable under the circumstances shall be payable in case of expropriation, which shall be allowed only in the public interest and in accordance with the law, which shall also set out the basis of compensation;

(b) All refugees and/or *sinistrés* must be able to recover their property, especially their land;

(c) If recovery proves impossible, everyone with an entitlement must receive fair compensation and/or indemnification;

(d) Refugees who do not return may receive a just and equitable indemnification if their land had been expropriated without prior indemnification and in contravention of the principle set out in subparagraph

(d) of the present article;

(e) The policy with respect to distribution of State-owned land shall be reviewed so that priority can be given to the resettlement of *sinistrés*;

(f) An inventory of destroyed urban property shall be drawn up with a view to making it habitable in order to redistribute it or return it as a priority to the original owners;

(g) A series of measures shall be taken in order to avoid subsequent disputes over land, including the establishment of a register of rural land, the promulgation of a law on succession and, in the longer term, the conduct of a cadastral survey of rural land;

(h) The policy of distribution or allocation of new lands shall take account of the need for environmental protection and management of the country's water system through protection of forests;

(i) Burundi's Land Act must be revised in order to adjust it to the current problems with respect to land management;

(j) The Sub-Commission on Land established in accordance with article 3 (b) of the present Protocol shall have the specific mandate of:

(i) Examining all cases of land owned by old caseload refugees and state-owned land;

(ii) Examining disputed issues and allegations of abuse in the (re)distribution of land and ruling on each case in accordance with the above principles;

(k) The Sub-Commission on Land must, in the performance of its functions, ensure the equity, transparency and good sense of all its decisions. It must always remain aware of the fact that the objective is not only restoration of their property to returnees, but also reconciliation between the groups as well as peace in the country.

Article 9

National Fund for *Sinistrés*

A National Fund for *Sinistrés* shall be established, and shall derive its funding from the national budget and from grants by bilateral and multilateral aid agencies or assistance from non-governmental organizations.

Article 10

Vulnerable groups

The Government shall ensure, through special assistance, the protection, rehabilitation

and advancement of vulnerable groups, namely child heads of families, orphans, street children, unaccompanied minors, traumatized children, widows, women heads of families, juvenile delinquents, the physically and mentally disabled, etc.

CHAPTER II
PHYSICAL AND POLITICAL RECONSTRUCTION

Article 11

Reconstruction programme

1. The transitional Government shall initiate and finance, with the support of the international community, a programme of physical and political reconstruction that takes a comprehensive approach incorporating

rehabilitation, peace building, and promotion of the rights and freedoms of the human person, economic growth and long-term development.

2. The reconstruction programme shall be conducted and carried out in accordance with a realistic timetable that takes account of local capabilities and external inputs. The programme must be designed with a view to equity so that all categories of the population may benefit from it.

Article 12

Physical reconstruction

Physical reconstruction aims at assisting in the return of the refugees and *sinistrés*, as well as at the rebuilding of destroyed physical property. Physical reconstruction shall be conducted, transparently and equitably, in such a way as to:

(a) Take into account both those who are being resettled or reintegrated and the communities receiving them;

(b) Contribute to correcting the imbalances relating to public infrastructures, including school infrastructures;

(c) Solve the problems relating to the repayment of loans that some Burundians had borrowed from banks and financial institutions for which the object financed has been destroyed;

(d) Ensure sound management of rebuilt infrastructures;

(e) Make use of human capital as an essential element of reconstruction;

(f) Create conditions conducive to reconstruction and the reactivation of production activities;

(g) Enhance the intervention capacity of the communes;

(h) Draw on national solidarity.

Article 13

Political reconstruction

Physical reconstruction and political reconstruction must be mutually supportive. Political reconstruction is aimed at making national reconciliation and peaceful coexistence possible, and must be directed towards the establishment of the rule of law. In this context, the following programmes and measures shall be undertaken:

(a) Launching of a multi- faceted national reconciliation programme;

(b) Promotion of the rights and freedoms of the human person;

(c) Education of the population in the culture of peace;

(d) Initiation of tangible actions for the advancement of women;

(e) Reform of the judicial system;

(f) Support of democratization, including strengthening of the parliamentary system and support for the political party system;

(g) Support for the development and strengthening of civil society;

(h) Provision of support for independent media.

CHAPTER III
ECONOMIC AND SOCIAL DEVELOPMENT

Article 14

Development programme

The transitional Government shall launch a long-term economic and social development programme. With the support of international agencies, it shall begin work on remedying the economic situation, reversing the trends resulting from the crisis, particularly the intensification of poverty, and taking up the challenges that impede economic development.

Article 15

Principal objectives

The Government shall endeavour to correct the imbalances in distribution of the country's limited resources and to embark on the path of sustainable growth with equity. It shall set itself the following principal objectives:

(a) Increasing rural and urban household income;

(b) Providing all children with primary and secondary education at least to the age of 16;

(c) Reducing the infant mortality rate by at least half;

(d) Giving the entire population access to health care;

(e) Improving the well-being of the population in all areas.

Article 16

Guidelines governing development

In pursuit of these objectives, the Government shall follow the guidelines set out hereunder on the basis of the measures specified in the report of Committee IV (see Annex IV):

(a) Working towards macro-economic and financial stabilization;

(b) Attempting to solve the problem of external and domestic public debt;

(c) Initiation of structural reforms in the social sectors;

(d) Creation of an environment conducive to the expansion of the private sector;

(e) Efforts to create new jobs and compliance with the criteria of equity and transparency in employment;

(f) Ensuring good governance in the management of public affairs;

(g) Rendering operational the Court of Audit established under the provisions of Chapter I of Protocol II to the Agreement;

(h) Transformation of the communes into focal points for development and promotion of greater public access to State services by means of a decentralization policy;

(i) Promotion of the role of women and youth in development, with the aid of specific measures to benefit them;

(j) Initiation of Burundi's integration into the region;

(k) Equitable apportionment of the benefits of development.

Article 17

Implementation

1. For the implementation of the reconstruction and development measures, an Inter-Ministerial Reconstruction and Development Unit shall be created to which the Ministries of Planning, Finance and Reintegration shall second personnel. Support for this Unit shall be sought from the World Bank, the United Nations Development Programme, the Office of the United Nations High Commissioner for Refugees, the European Commission and others. It shall have the following mandate:

(a) Preparation, within six weeks of the signing of the peace agreement, of an emergency reconstruction plan that will set the priorities for reconstruction and provide an initial estimate of costs. In preparing this plan, the National Commission for the Rehabilitation of *Sinistrés* shall be consulted and invited to submit proposals. This emergency plan shall also serve as the basis for discussion at a donor conference;

(b) Subsequently, preparation of a detailed reconstruction plan covering the transition period as set forth in Chapter II of Protocol II to the Agreement;

(c) At the same time, preparation of a medium- and long-term development plan.

2. The three plans shall be submitted to the National Assembly for approval. They will be guided by the measures proposed by Committee IV (see Annex IV,

chapters II and III) while adapting the priorities in response to developments in the situation and bearing in mind opportunities for financing.

3. Donors will be involved in the work of the Unit, and may request an international auditing company to monitor all financial operations and accounts that may be established.

PROTOCOL V

GUARANTEES ON IMPLEMENTATION OF THE AGREEMENT

PREAMBLE

We, the Parties,

Aware of the importance of guarantees in any peace process, and particularly in the implementation of peace agreements,

Having learned the lessons from the failure of previous agreements in Burundi,

Desirous that peace and reconciliation should be based on an agreement that is clear, precise, specific, unequivocal, comprehensive and implementable in

Burundi in accordance with the implementation timetable contained in Annex V to the Agreement,

Having expressed a solemn commitment to assume joint responsibility for the content of the Agreement,

Concerned also about the negative impact of the conflict on Burundian women and children,

Recognizing the unique potential of women to contribute to the healing, reconstruction and development of Burundian society,

Aware that the Burundian people is the focus and beneficiary of the Agreement concluded in its name,

Confident of the will and ability of Burundians to restore peace and harmony in their country, with the support of the international community,

Resolved to ensure the effective implementation of the Agreement,

Have agreed as follows:

Article 1

Acceptance and support of the Agreement by the Burundian people

All the Parties commit themselves to undertake a broad campaign to inform and sensitize the population about the content, spirit and letter of the Agreement.

Article 2

Transitional institutions

1. The transitional institutions shall be established and operate in accordance with the relevant provisions of Chapter II of Protocol II to the Agreement.

2. The men and women called upon to lead the transition must, at all times, show integrity, determination, patriotism and competence, and devote themselves to the interests of all Burundians without any discrimination. They must take a solemn oath before assuming their duties.

3. The duration of the transition period shall be as specified in article 13 of Protocol II to the Agreement.

Article 3

Implementation Monitoring Committee

A committee to follow up, monitor, supervise and coordinate the implementation of the Agreement, hereinafter referred to as the Implementation Monitoring Committee, shall be established.

1. Role of the Implementation Monitoring Committee

The functions of the Implementation Monitoring Committee shall be to:

(a) Follow up, monitor, supervise, coordinate and ensure the effective implementation of all the provisions of the Agreement;

(b) Ensure that the implementation timetable is respected;

(c) Ensure the accurate interpretation of the Agreement;

(d) Reconcile points of view;

(e) Arbitrate and rule on any dispute that may arise among the signatories;

(f) Give guidance to and coordinate the activities of all the commissions and sub-commissions set up pursuant to each protocol for the purpose of implementing the Agreement. These commissions and sub commissions shall include the following:

- The Technical Committee to implement the procedures for the establishment of a national defence force;

- The Technical Committee to implement the procedures for the establishment of the national police;

- The Ceasefire Commission;

- The Reintegration Commission;

- The National Commission for the Rehabilitation of *Sinistrés*;

(g) Assist and support the transitional government in the diplomatic mobilization of the financial, material, technical and human resources required for the implementation of the Agreement;

(h) Decide on the admission of new participating parties in accordance with article 14 of Protocol II to the Agreement;

(i) Perform any other duty specifically allocated to it by the Agreement.

2. Composition and structure of the Implementation Monitoring Committee

(a) The Implementation Monitoring Committee shall have the followingcomposition:

(i) Two representatives of the Parties;

(ii) One representatives of the Government;

(iii) Six Burundians designated for their moral integrity;

(iv) Representatives of :

- The United Nations;

- The Organization of African Unity;

- The regional Peace Initiative on Burundi;

(b) The Implementation Monitoring Committee shall be chaired by the representative of the United Nations, who shall act in consultation with the Government, the Organization of African Unity and the Regional Peace Initiative on Burundi;

(c) The Implementation Monitoring Committee shall be based in Bujumbura and shall have an Executive Council, to which it may delegate such of its powers as it deems appropriate;

(d) There shall be a secretariat to service the Implementation Monitoring Committee and the Executive Council.

3. Functioning and powers of the Implementation Monitoring Committee

(a) The Implementation Monitoring Committee shall begin its operations upon the appointment of its chairperson, and its mandate shall end when the Government elected during the transition period takes office. It shall draw up its own rules of procedure and work programme.

(b) The Implementation Monitoring Committee shall possess the requisite authority and decision-making powers to perform its functions impartially, neutrally and effectively.

(c) Decisions of the Implementation Monitoring Committee shall be taken by the Parties, by consensus or failing that by a **four-fifths** majority.

Article 4

The Facilitator

The Facilitator shall continue in his role as moral guarantor, recourse authority and conciliation agent.

Article 5

Commissions

1. The Implementation Monitoring Committee, in collaboration with the Government, shall establish commissions and sub-commissions responsible for sectoral activities as provided for in paragraph 1 (g) of article 3. Their activities shall be coordinated by the Implementation Monitoring Committee, to which they shall report.

2. The Implementation Monitoring Committee shall, when setting up commissions and sub commissions, specify their composition, functions, structures, location, decision-making process and leadership, as well as the timetable for the completion of their activities.

3. International Judicial Commission of Inquiry

(a) The transitional Government shall address the request referred to in article 6, paragraph 10, of Protocol I to the Agreement to the United Nations Security Council within 30 days from its installation.

(b) International criminal tribunal The Government of Burundi shall address the request referred to in article 6, paragraph 11, of Protocol I to the Agreement to the United Nations Security Council within 15 days after publication of the report of the International

Judicial Commission of Inquiry.

4. National Truth and Reconciliation Commission

The transitional Government, in consultation with the Bureau of transitional National Assembly, shall establish the National Truth and Reconciliation Commission pursuant to article 8 of Protocol I to the Agreement not later than six months after taking office. The Commission shall begin work within 15 days after its establishment.

5. Technical Committee to implement the procedures for the establishment of a national defence force

(a) The establishment of the national defence force, its name, its strength, its training, its conditions of service and its functioning shall be as defined in the relevant provisions of Chapter II of Protocol III to the Agreement and in organic laws, regulatory texts and disciplinary rules adopted pursuant to article 11, paragraph 5, and article 19 of that Protocol.

(b) The organic laws, regulatory texts and disciplinary rules referred to above shall be adopted by the appropriate transitional institutions within 30 days from the adoption of the Constitution.

(c) The Technical Committee to implement the procedures for the establishment of a national defence force referred to in article 14, paragraph 1 (d) of Protocol III to the Agreement shall be constituted within 15 to 30 days after the adoption of the texts referred to in paragraph (b) above. Its work shall begin within seven days after its constitution, and shall be concluded before the start of the electoral process.

6. Technical Committee to implement the procedures for the establishment of the national police

(a) The creation, name, missions, composition, strength, training, conditions of service and functioning of the national police shall be as defined in the relevant provisions of article 14, paragraph 2, article 15, article 17, paragraph 3, and article 20 of Protocol III to the Agreement.

(b) The Technical Committee to implement the procedures for the establishment of the national police set up pursuant to the provisions of article 14, paragraph 2

(c) of that Protocol shall be constituted within 15 to 30 days from the date when the transitional Government takes office. Its work shall begin within seven days after its constitution, and shall be concluded before the start of the electoral process.

7. Ceasefire Commission

(a) The ceasefire, as defined in article 25 of Protocol III to the Agreement, shall take place on the date of signature of the Agreement.

(b) The Ceasefire Commission provided for in article 27, paragraph 1 of Protocol III to the Agreement shall be established by the Implementation Monitoring Committee on the day the Committee starts its activities. It shall begin its work upon the appointment of its chairperson.

(c) In conformity with article 27, paragraph 1 of Protocol III, the Ceasefire Commission shall consist of representatives of the Government, the combatants of the political parties and movements, the United Nations, the Organization of African Unity and the Regional Peace Initiative for Burundi.

(d) The Ceasefire Commission may establish offices in the military regions of the country, as well as in the quartering locations and at other points as its functions may require.

(e) The functions of the Ceasefire Commission shall be as defined in article 21, article 27, paragraphs 1(d), 2, 3 and 4 and article 28 of Protocol III of the Agreement.

(f) The operations consisting of the ceasefire, disengagement, quartering and demobilization of the forces shall be completed within six months from the commencement of the activities of the Ceasefire Commission.

(g) Deployment and operations of the international peacekeeping force provided for in article 27, paragraph 5 of Protocol III to the Agreement shall commence as soon as possible after the establishment of the Ceasefire Commission. They shall be conducted in coordination and cooperation with the Ceasefire Commission.

(h) In performing their duties, the members of the Ceasefire Commission as well as those of the international peacekeeping and security force shall enjoy complete freedom of movement throughout the territory of Burundi.

(i) The amnesty provided for in article 26(l) of Protocol III to the Agreement shall go into effect on the date of signature of the Agreement.

8. Reintegration Commission

(a) The organ provided for in article 21, paragraph 8 of Protocol III to the Agreement, hereinafter referred to as the Reintegration Commission shall have the role of organizing, supervising, monitoring and ensuring the effective economic and social reintegration of the troops and combatants who, as a result of the demobilization process carried out in conformity with article 21 of Protocol III to the Agreement, have become civilians.

(b) The Reintegration Commission shall consist of representatives of the Government, the United Nations and the Organization of African Unity. It shall be chaired by the Government.

(c) The Reintegration Commission shall commence its activities on the day of its establishment. These activities must be completed before the commencement of the electoral process.

9. National Commission for the Rehabilitation of *Sinistrés*
The organ provided for in article 3, paragraph (a) of Protocol IV to the Agreement, shall be constituted within 30 days after the signature of the Agreement. It shall begin its work upon the election of its chairperson and shall report to the Implementation Monitoring Committee. It shall be based in Bujumbura. It shall be in place until the end of the transition period.

Article 6

Genocide, war crimes and other crimes against humanity

The Implementation Monitoring Committee shall ensure implementation of the measures specified in Protocol I to the Agreement relating to the prevention, suppression and eradication of acts of genocide, war crimes and other crimes against humanity.

Article 7

Role of the international community

1. The involvement of the international community in the implementation of the Agreement is necessary, both as a moral and diplomatic guarantee and as a provider of technical, material and financial assistance.

2. In this respect, the Burundian Government shall immediately following the signature of the Agreement send formal requests to the countries and organizations agreed upon by the Parties inviting them to participate in and render their financial, technical and material support to the implementation of the Agreement as provided for in the relevant provisions of the present Protocol and of Protocols I, II, III and IV.

Article 8

Peacekeeping

Immediately following the signature of the Agreement, the Burundian Government shall submit to the United

Nations a request for an international peacekeeping force in conformity with and for the purposes set forth in article 27, paragraph 5 of Protocol III to the Agreement. Account must be taken of United Nations practice in this respect. This force shall be responsible *inter alia* for:

(a) Ensuring respect for the ceasefire;

(b) Supervising integration;

(c) Providing technical support for demobilization aid and training;

(d) Ensuring protection of the institutions and of any public figure who so wishes;

(e) Assisting in the establishment and training of an ethnically balanced special unit for the protection of the institutions.

Article 9

Financial guarantees

Implementation of all the reforms and programmes contained in the Agreement will require financial support from donors. In this context, the Facilitator, in coordination with the Implementation Monitoring Committee and the transitional Government, shall take the necessary steps for a donors' conference to be convened to raise funds for the reconstruction of Burundi.

Article 10

Role of the region

1. The Parties urge the heads of State of the countries of the region to continue to provide their support for the peace process in Burundi.

2. The heads of State of the region shall also constitute guarantors of the Agreement.

ANEXURE THREE
THE 2005 CONSTITUTION OF BURUNDI
CONSTITUTION OF BURUNDI

We, the People's Representatives to the National Assembly,

PREAMBLE.

Whereas given the seriousness of the multidimensional crisis affecting our country, required to reaffirm faith in the nation of Burundi and engage proactively in rebuilding the nation-state as a unit;

Recognizing the need for all institutions and political organizations engage in a way that gives priority to peace;

Convinced of the urgency to create the conditions for a long lasting peace that is involving of all forces committed to building a lasting peace for our Country;

Noting that genocide has become a dramatic reality in Burundi and in the sub region of the Great Lakes, it is necessary that society, especially institutions and political organizations, resolutely fighting against the ideology of Genocide and adopt strategies to eradicate it;

Determined to fight against all forms of exclusion and to seek proactive solutions wherever relevant problems exist.

Reaffirming the commitment to forge a democratic system reassuring for everyone inspired by the realities of our country and based on the values of assembly, participation and consensus than confrontation and opposition;

Determined to promote good governance and sound management of the State;

Affirming the need for a transitional period to consolidate peace and security, stabilize the country and educate people for peace and democracy;

Proclaiming our commitment to respect fundamental rights of the person, human as a result of the Universal Declaration of Human Rights of December 10, 1948, the International Covenants on Human Rights of 16 December 1966, the African Charter on Human and Peoples Rights of 18 June1981 and the Charter of National Unity;

Recognizing the urgent need to promote economic development and of our country and safeguard our national culture;

Reaffirming the importance in international relations, the right of peoples to self-determination;

Considering that relations between peoples should be characterized by peace, friendship and cooperation under the UN Charter of 26 June1945;

Reaffirming our commitment to the cause of African Unity in accordance with the

Charter of the Organization of African Unity May 25, 1963; given the current constitutional impasse;

Adopt the present Constitutional Act of Transition.

TITLE I
GENERAL PROVISIONS.

Article 1.

This Constitutional Act identifies and organizes the functioning of institutions of the Republic during the transition period.

Article 2.

The institutional system covers the transition period takes effect from the date of promulgation of this Constitutional Act until the date of enactment the future constitution.

Article 3.

The transitional institutions are tasked with the following priorities:

- Restore and consolidate peace and security;

- Stabilize the country and reconcile the people of Burundi;

- Strengthen the national consciousness of ethnic awareness;

- Educate politicians and the public about values of peace and democracy;

- To combat the ideology of genocide and all forms of exclusion;

- Fighting against impunity for crimes and promote a fair justice system and reconciliation;

- Repatriate refugees, resettlement, reintegration and rehabilitation of all victims;

- Reviving the economy;

- Promote and strengthen good governance and sound management of the State;

- Promote a process to negotiate a lasting solution to the conflict;

- Prepare and implement a democratic system suited to the realities of country.

PART II
THE STATE AND SOVEREIGNTY OF THE PEOPLE

Article 4.

Burundi is a unitary republic, independent and sovereign, secular and Democratic. Its principle is government of the people, by the people and for the people. Its democratic system must be consistent with the fundamental values of the company that is national unity, social peace, development, independence and national sovereignty.

Article 5.

National sovereignty belongs to the people whose exercise is through its representatives, either directly by way of referendum. No part of the people, no individual can assume the exercise of sovereignty on behalf of the people.

Article 6.

The Republic of Burundi is divided into provinces and municipalities. The law determines their organization and operation and other administrative constituencies. It may change the boundaries and numbers. The national territory is inalienable and indivisible, subject to the provisions of Title X of this Act Constitutional.

Article 7.

Burundi's capital, Bujumbura is fixed. It can be transferred to any other instead of the Republic by the Act.

Article 8.

The flag of Burundi is a tricolor of green, white and red. It has the shape of a rectangle divided by a saltire, with its center a white disk hit three red stars to six branches that form an equilateral triangle inscribed in a fictitious imaginary circle having the same center as the disk and whose base is parallel to the length of the flag. The law specifies the dimensions and other details of the flag.

Article 9.

The motto of Burundi: Unity, Work, Progress. The emblem of the Republic is a shield which hits the head of a lion and three lances, surrounded the national currency. The national anthem is bwacu Burundi. The seal of the Republic is determined by law.

Article 10.

The national language is Kirundi. The official languages are Kirundi and other Languages specified by law.

Article 11.

The quality of Burundians is acquired, retained and lost under the conditions determined by law.

TITLE III
RIGHTS OF THE HUMAN PERSON, THE DUTIES OF THE INDIVIDUAL AND CITIZEN

Article 12.

The rights and duties proclaimed and guaranteed by the Universal Declaration of Human Rights, the International Covenants on Human Rights, the African Charter on Human and Peoples Rights and the Charter of national unity is guaranteed by the present Constitutional Act. No restriction of these rights may be imposed by law.

1. RIGHTS OF THE HUMAN

Article 13.

The human person is sacred and inviolable. The State has an absolute obligation to respect and protect.

Article 14.

Everyone has the right to development and full development of his person in compliance with this constitution, public order, morality and rights of others.

Article 15.

Everyone has the right to life, security of person and bodily integrity.

Article 16.

The freedom of the human person is inviolable. Restrictions may be to that freedom under the law. All persons deprived of their liberty shall be treated with humanity and with respect for the inherent dignity of the human person.

Article 17.

All men are equal in dignity, rights and duties, without distinction of sex, origin, ethnicity, religion or opinion. All men are equal before the law and are entitled without discrimination to the equal protection of the law.

Article 18.

No person may be charged, arrested or detained except in cases determined by law enacted prior to the acts alleged against him. The right of defense is guaranteed in all courts. No one shall be deprived, against his will, the judge that the law assigns it.

Article 19.

Everyone charged with a crime is presumed innocent until proved guilty in a legally established and public trial during which all guarantees necessary for their defense have been assured.

Article 20.

No person shall be sentenced for actions or omissions which, when they were committed did not constitute an offense. Similarly, it can be inflicted heavier penalty than was applicable when the offense was committed.

Article 21.

No one shall be subjected to security measures in the cases and manner provided by law including for reasons of public order or state security.

Article 22.

No one shall be subjected to torture or ill-treatment or cruel, inhuman or degrading.

Article 23.

No person shall be subjected to arbitrary interference with his privacy, family, home or correspondence, nor to attacks upon his honor and reputation. It can be ordered searches and searches of premises in the forms and conditions provided by law. The secrecy of correspondence and communication is guaranteed in respect of forms and conditions determined by law.

Article 24.

All Burundians have the right to move and settle freely within the National territory and leave and return. The exercise of this right may be limited by law for reasons of public order or state security, to deal with Hazard or to protect people in danger.

Article 25.

No citizen may be forced into exile.

Article 26.

The right to asylum is recognized in the conditions defined by law. Extradition is permitted within the limits prescribed by law. Burundians can not be extradited abroad.

Article 27.

Everyone has the right to freedom of thought, conscience, religion and worship in respect of public order and law. The exercise of religion and expression, beliefs must be in accordance with the principle of the secular state.

Article 28.

Everyone has the right to freedom of opinion and expression in respect of Public order and the law. Freedom of press is recognized and guaranteed by the state.

Article 29.

Everyone has the right to property. No one shall be deprived of his possessions except for public interest in cases and manner established by law and subject to a just and prior compensation or pursuant to a court decision casting res judicata.

Article 30.

Freedom of assembly and peaceful association is guaranteed under the conditions set by law.

Article 31.

All Burundians have the right to participate, either directly or indirectly by its representatives, management and administration of state affairs subject to legal requirements, including age and capacity. While Burundi is also entitled to access to public service in his country.

Article 32.

The family is the natural unit and basis of society. The family and marriage must be under the special protection of the state. Parents have the natural right and duty to educate and raise their children. They are supported in this task by the State and public authorities. Every child is entitled to his family, society and state, to special protection measures required by his status as a minor.

Article 33.

Everyone is entitled to the exercise of the economic, social and cultural rights which are indispensable for his dignity and the free development of his person, through national effort and given the resources.

Article 34.

Every citizen is entitled to equal access to education, and culture. The State has the duty to organize public education. However, the right to establish private schools is guaranteed under conditions fixed by law.

Article 35.

The State grants all citizens the right to work and strives to create conditions which render the enjoyment of this right effectively. It recognizes the right of everyone to the enjoyment of working conditions and fair and satisfactory guarantees to Worker fair compensation for its services or its production.

Article 36.

Equally qualified person is entitled without any discrimination, to Equal pay for equal work.

Article 37.

Any worker may defend in the manner prescribed by law, their rights and interests, either individually or collectively or through trade union action. The right to strike is exercised under the conditions defined by law.

Article 38.

Everyone is entitled to the protection of moral and material interests resulting from any scientific, literary or artistic production of which he is the author.

Article 39.

Any alien in the territory of the Republic shall enjoy the protection granted to persons and property under this Act and the Constitution.

Article 40.

In exercising its rights and the enjoyment of his freedoms, everyone shall be subject to limitations as are determined by law solely for the purpose of securing due recognition and respect for rights and freedoms of others and of meeting the just requirements of morality, public order and general welfare in a democratic society.

Article 41.

The judiciary, custodial rights and public freedoms, ensures compliance such rights as provided by law.

Article 42.

No one can abuse the rights recognized by the Constitutional Act or by law to undermine national unity, territorial integrity or independence of Burundi, undermine the republican regime, the secular state or violate any other so this Constitutional Act.

2. DUTIES OF THE INDIVIDUAL AND CITIZEN

Article 43.

Every citizen has duties towards the family and society, the State and other jurisdictions.

Article 44.

Each Burundian has the duty to preserve and strengthen national unity accordance with the Charter of National Unity.

Article 45.

Everyone must respect the laws and institutions of the Republic.

Article 46.

Each Burundian has the duty to preserve the harmonious development of the family and work for the cohesion and respect for this family, meet at any time his parents to feed them and assist them when necessity.

Article 47.

Each individual has the duty to respect and consider his fellow man without discrimination, and to maintain relations with him that can promote, protect and enhance respect and mutual tolerance.

Article 48.

Each Burundian must ensure, in its relations with society, preservation and strengthening of Burundian cultural values and contribute to the establishment a morally healthy society.

Article 49.

The public property is sacred and inviolable. Everyone is obliged to comply and scrupulously protected. Each Burundi has the duty to defend heritage of the nation. Any act of sabotage, vandalism, corruption, misappropriation, embezzlement or any other act prejudicial to the public good is punishable as provided by law.

Article 50.

All citizens are required to fulfill their civic obligations. Everyone has the duty to work for the common good and to fulfill its obligations professional. All are equal before the public burdens. It can not be established exemption by law. The state may proclaim the solidarity of all before the expenses resulting from natural disasters and national.

Article 51.

All Burundians are responsible for public office or elected to political office is duty to perform with knowledge, honesty, dedication and loyalty in the General interest.

Article 52.

Each Burundi has the duty to defend national independence and integrity of land. Every citizen has the sacred duty to watch and participate in the defense of its country. All Burundians, any alien who is on the territory of the Republic the duty not to compromise the security of the state.

Article 53.

Everyone has the duty to contribute to safeguarding peace, democracy and social justice.

Article 54.

All Burundians have the duty to contribute his work to the construction and prosperity.

TITLE IV
POLITICAL PARTIES.

Article 55.

The multiparty system is recognized in the Republic of Burundi.

Article 56.

The political party is a non-profit organization with legal personality and composed of citizens around a democratic society based on unity national program with a specific political objectives dictated by the interests of achieve the interest and development of all.

Article 57.

Political parties are recognized under this Act and the Constitutional law. To be approved, they are required including adherence to the Charter of the Unit National and adhere to the following fundamental principles: respect, safeguarding and consolidation of national unity, protection and promotion of human fundamental human; promoting a state based on respect and defense of democracy, defending territorial integrity and sovereignty national, the prohibition of intolerance, ideology of genocide, the ethnicity of regionalism, xenophobia, the use of violence in all its forms. The Political parties are required to comply with the Charter of National Unity and principles outlined above, during their operation.

Article 58.

Political parties, their organization and membership bodies Leaders must address both the stage of approval in their functioning, democratic principles and the ideal of national unity by taking account of the various components of the Burundian population.

Article 59.

The political parties involved, by peaceful means in political life through their governing bodies at national, provincial and municipal.

Article 60.

Without prejudice to Article 30, and given the imperatives of restoration of peace and national cohesion, political parties are not allowed to organize demonstrations and public meetings. Only authorized meetings of governing bodies of political parties Levels National, provincial and municipal.

Article 61.

It is forbidden for political parties to identify themselves in the form in action or other manner whatsoever, including ethnicity, region, religion, a sect or sex.

Article 62.

Members of the armed forces, police and magistrates in activity are not allowed to join political parties.

Article 63.

The external funding of political parties is prohibited unless otherwise. Exceptional established by law. Is also prohibited any funding likely to undermine the independence and sovereignty. The law identifies and organizes the funding of political parties.

Article 64.

The conditions under which political parties are formed, exercise and stop their activities are determined by law.

TITLE V
THE EXECUTIVE

1. THE PRESIDENT OF THE REPUBLIC

Article 65.

The President of the Republic, Head of State, embodies national unity, ensures compliance with the Charter of National Unity and the Constitutional Act and ensures its Arbitration continuity of the state and the smooth running of government. It is guarantor of national independence, territorial integrity, respect for treaties and international agreements.

Article 66.

Upon entry into force of this Constitutional Act, the President of the Republic reads the solemn oath below, received by the Constitutional Court to the Transitional National Assembly: "Before the people of Burundi, the only holder of national sovereignty, I swear fidelity to the Charter of National Unity, the Constitutional Act and the Act and pledge to devote all my strength to defend the supreme interests of the nation to ensure national unity and security for all, social peace, justice social and national development, promote and defend the rights and safeguard the integrity and independence of the Republic ".

Article 67.

During their appointment and the end thereof, the President of the Republic, Vice-Presidents and members of the Government are required to honor the written statement of their property and assets sent to the Supreme Court.

Article 68.

The President of the Republic shall exercise the regulatory power and shall execute laws. It exercises its powers by decree countersigned as appropriate by the Vice - President and the Ministers concerned. The countersignature is not involved in the acts of the President of the Republic under Articles 71, 74, 76, 83, 123, 124 of this Constitutional Act of Transition. The President of the Republic may delegate his powers to Vice-Presidents except those listed in the preceding paragraph.

Article 69.

The President of the Republic, after consultation with the Vice-Presidents, appoints the members of government and put an end to their functions.

Article 70.

The President of the Republic chairs the Council of Ministers.

Article 71.

The President of the Republic is the Head of State. He declares war and signs the armistice after consulting the Government, the President of the National Assembly and National Security Council.

Article 72.

The President of the Republic shall appoint senior civilian and military officers. An organic law defines the categories of posts referred to in the preceding paragraph.

Article 73.

The President of the Republic accredits and recalls ambassadors and envoys extraordinary to foreign states and receives letters of credence and recall ambassadors and special envoys of foreign states.

Article 74.

The President of the Republic has the prerogative of mercy.

Article 75.

The President of the Republic shall establish the national orders and decorations Republic.

Article 76.

Once the institutions of the Republic, the independence of the Nation, the integrity of territory or the fulfillment of its international commitments are threatened with serious and immediate and regular operation of government is interrupted, the President of the Republic may decree-law state of emergency and take all measures required by these circumstances, after formal consultation of the President of the National Assembly, National Security Council and Constitutional Court. He informs the nation by a message. These measures must be inspired by the desire to provide the government the means to accomplish their mission.

Article 77.

The office of President of the Republic is incompatible with the exercise of any other elective public office, any public employment and professional activity. They are also incompatible with the position of leader of a political party.

Article 78.

The President of the Republic is criminally responsible for acts performed in the exercise of his functions in case of high treason. It is high treason when in violation of the Charter of National Unity, of the Or constitutional law, the President of the Republic guilty of deliberately act contrary to the best interests of the nation that seriously undermines the unity national, social peace, national development and seriously jeopardizes human rights, territorial integrity, independence and sovereignty national. The acts constituting treason could be attributed to the President of the Republic and the penalties are determined by law. The President of the Republic may be impeached by the Assembly acting national show of hands, a majority of three quarters of its members. The instruction can be conducted by a team of at least three judges of General Procuracy of the Republic.

Article 79.

Except for acts within its jurisdiction, discretionary acts, or Administrative the President of the Republic may be challenged before the courts.

Article 80.

At the expiration of his duties, the President of the Republic is entitled, unless conviction for high treason, a pension and all other privileges and facilities determined by law.

Article 81.

In case of absence or temporary incapacity of the President of the Republic, 1st

Vice President manages the daily business. In case of vacancy caused by resignation, death or any other cause of termination of his duties, the acting is provided by the 1st Vice-President or, if it is in turn unable to perform these functions, by 2nd Vice-President. The vacancy is found by the Constitutional Court within three days before the

1st Vice-President or in his absence by the 2nd Vice-President. The interim authority can not form a new government. The Government is considered resigned and can only ensure just the current business until the formation of a new Government. Within a period not exceeding three months, the Government and National Assembly. Transition designates by consensus a new President of the Republic. A law establishes the procedure for appointing the new President of the Republic.

2. VICE-PRESIDENTS

Article 82.

In exercising his functions the President of the Republic shall be assisted by two Vice-Presidents. The First Vice-President coordinates the political and Administrative. The

Second Vice-President coordinates the economic and social fields.

Article 83.

The Vice-Presidents are appointed and removed from office after consultation by the President of the Republic with the President of the National Assembly and members of the National Assembly. Their designation is made by a decree of the President of the Republic.

Article 84

The 1st Vice-President chairs the Council of Ministers by express delegation of President and a specific agenda. In the absence of the 1st Vice - President, the President confers the delegation to 2nd Vice-President.

Article 85

The Vice-Presidents shall by order, each in its sector, ensure all measures for the implementation of presidential decrees. Ministers responsible for implementing them countersign the orders of Vice-Presidents.

Article 86.

Upon taking office the Vice-presidents lend a solemn oath below: "Before the people of Burundi, the only holder of national sovereignty, I swear fidelity to the Charter of National Unity, the Constitutional Act and the law and undertake to devote all my strength to defend the supreme interests of the nation, to ensure national unity, security for all, social peace, social justice and developing countries, to promote and defend human rights and safeguard the integrity and independence of the Republic. I swear, in addition, fidelity and loyalty to the President of the Republic".

3. GOVERNMENT

Article 87.

The Government consists of the Vice-Presidents, Ministers and, where appropriate, Secretaries of State. It must be composed in a spirit of national unity by taking account of the various components of the Burundian population.

Article 88.

The government determines and conducts the policy of the Nation under the decisions taken by the Council of Ministers.

Article 89.

Cabinet deliberates on the mandatory policy of the State, draft treaties and international agreements, bills, projects presidential decrees, draft Orders of the Vice-Presidents and projects. Orders of Ministers in the nature of general rules.

Article 90

The Government is responsible to the President of the Republic. Cabinet members are politically united. In case of termination of a Vice-President for any reason whatsoever, his replacement has the right to have a change in the composition of Government. This change does not affect the other Vice-President.

Article 91.

Ministers are the heads of departments that were entrusted to them. They shall, by ordinance, all measures of implementation of decrees Presidential decrees and Vice-Presidents.

Article 92.

State Secretaries to assist Ministers which their department is attached. They participate in the deliberations of the Law Council of Ministers.

Article 93

Cabinet members are criminally liable for acts performed in exercising their functions and recognized as crimes or offenses when they were committed.

Article 94.

The office of member of the Government is incompatible with the exercise of all work including the exercise of a parliamentary mandate.

TITLE VI
THE LEGISLATIVE POWER

Article 95.

Legislative power is exercised by a unicameral Assembly called National Transition whose members carry the title of "parliamentary".

Article 96.

The Transitional National Assembly is composed of members of the Assembly National office at the time of the adoption of this Act or the Constitutional their deputies and embers from political parties and society calendar. Political parties referred to in the preceding paragraph are those approved before the promulgation this transitional constitution and were not represented at the National Assembly. Each of these parties is represented by a Member.

Article 97.

Parliamentarians from these political parties are nominated by the bodies leaders nationally in the formal meeting held for that purpose and in compliance statutory rules on meetings and decisions.

Article 98.

The previous article will apply to the replacement of parliamentary and their deputies from political parties represented in the National Assembly in function before the promulgation of this Constitutional Act but lists election districts are exhausted.

Article 99.

The parliamentary representatives of civil society are twenty in number eight. They are designated by a consultation of the President of the Republic, the President of National Assembly and the Chairman and Vice-Chairman of Bashingantahe for national unity and reconciliation.

Article 100.

The mechanisms of enlargement of the Transitional National Assembly and the

Replacement of parliamentarians in case a vacancy shall be determined by the law.

Article 101.

The Act establishes the system of allowances and benefits for parliamentarians and the system incompatibilities.

Article 102.

The parliamentary mandate is national in character. Any imperative mandate is null.

The parliamentary vote is personal.

The Procedure of the National Assembly may authorize the exceptionally delegation to vote. In this case, no person may act on behalf of more than one term.

Article 103.

Parliamentarians can not be prosecuted, arrested or searched, detained or tried for opinions expressed or votes cast during the sessions. Except in cases of flagrante delicto, MPs can not, for the duration of sessions, be prosecuted without the authorization of the Office of the National Assembly. Parliamentarians can, out of session, be arrested without the authorization of Office of the National Assembly, except in cases of flagrante delicto, tracking already authorized or a final sentence.

Article 104.

The parliamentary mandate is incompatible with any other character in public. The law may exempt certain categories of local or state officials plan incompatible with the parliamentary mandate.

Article 105.

A parliamentarian appointed to the Government or any other public office is incompatible with the parliamentary mandate he accepts and ceases immediately His seat in the National Assembly and shall be replaced. He resumes his duties as soon as causes of conflict have disappeared and provided that the mandate he has exercised is still ongoing.

Article 106.

The National Assembly enacts laws and controls the action of the Government.

Article 107.

Are within the law:

1. The guarantees and fundamental obligations of a citizen:

• Backup of individual liberty;

• Protection of civil liberties;

• Constraint imposed in the interest of national defense and public safety to citizens in their persons and their property.

2. The status of persons and property:

• Nationality, condition and capacity of persons;

• Matrimonial property regimes, inheritance and gifts;

• Plan of property, real rights and civil obligations and commercial.

3. The political, administrative and judicial:

• Organization's General Administration;

• Territorial organization, creation and modification of constituency's administrative divisions and the election;

• Electoral system;

• General rules of organization of national defense;

• Statute of military personnel, public security forces and assimilated;

• General Principles of Civil Service;

• Regulations of the Public Service;

• State of emergency;

• Framework organic facilities and utilities autonomous;

• Organization of courts of all orders and proceedings in such courts,

• Creation of new types of courts, determining the status of the judiciary, ministerial offices and court officers;

- Determination of crimes and their punishment is applicable;

- Organization of Bar;

- Plan prison;

- Amnesty.

4. The environmental protection and conservation of natural resources;

5. Financial issues and heritage:

- Plan to issue currency;

- State budget;

- Definition of the base and tax rates and taxes;

- Alienation and managing the state;

6. Nationalization and denationalization of enterprises and transfers corporate ownership from public to private sector;

7. The system of education and scientific research;

8. The objectives of the economic and social state;

9. Labor laws, social security, trade union law including conditions for exercising the right to *strike.*

Article 108.

Materials other than those in the field of law are lawful.

Article 109.

The Finance Act determines, for each year, resources and expenses state.

Article 110.

The Transitional National Assembly has before it the draft finance law soon the opening of its session in October.

Article 111.

The Transitional National Assembly passes the budget. If she has not ruled on the 31 December, the budget last year was taken by twelfth Provisional.

At the request of the Government, the Transitional National Assembly is convened in extraordinary session within 15 days to review the bill Finance.

If the Transitional National Assembly has not approved the budget at the end of this session it is definitively established by Legislative Decree issued by the Council of Ministers.

Article 112.

The National Assembly elects a Bureau comprising the President, 1st and 2nd Vice - President, the Secretary General and Deputy Secretary-General.

The President and other officers of the National Assembly are elected for the duration of the transition under the conditions laid down by the Rules of that Assembly.

Article 113.

The parliamentary mandate is terminated by death, resignation, incapacity Permanent, no more unjustified quarter sessions or one session when the Parliamentary falls into one of the cases of disqualification under the Act.

Article 114.

The National Assembly meets annually in two ordinary sessions. The first session begins the first Monday in April and the second the first Monday of October each year. The total duration of each session can exceed two months. Special sessions, not exceeding a period of fifteen days may be convened at the request of the President of the Republic, the Government or application of the absolute majority of members of the National Assembly on a specific agenda. Special sessions are opened and closed by decree of President of the Republic.

Article 115.

The National Assembly may deliberate validly unless two-thirds of MPs are present. Laws are passed by an absolute majority of MPs. Organic laws are passed by two-thirds majority of parliament present, though this majority can be less than the absolute majority of Member of the Assembly.

Article 116.

Except in cases of force majeure duly noted by the Constitutional Court, the Proceedings of the National Assembly shall be valid only if held in held its regular sessions.

Sittings of the National Assembly are public. However, the Assembly may meet in closed session if necessary. The minutes of the proceedings of the National Assembly shall be published in newspaper Parliamentary.

Article 117.

The National Assembly adopts the Rules setting other rules of its organization and its functioning.

Article 118.

A court of accounts, Examining, liquidation and arrested accounts of all public services will be created and organized by law. The court shall, at the end of each fiscal year if the Finance Act was properly executed by the Government and reports to the Assembly National.

TITLE VII
RELATIONS BETWEEN THE EXECUTIVE AND THE LEGISLATURE.

Article 119.

The agenda of the National Assembly has prioritized and in order that the Government has set the discussion of Bills tabled by the Government and proposals for laws submitted by members of the National Assembly.

Article 120.

The legislative initiative belongs jointly to the National Assembly, the President Republic and the Government.

Article 121.

The Government has the right to propose amendments to bills submitted by members of the National Assembly. Parliamentarians have the right to propose amendments to bills

Tabled by the Government. However, proposals and amendments made by members of the Assembly National is not admissible where their adoption would result in either

a significant decrease of public resources or the creation or aggravation an important public office, unless such proposals or amendments are backed proposals for offsetting revenue. When the Assembly has entrusted the examination of a draft to a committee

Parliament, the Government may, after the opening of the trial, opposing consideration of any amendment that has not been previously submitted to this Committee. If the Government requests, the Assembly voted by a single vote on all or Part of the text by retaining only the amendments proposed or accepted by him.

Article 122.

The Government may, for the implementation of its program, ask the Assembly National authority to make laws by decree for a limited period, the measures which are normally a matter of law. These legislative decrees must be ratified by the National Assembly during the session next. In the absence of a ratification bill, they are struck by sunset.

Article 123.

The President of the Republic promulgates the laws adopted by the National Assembly within thirty days of their submission, he makes no request a second reading or grasps the Constitutional Court in unconstitutional. The request for reconsideration may cover all or part of the law. After a second reading the same text can not be enacted unless it has been voted a majority of 2 / 3 of members present for ordinary legislation, and a three-fourths majority of members present for the organic laws. When the text deals with security aspects identified as important by the Government, the law is enacted if it was passed by a majority of four fifths of MPs.

Article 124.

The President of the Republic may, after consultation with the Vice-Presidents and President of the National Assembly, submit to referendum any draft constitutional, legislative or otherwise likely to have profound implications life and the future of the nation or the nature or operation of institutions Republic.

Article 125.

The President of the Republic shall communicate with the National Assembly through message that is read by a member of the Government. These messages do rise to any debate.

Article 126.

Cabinet members may attend meetings of the Assembly National, they are heard when they ask. They may be assisted by experts.

Article 127.

Parliamentarians have the right to discuss the action and policy Government.

Article 128.

The National Assembly can learn about government action through the oral or written questions addressed to members of the Government. The Government shall provide the National Assembly that all explanations it requested its management and its actions.

Article 129.

The National Assembly has the right to form committees responsible for investigating specific articles of government action and to submit its conclusions.

TITLE VIII
THE JUDICIARY

Article 130.

Justice is administered by courts and tribunals throughout the territory of the Republic behalf of the Burundian people. The role and functions of the Public Ministry are filled by the magistrates Parquet. However, judges in courts of residence satisfy themselves with their court duties of the Public Prosecutor under the supervision of attorney

Republic. The organization and jurisdiction are set by law.

Article 131.

The court hearings are public, unless closed by delivery court, where advertising is dangerous to public order or morality.

Article 132.

Any judicial decision is justified, his device is delivered in open court public.

Article 133.

The judiciary is independent of the legislative and executive branches. In exercising its functions, the judge is subject only to the Constitutional Act and law.

Article 134.

The President of the Republic, Head of State is the guarantor of the independence of the judiciary. He is assisted in this task by the Supreme Council of Judicial whose composition, organization and functioning are determined by law.

THE SUPREME COURT

Article 135.

The Supreme Court is the highest ordinary court of the Republic. It guarantees the enforcement by the courts. It includes:

• A Chamber of Cassation, which hears appeals in cassation against the decisions made ultimately by courts other than those referred Article 136, paragraph 1.

- An Administrative Division which decides on appeals against decisions made by the administrative courts and other remedies the laws. A House judiciary who knows offenses committed by political representatives and public litigants in the Supreme Court first and last resort.

Article 136.

Decisions of the Administrative Division and the Judicial Chamber of the Court Supreme and decisions of courts of equal rank as chambers of

Supreme Court of Cassation are likely before the combined chambers of the Court Supreme. Decisions of the Chamber of Cassation and the Supreme Court all rooms

met are likely to appeal, except for clemency or a retrial.

Article 137.

Justices of the Supreme Court are appointed by the President of the Republic.

Article 138.

The Act specifies the composition and organization of the Supreme Court. It determines also the operating rules and procedures applicable to this Court.

Article 139.

The Supreme Court full bench is united to try the President of the Republic for high treason, the President of the National Assembly for crimes committed during their term. The investigation and trial took place drop everything.

Article 140.

The persons referred to in the preceding article shall be suspended from their duties if convicted.

Article 141.

The Supreme Court is competent to receive written statements of assets and Heritage President of the Republic, Vice-Chairpersons and Members Government.

THE CONSTITUTIONAL COURT.

Article 142.

The Constitutional Court is the court of the State in constitutional matters. She shall determine the constitutionality of laws and interpretation of the Constitutional Act of Transition.

Article 143

The Constitutional Court is composed of an odd number of at least 5 members appointed by the President of the Republic for a term of 4 years renewable. Members of the Constitutional Court must be lawyers with experience affirmed.

They are chosen from among persons recognized for their moral integrity, their impartiality and independence. The Constitutional Court consists of judges, permanent and non permanent. The permanent members are professional magistrates.

Article 144.

The Constitutional Court is competent to:

• To decide on the constitutionality of laws and regulatory acts taken in materials other than those in the area of the law of demand President of the Republic, the President of the National Assembly, to fourth parliamentarians or persons and body referred to in Article

This Constitutional Act.

• Interpreting the Constitutional Act, at the request of the President of the Republic, the President of the National Assembly or one quarter of parliamentarians;

• Decide on the regularity of the procedure for appointing members of the Transitional National Assembly;

• Receive the oath of the President of the Republic and Vice-Presidents;

• Declare the vacant post of President of the Republic.

Article 145

Organic laws before their promulgation and the Rules of the Assembly National before its implementation are necessarily subject to supervision constitutionality.

Article 146

The Constitutional Court is competent to adjudicate on cases referred Articles 76 and 116.

Article 147

Any natural or legal person and the prosecution can seize the Constitutional Court on the constitutionality of laws, either directly by way of action or indirectly by the procedure of unconstitutionality invoked in a case before another court. This should defer proceedings until the decision of the Constitutional Court must act within thirty days.

Article 148

A provision declared unconstitutional may not be promulgated or application. Decisions of the Constitutional Court are not subject to any constitutional complaint.

Article 149

A law determines the organization and functioning of the Constitutional Court, and the procedure applicable before it.

TITLE IX
NATIONAL BOARD

1. Abashingantahe COUNCIL FOR NATIONAL UNITY AND RECONCILIATION.

Article 150

The Abashingantahe Council for National Unity and Reconciliation is a body

Advisory include:

- conduct reflections and advice on all matters essential for unity, peace and national reconciliation in especially those related to priority tasks of the institutions transition;

- regularly monitor the evolution of Burundian society's point of view the question of national unity and reconciliation;

- produce a periodic report on the status of national unity and reconciliation and to bring to the attention of the nation;

- make proposals for improving the situation of the unit and national reconciliation in the country;

- devise and initiate actions necessary to rehabilitate Ubushingantahe the institution into an instrument of peace and social cohesion;

- to provide advice and proposals on other matters affecting the nation; The Abashingantahe Council for National Unity and Reconciliation is accessed by the President of the Republic, the Government and the National Assembly. On its own initiative, may also issue opinions and make them public.

Article 151.

The Abashingantahe Council for National Unity and Reconciliation is composed individuals recognized for their moral integrity and their interest in the life Nation and especially to his unit. The President of the Republic appoints the Council of Bashingantahe for National Unity and Reconciliation.

Article 152

A law determines the composition, organization and functioning of the Council Bashingantahe for national unity and reconciliation. This law also stipulates the establishment, composition, organization and operation of Abashingantahe Council for National Unity and reconciliation at various administrative levels and organic links.

2. THE ECONOMIC AND SOCIAL COUNCIL

Article 153.

The Economic and Social Council is a consultative body with jurisdiction over all aspects of economic and social development. It must be consulted on any proposed development plan and on any regional integration project or sub-regional.

The Economic and Social Council may, on its own initiative, as recommendations, attracting the attention of the National Assembly or the Government on reform of economic and social order which it deems consistent or contrary to public interest.

It also gives advice on all matters brought to its consideration by the President of the Republic, the Government, and the National Assembly or by another public institution.

Article 154

The Economic and Social Council is composed of members chosen for their competence in the various socio-professional sectors of the country. Members of the Economic and Social Council are appointed by the President of the Republic.

Article 155.

An organic law defines the composition and determines the organization and functioning of Economic and Social Council.

3. NATIONAL SECURITY COUNCIL

Article 156.

The National Security Council is an advisory body to assist the President of the Republic and the Government in developing the policy Security in monitoring the situation in the country security and the development of defense strategies in case of crisis. The board can be accessed on any other matter related national security.

Article 157.

Members of the National Security Council are appointed by the President of the Republic.

Article 158.

An organic law defines the composition and determines the organization and functioning of the National Security Council.

4. NATIONAL COUNCIL OF THE COMMUNICATION

Article 159.

The National Council of Communication ensures freedom of communication audiovisual and written in compliance with the law, public order and good mores.

The National Council of Communication is an independent body. It is guided by principles of neutrality, objectivity, impartiality and concern for preserving interest.

The Council has powers of decision in particular on respect for freedom of Press. It also plays an advisory role to the Government's communication.

Article 160.

Members of the National Communication are appointed by the President Republic.

Article 161.

An Act specifies the composition and determines the organization and functioning of National Council of Communication.

TITLE X
TREATIES AND INTERNATIONAL AGREEMENTS

Article 162.

The President of the Republic of senior management of international negotiations. He signs and ratifies international treaties and agreements.

Article 163.

Peace treaties and trade treaties, treaties relating to the organization international treaties that commit the finances of the State, to amend the legislative provisions and those relating to personal status can be ratified only by a law.

Article 164.

The Republic of Burundi may create with other State agencies international management or joint coordination and free cooperation. She may conclude association agreements or community with other states.

Article 165.

The treaties take effect only after having been duly ratified and subject their application by the other party to bilateral treaties and the achievement of conditions of enforcement provided by them for multilateral treaties.

Article 166.

The facility agreements of foreign military bases on national territory and than allowing the storage of toxic waste and other materials that can be seriously affect the environment are prohibited.

Article 167.

No Sale, no exchange, no addition of territory shall be valid without the consent of the Burundian people called to vote in a referendum.

Article 168.

When the Constitutional Court before the President of the Republic, President of the National Assembly or one quarter of MPs said that international commitment includes a clause contrary to the Constitutional Act, authorization to ratify this commitment can only occur after revision of Constitutional Act.

TITLE XI
THE REVIEW OF THE CONSTITUTIONAL ACT

Article 169.

The initiative for the revision of the Constitutional Act belongs jointly to President of the Republic after consultation with the Government and Assembly National acting by an absolute majority of its members. The draft or proposed amendment is adopted by a majority of four fifths of the members of the National Assembly.

TITLE XII
THE FINAL AND TRANSITIONAL PROVISIONS

Article 170.

After its adoption by the National Assembly based on this Act

Constitution was promulgated by decree-law of President of the Republic.

Article 171:

Upon entry into force of the Constitutional Act, the President of the Republic functions assume the powers conferred by it to the presidential institution. Pending the establishment of the Constitutional Court, the oath of the President Republic under Article 66 of the Constitutional Act will be received by the Court Supreme.

Article 172:

Pending the appointment of the new Government, the present Government remains office.

Article 173

Notwithstanding the provisions of Article 112, the President of the Assembly National Service serves as the Chairman of the National Assembly Transition from the entry into force of this Constitutional Act.

Article 174

Notwithstanding Article 83 and pending the election of officers of the Assembly National Transition, Vice-

Presidents are appointed after consultation of President of the Republic, the President and officers of the previous Assembly and the Presidents of Parliamentary Groups.

Article 175

Until the actual establishment of the Transitional National Assembly, the current National Assembly remains in office. The Office of the National Assembly office chair works thereof until the adoption of internal rules governing the National Assembly Transition and the establishment of a new Office.

Article 176

Insofar as they are not contrary to this Act constitutional, international commitments of the government of Burundi and all laws and regulations prior to signing remain in force until they amendment or repeal.

Article 177

This Act Transitional Constitution provides for the future and not retroactive application.

The Constitution of the Republic of Burundi, adopted March 9, 1992 and promulgated March 13, 1992 and Decree-Law No. 1/001/96 of 13 September 1996 Institutional system of transition are repealed. This Constitutional Act shall enter into force on the day of its promulgation.

www.ingramcontent.com/pod-product-compliance
Lightning Source LLC
Chambersburg PA
CBHW030344190426
43201CB00041B/87